Retracing the Keowee Trail

Retracing the Keowee Trail

A Deep Map of the Cherokee Path
in the History of the Carolinas

STUART TAYLOR

CASCADE *Books* • Eugene, Oregon

RETRACING THE KEOWEE TRAIL
A Deep Map of the Cherokee Path in the History of the Carolinas

Copyright © 2024 Stuart Taylor. All rights reserved. Except for brief quotations in critical publications or reviews, no part of this book may be reproduced in any manner without prior written permission from the publisher. Write: Permissions, Wipf and Stock Publishers, 199 W. 8th Ave., Suite 3, Eugene, OR 97401.

Cascade Books
An Imprint of Wipf and Stock Publishers
199 W. 8th Ave., Suite 3
Eugene, OR 97401

www.wipfandstock.com

PAPERBACK ISBN: 979-8-3852-2576-7
HARDCOVER ISBN: 979-8-3852-2577-4
EBOOK ISBN: 979-8-3852-2578-1

Cataloguing-in-Publication data:

Names: Taylor, Stuart.
Title: Retracing the Keowee trail : a deep map of the Cherokee path in the history of the Carolinas / Stuart Taylor.
Description: Eugene, OR : Cascade Books, 2024 | Includes bibliographical references.
Identifiers: ISBN 979-8-3852-2576-7 (paperback) | ISBN 979-8-3852-2577-4 (hardcover) | ISBN 979-8-3852-2578-1 (ebook)
Subjects: LCSH: Indians of North America—History. | Indians of North America—Relocation. | Indian Removal—(United States :—1813–1903).
Classification: E98.F39 T37 2024 (print) | E98.F39 T37 (ebook)

Cover design by Ms. Sarah Jane Walter Winter.

This book is dedicated to my grandparents,
Hazael Gilreath and John S. Taylor.

Table of Contents

List of Illustrations | ix

Preface | xi

Introduction | 1

Chapter 1: Five Centuries of Indigenous Resistance to the European Conquest of North America | 14

Chapter 2: Celtic Origins and the Migration Journey of My Scots Irish Ancestors | 24

Chapter 3: The Cherokee Nation Encounters the Colony of South Carolina | 42

Chapter 4: A Vicious Cycle of Violence: The Cherokee War of 1760–61 | 80

Chapter 5: Waves of Scots Irish Settlers Come to the Carolina Up-Country | 93

Chapter 6: Bartram's Travels on the Keowee Trail | 107

Chapter 7: The American Revolution and Other Struggles for Freedom | 120

Chapter 8: Slavery and the Rise and Fall of Southern Abolitionism | 160

Chapter 9: A Shaking of the Foundations | 171

Chapter 10: The Ghost Dance | 176

Chapter 11: A Reckoning with Settler Colonialism | 185

Chapter 12: The Haunted History of the South | 192

Chapter 13: Healing the Family Tree | 197

Chapter 14: Doing History | 225

Chapter 15: Coming Full Circle | 236

Postscript: The Anderson Diaspora | 249

Epilogue: The Unfinished Revolution | 253

Acknowledgments | 257

Bibliography | 259

List of Illustrations

Hazael Gilreath and John S. Taylor v
Contemporary Map Including Cherokee Path xiii
Cherokee Path 2
Family Reunion 6
Nazareth Presbyterian Church, Spartanburg County, South Carolina 6
William Anderson Grave 7
Tyger Jim 7
Departure of Columbus 17
Discovery of Mississippi 18
American Progress 18
Philadelphia Wagon Road 31
Hunter's Map of the Cherokee Path (1730) 43
Mepkin 44
Oconee Station 51
Judaculla Rock 60
Connestee Marker 65
John S. Taylor Dedicating Keowee Marker 78
Keowee Marker 78
Forks of Yadkin 82
Long Canes Massacre Headstone 86
Fort Prince George 87
Boone Escorting Settlers through the Cumberland Gap 105
Hampton Massacre Marker 130
Tamassee 133

David Anderson Grave 144
Andrew Pickens Portrait 148
Old Stone Church 158
Pickens Grave 158
Gilreath Mill Photo 202
Gilreath Mill Drawing 203
Photo of Mariah and Five Gilreath Sisters 204
Janie Gilreath as Cateechee (Keowee Trail Pageant Brochure) 204

Preface

Osage author William Least Heat-Moon has suggested that when we enter a land we deeply love, we begin to "pick up the scent of our histories" and, traveling vertically, "we end up following road maps in the marrow of our bones and in the thump of our blood."[1] In writing this book, tracing the deep history of the South and my ancestors' fraught relationship to both its original inhabitants and those my people held in bondage, I am also seeking to map my own deep and conflicted history as a southerner. William Zinsser has said that "writing is how we think our way into a subject and make it our own. Writing enables us to find out what we know—and what we don't know—about whatever we're trying to learn."[2] This observation seems especially apt when writing a deep history of one's own origins. I write because I love this land, its rivers, forests, and pastures, its foothills, and its mountains. I write to remember, for memory is always another form of imagination by which we can reenter the past. I write to travel back in time, to listen to voices long silenced. I write because my history—southern history—is haunted, and it is time to meet the ghosts that haunt it. Being haunted is another name for writing. I write in the hope of connecting with other southerners who also love our land, our history, and yet choose to name and face the whole truth of our past for the sake of justice and healing in our future. I write hoping that in some small way I may be able to detoxify the groundwaters of our collective culture. I write to honor my grandparents and all of my ancestors behind them by owning all that they represent. I write to bear witness to Southern history. I write to heal the family tree. So let us begin.

For century upon century a great nation thrived in the Southern Appalachian Mountains. They called themselves the *Ani-Yun-Wiya*, meaning the original or principal people. Known as the Cherokee, they

1. Least Heat-Moon, *Prairyerth*, 273.
2. Zinsser, *Writing to Learn*, 16.

inhabited a homeland that included thriving villages, abundant agricultural fields, a network of trading paths, and vast hunting grounds across what is now upstate South Carolina, western North Carolina, northern Georgia, southwestern Virginia, and eastern Tennessee. European explorers—Spanish, French, and English alike—encountered a nation rooted in its own history, inhabiting a vast homeland, connected by a common culture, united by strong bonds of kinship that held them together and made them a people. Over the centuries of their encounter with Europeans, waves of conquest washed over the Cherokee Nation and provoked their resistance. In the course of this book, we will examine various dimensions of this history of conquest and resistance:

- The Doctrine of Discovery laid a theological foundation for the conquest of Indigenous peoples, first articulated by the church, and encoded politically by colonial powers as a rationale for empire-building.
- The next wave of conquest was spread through the ravages of epidemic disease that reduced the Cherokee population by more than half.
- Another wave of conquest was met by the Cherokee in the assaults on their culture as they struggled with the impact of colonial capitalism on their political economy.
- Wars of conquest were launched against the Cherokee nation destroying villages and further displacing people.
- The civilization project envisioned by the founding fathers of the new American nation was designed to ensure that the only way the Indian could survive was to cease to be an Indian. Christian missionaries among the Cherokee consciously contributed to the erosion of Cherokee identity.
- Treaty after treaty demonstrated the sole purpose of US policy toward the Cherokee Nation was to dispossess them of their land.
- Finally, these successive waves of conquest culminated in the brutal dispossession of the Cherokee and all the "civilized" tribes from their homeland on a forced march that killed thousands that has now become known as the Trail of Tears. My Scots Irish ancestors participated in this conquest.
- Dispossession of Native peoples proceeded across the continent hand in hand with the consolidation of slavery and the advancement of the plantation economy. Therefore it is imperative to address how these two narratives are interwoven.

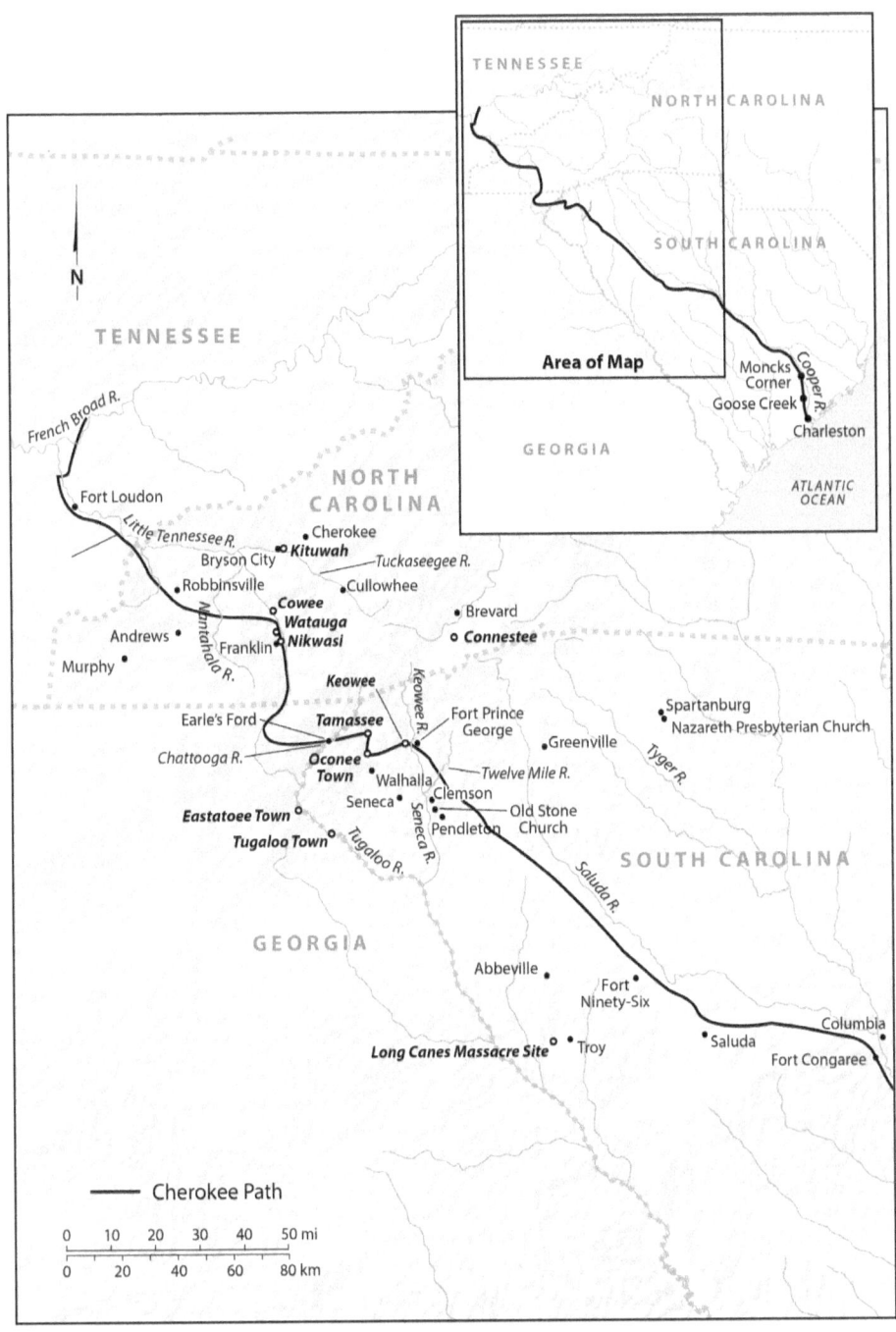

Contemporary Map Including Cherokee Path
Courtesy of Bill Nelson of Bill Nelson Maps with special thanks to Dennis Chastain

Introduction

THE KEOWEE TRAIL

THE CENTRAL FACT AND metaphor of this story is the Keowee Trail: the long, winding path that connected colonial Charles Town on the coast of South Carolina to Keowee, the mother town of the Lower Towns of the Cherokee Nation. The Keowee Trail or, as it is now more commonly known by historians, the Cherokee Path, served as a conduit for a burgeoning deerskin trade between the colony and the Cherokee. Following that path, colonial traders arrived to establish trading posts to facilitate a commercial exchange that would utterly transform the Cherokee Nation. These traders sometimes married Cherokee women, creating interracial family bonds. And tragically, epidemic disease also made its way up the trail, depopulating Cherokee communities in devastating waves of suffering and death. The Cherokee were—and are—a sovereign nation with whom my ancestors and people like them fought a total war, destroying their way of life and displacing them from their homeland. I want to bear witness to what I have learned about the colonial history of up-country South Carolina in this increasingly conflictual encounter between the original inhabitants and settlers like my Anderson ancestors.

The dispossession of Native Americans was the prelude to the extension of the plantation economy across the southeast. I intend to point out the ways in which my ancestors may have related to enslaved African workers and helped consolidate the institution of slavery and its spread across the South. But in the scope of this book, my treatment of slavery will be only preliminary at best. In a less sustained way, I will begin to trace the experience of enslaved African Americans because dispossession of Native peoples was closely followed by the plantation economy and the institution of slavery especially in the southern colonies. I hope to undertake a more thorough reckoning in a second volume to follow this one using my family history as an entryway into the emergence of slavery, the Civil War, and Reconstruction. A more complete treatment of slavery and my ancestors' involvement in enslaving African Americans will have to wait for a hoped-for volume two.

In his book *Unworthy Republic,* the historian Claudio Saunt asserts that the period of the Civil War and Reconstruction, though delayed, incomplete, and ambiguous at best, provided at least some kind of historical reckoning in the US with the legacy of slavery. But he notes that, sadly, there has been no similar reckoning with the conquest of Native peoples and little serious reflection on its centrality to the rise of our nation. White descendants of European settlers have had only minimal sustained engagement with the peoples who lost their homelands. This, Saunt claims, is the war the enslavers won. In this volume, we will further utilize Saunt's historical perspective to understand this war the enslavers won.

This story of my Anderson ancestors will include their initial settlement in colonial Carolina and their participation in the conflicts engendered by the American Revolution in a violent struggle between the revolutionaries and those loyal to the British Crown. This struggle for independence was a crisis for all those who inhabited Carolina, whatever their race. The years beyond the American Revolution utterly transformed the Cherokee Nation, leading up to their almost complete dispossession from their homeland in 1838, in what is remembered as the Trail of Tears.

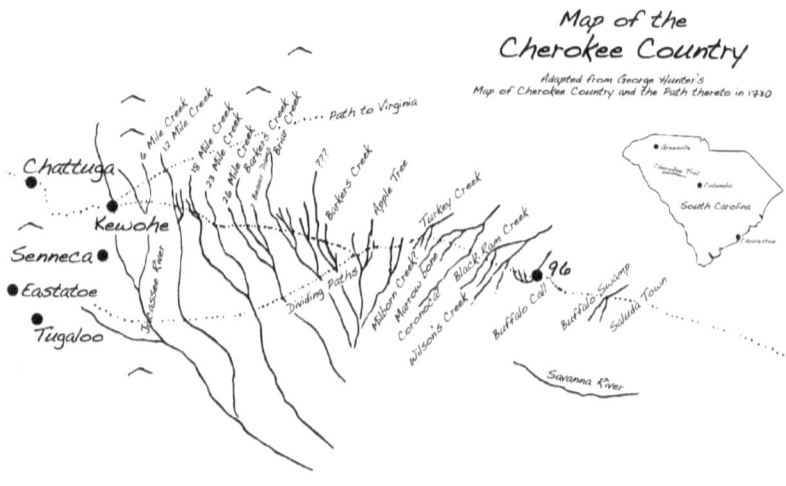

Cherokee Path[1]

1. From the South Caroliniana Library, University of South Carolina, Columbia, South Carolina. https://core.ac.uk/download/pdf/49236868.pdf.

THE DEEP MAP

I will approach this complex story through what William Least Heat-Moon describes as a "deep map": a way of exploring a historical time and space using multiple venues and vantage points, interweaving memoir and biography, stories and memories, folklore, art, photography, actual maps, and museum artifacts, as well as archeology and natural history. I first learned of the concept of deep mapping from the Cherokee scholar Deborah Kirk in a workshop at the 2022 Trail of Tears Conference in Cherokee, North Carolina. She described a deep map as an open-ended act of remembering a multi-layered landscape—an approach she believes is the most effective and collaborative way that the Cherokee people and their allies can tell the story of the Trail of Tears. That deep map is also the best image I have found to describe my own approach and purpose. My point of departure for this narrative is a literal map from colonial South Carolina, drawn in 1730 by George Hunter, depicting the Keowee Trail. This map traces what was known then as the Cherokee trading path that led from colonial Charles Town, on the South Carolina coast, to Keowee in the Appalachian foothills and on beyond into the mountainous heartland of the Cherokee Nation.

The deep map of many layers and perspectives that I will draw here will include elements of personal memoir as I share the story of my family. Beginning with my grandparents and their formative influence on me, I trace the history of the Anderson family: my Scots Irish ancestors who migrated to America in the mid-eighteenth century. Interwoven with that story is the history of two Presbyterian churches that my ancestors established and the role these congregations played in shaping the culture of the colonial up-country. I will also weave a portrait of the encounter between Scots Irish settlers like my ancestors and the Cherokee Nation, beginning in the colonial period of the mid-eighteenth century and moving through the American Revolution and the early nineteenth century, the period of Indian removal. Finally, as an integral dimension of this deep map approach, I will recount moments of my own journey of discovery along the Cherokee Path, at destinations where Indigenous communities existed or significant events occurred, in a trail journal interspersed throughout this narrative.

MY SCOTS IRISH ANCESTORS

In 1761, my ancestors William and Rebecca Anderson were members of a group of Scots Irish Presbyterian families who left Pennsylvania and began the long journey down the Great Wagon Road, through the Shenandoah Valley and into the Carolinas. Finally settling in the South Carolina up-country frontier, they would claim and occupy land that had long been recognized as Cherokee territory. Prior to their arrival, colonial South Carolina military forces had launched a series of devastating scorched-earth invasions of the Lower Towns of the Cherokee Nation, seizing more of their lands for further settlement. Grappling with my Anderson family history provides a complex historical perspective on Scots Irish migration, the mythology of settler identity, and the evolving conflicts between settlers and the Cherokee Nation.

I got my love of history from my grandfather, John Stuart Taylor Sr. (I am J. Stuart Taylor III), but the genetic heritage and bloodline of my Anderson ancestors came to me from my grandmother, Hazael Gilreath Taylor. It was through her that I am descended from the Andersons. Both her mother, Maria Jane Anderson, and her father, Jefferson Davis Gilreath, came from Scots Irish families that arrived in the Carolinas in the early to mid-eighteenth century. From their union, five daughters were born: Mary, the eldest, then my grandmother Hazael, followed by Jane, Elizabeth, and Earline. Here, briefly, is my lineage:

- William Anderson: 1706–1785, Married Rebecca Denny
- Major David Anderson: August 25, 1741 (Pennsylvania)–May 30, 1827, Married Miriam Mayson
- James Mason Anderson (Tyger Jim): January 28, 1784–June 24, 1870, Married Mary Polly Miller
- William Washington Anderson: April 14, 1819 (Spartanburg, South Carolina)–December 23, 1895, Married Jane Cauble
- Maria Worthington Anderson: April 11, 1868 (Greenville, South Carolina)–January 16, 1955, Married Jefferson Davis Gilreath
- Hazael Earl Gilreath: February 14, 1892 (Greenville, South Carolina)–January 10, 1975, Married John Stuart Taylor
- John Stuart Taylor Jr.: January 25, 1924 (Greenville, South Carolina)–November 9, 1997, Married Mary Stuart Hatch
- John Stuart Taylor III: July 23, 1954 (Greenville, South Carolina)

Because my Anderson ancestors were Scots Irish Presbyterians, my family history is inextricably woven into the story of the Presbyterian Church in the history of South Carolina. But it is not necessary to be a Presbyterian, or even a person of faith, to interact with this story. (Whether or not you hold to a faith tradition, to get to the bottom of American history, it will prove necessary to grapple with the historical role of the Christian church in its complicity in the conquest of Native peoples.) My ancestors are buried in the graveyards of two Presbyterian congregations that feature prominently in this story. The first, Nazareth Presbyterian Church in Spartanburg County, is associated with my grandmother's Anderson ancestors. The other, about fifty-seven miles west, was once known as Hopewell Keowee, but is now just called the Old Stone Church. This was the congregation later relocated to the village of Pendleton, where my grandfather was baptized and raised in the faith, and where both my grandparents are buried. I want to examine the attitudes among my Presbyterians forebears toward the racial other, whether that be the Cherokee Indians or the enslaved Africans brought in just as Natives were being pushed out.

Since 1896, Anderson family reunions have been held every few years at Nazareth Presbyterian Church. As these kinfolks have gathered for picnics on the grounds, they have been surrounded by our Anderson ancestors who lie in the ancient graveyard all around them. My great-grandmother, Maria Worthington Anderson Gilreath, attended the Anderson reunion at Nazareth on August 21, 1954, just a little less than a month after I was born. At seventy-two, she was the oldest member of the family in attendance. She died six months later, on January 16, 1955, at her home on Mill Rocks. At that same reunion, Edward Lee Anderson was commissioned to write an updated history of the Andersons. Published the following year as *A History of the Anderson Family 1706–1955*, it is an essential resource for the historical and genealogical information I draw on.

One of my earliest memories, however faint, is of going to those Anderson family reunions. I recently returned there with my sister and cousin for the first time in decades to view the interior of the old church and to see if we could locate those ancestral graves. Our search through the graveyard was rewarded on that hot June day. From a white gravestone we read: "In memory of William Anderson and his wife Rebecca, the former of whom was born in 1706 and was murdered by a party of Tories near the end of the Revolution. The latter was born in 1710 and died in 1809. Erected by their affectionate daughter." In another section of the graveyard, we found the gravestones of "Tyger" Jim Anderson and his wife Polly. Tyger Jim, so named for living on the Tyger River, was distinguished from his cousin "Enoree" Jim, who lived on the Enoree River. Tyger Jim and Polly were my great-great-great-great-grandparents.

Family Reunion

Nazareth Presbyterian Church, Spartanburg County, South Carolina

INTRODUCTION 7

William Anderson Grave

Tyger Jim

The stories of these ancestors are all, in themselves, historically fascinating. But what I seek to do here is more than documenting an interesting family history. There are countless amateur genealogists doing that work, and I understand their curiosity and enthusiasm for knowing more about their family histories. But even as I recount the migration story of my Scots Irish forebears with some measure of ethnic pride and admiration for their courage and determination, I would not be telling the whole story if I stopped there. My narrative concerns not just those Presbyterians who settled in South Carolina but also the Cherokee people with whom they coexisted. Cherokee history is, after all, American history. This story will describe the interactions between my Scots Irish ancestors with the Cherokee Nation and consider the impacts of that prolonged encounter.

It is not my role to tell the Cherokee story. But it is my responsibility to recount how the history of my ancestors affected that story. This deep map of the colonial history of the Carolinas leads to a reckoning with the destructive legacy of settler colonialism that resulted not only in the dispossession of the Cherokee from their land but also in the advancement of slavery and the exploitation of African people as enslaved workers. In the context of one family history, I am seeking to come to terms with the white supremacy that underlies not only the history of the South Carolina up-country but the entire narrative of American history.

INHERITING MY GRANDFATHER'S LOVE OF HISTORY

The man who was my grandfather is present in me as I felt his father to always be present in him. You work your way down into the interior of the present until finally you come to the beginning. —WENDELL BERRY

My grandfather, John S. Taylor Sr.—or Poppy, as his grandchildren called him—was a lover of history, not credentialed by academic degrees but serving his community as public historian. Only gradually did I become aware of the scope of his work to commemorate Cherokee history. We have a Kodak snapshot of him from 1935 on an outdoor podium surrounded by listeners as he spoke at the dedication of a historical marker commemorating the site of the Cherokee village of Keowee. Across from the village site on the Keowee River was the British colonial outpost Fort Prince George. From an archive of my grandfather's papers, I have the transcript of the talk he gave that day, which we will consider in due course. I also found there a copy of a 1730 map of the Keowee Trail created by George Hunter, the surveyor for the colony of South Carolina, that traces the Cherokee Path from Charles Town to Keowee, the principal village of the Lower Towns of the Cherokee Nation.

Since my earliest years I have been fascinated by the history of the Cherokee people. As a boy, I was enthralled with my grandfather's collection of Native artifacts, which included pipes, bowls, arrowheads, and spear points gathered from across the Carolinas and Georgia. (It needs to be said that these kinds of collections are frowned upon today.) While hiking and camping in the more mountainous areas of the Carolinas, I became interested in the specific locations of Cherokee settlements. I pored over maps that showed where these towns might have been. Like so many southern boys, I had a longing to have lived in ages past. And to this day I have that incurable nostalgia of the lover of history who wishes he could travel back in time and know the Cherokee then.

Over the years, I read various histories of the Cherokee, each filling out in growing detail a sense of their story and culture. It was the voice of Swimmer, a Cherokee elder interviewed by the anthropologist James Mooney for his classic *Myths of the Cherokee*, that most vividly revealed to me the identity of this people that I so admire. Swimmer eluded capture during Cherokee removal and the Trail of Tears. Learning the Cherokee syllabary, he began to record in his notebooks the sacred stories, rituals, and traditional practices of his people. He was recognized by his tribe as a shaman, healer, and keeper of tradition. In 1887, when the Smithsonian Institution sent Mooney to document Cherokee life, the ethnologist came to rely on Swimmer as his primary source. When Swimmer died at the age of sixty-five, Mooney declared that half of the knowledge of Cherokee tradition died with him. Perhaps Swimmer understood the necessity of his partnership with Mooney in preserving the traditions of his people for posterity. I am grateful that he did.

THE BURIED PAST

I have seen a letter my grandfather wrote to the editor of my hometown's newspaper, the *Greenville News*, opposing the plans of Duke Energy to build a dam and flood the Keowee River basin, inundating Keowee and the very heart of the Lower Towns of the Cherokee. He was horrified at the idea of covering countless historical treasures under what would become the Lake Keowee watershed system. But his and others' protestations were never heeded. Archeologists were allowed only a year to do a rushed excavation of Keowee and Fort Prince George prior to the flooding. Today, this historic and beautiful valley lies beneath Lake Keowee, a portion of the vast Hartwell Reservoir. The granite marker to Keowee that my grandfather dedicated in 1935 was moved to a higher ridge above the lake in 1972.

All that history being submerged under water somehow symbolizes to me the willful forgetting that has buried the violent history of my home state in its early relations with the Cherokee. In an essay in a wonderful collection of reflections on William Bartram's legacy, John Lane, a well-known South Carolina naturalist, writes of his own sense of grief about Keowee. Bartram was a botanist who in 1775 explored and documented wilderness areas of the southeast. His journal of his observations about the Cherokee and the flora and fauna of the region as he journeyed up the Keowee Trail is one of the great classics of American literature, and we will return to it soon.

In his essay on Bartram, "Keowee," Lane recalls kayaking around Lake Keowee and grieving that "the old colonial fort has been lost under 200 feet of reservoir water" for decades.[2] The beautiful mountain vistas Bartram saw were still largely available to Lane, but he mourned for the vanished valley of the Keowee River: "I have privileged the past over the present. After all, isn't Lake Keowee a typical engineered/manufactured reservoir that's drowned a good river for utility, boondoggle, profit or all three?" As seen by Bartram and the few today who fervently wish to imagine it, "the Keowee River flowed through what was possibly the most beautiful river valley in the South." As Lane paddles his kayak around this part of the lake that engulfed Keowee and Fort Prince George, he reads Bartram's description of the Keowee vale as a "most charming situation . . . through which the beautiful river meanders, sometimes gently flowing, but more frequently agitated." The mountains beyond Bartram's gaze are "lofty, superb, misty and blue."[3] This is the physical setting of Keowee and the Lower Towns of the Cherokee Nation. I am certain that my grandfather shared this sentiment of "privileging the past over the

2. Lane, "Keowee," 382.
3. Lane, "Keowee," 388.

present" and felt great sadness for what was lost when the Keowee valley was drowned.

THE *KEOWEE TRAIL PAGEANT* OF 1921: A HISTORICAL PERFORMANCE

My grandfather was also the primary historian for a historical pageant performed in my hometown of Greenville on the weekend of November 8 in 1921: *Keowee Trail Pageant*. In our possession is an old pageant program some sixty pages long. Janie Gilreath, my great-aunt, had a starring role and served on the production committee. My grandfather, her brother-in-law, was on the history committee, and both served on the executive committee. From faded and crumbling newspaper articles of the *Greenville News* we learned that some 35,000 people came to the Greenville Fairgrounds to see this outdoor drama celebrating the settler history of South Carolina. The *Keowee Trail Pageant* involved hundreds upon hundreds of cast members and volunteer supporters, drawn from a wide range of community groups from all over a wide seven-county area. I take great pride in my family's part in remembering local history, but it is important to give the full truth of that history. Later, we will take a longer look at the *Keowee Trail Pageant* of 1921 and consider how it fell short of that truth.

When I began this writing project, I originally intended that the story of my Anderson ancestors and the early settler history of South Carolina would compose the first chapter of a family history that would trace the development of slavery on to the Civil War and Reconstruction, and beyond into the twentieth century and to the civil rights movement. The Anderson story refused to remain a chapter and grew into a book. Once that story is told, I can turn back to the other ancestors' stories especially as that history relates to the enslavement of African people. I want to immerse myself further in largely unexplored moments in my family history as my ancestors related to the racial other.

You see, my grandfather not only introduced me to Cherokee history, he also instilled in me early on a fascination for Civil War history by telling me stories of what he called the "Northern war of aggression against the Southern states for independence." When I went off to first grade, my grandfather donated a Confederate flag to the school. I will never forget a school-wide assembly at the flagpole as I raised that flag standing beside my grandfather. I owe a great deal to my grandfather for the love of history that he instilled in me. But that is not his only legacy to me, for he also introduced me to the ideology of the Lost Cause of the Confederacy, and deeper still, imprinted on me the racism of southern culture. My grandfather was a racist as almost every white who grew up in South Carolina had to be at some level. I do not say this about him as a condemnation, but only as a statement of fact. This legacy of racism of course did not begin with him but had deeper roots going to the very beginnings of American history. Exploring my family history seems to be one way to begin to dismantle the racism in my life and in the surrounding culture.

I intend to wrestle with my own history to bring greater clarity and truth to the way my ancestors and I have been involved in the oppression and suffering of those they regarded as the racial other. Revelations are springing from this process, and some are encouraging and life-giving. Others make me wonder how I could have lived so long and understood so little. My hope is that this effort sparks further conversation and inquiry. Maybe there are others who will be encouraged to dig into their own family history and grapple with the questions they discover there. I am sure that I will continue to need the critical insights of others to enlarge my view of our shared history.

I write of my family history in the hope that all our stories, as difficult and ambiguous as they are, will ultimately lead us to a more truthful reckoning—a truth-telling that owns all our history: the good, the ambiguous, the not so good, and the outright evil. May the truth-telling found here be one small contribution to the crafting of a larger national story that may lead us one day toward an America that fulfills the promise of the Declaration of Independence: a genuinely multiracial democracy, what Dr. King called the "Beloved Community."

FOLLOWING THE KEOWEE TRAIL

I am grateful to Dennis Chastain, a well-known South Carolina naturalist who is also a charismatic storyteller, historian, and local legend, for taking it upon himself to document the exact route of the Cherokee Path from Charleston to Keowee. He and his wife Jane, who devoted themselves over many years to locating traces of the original trail, kindly showed me some of those they have documented. Their quest took on a serendipitous quality as leads emerged and they discovered new contacts along the way. Using Hunter's map of the Keowee Trail and another drawn by Henry Mouzon in 1775, they carefully followed the route of the Cherokee Path from King Street in Charles Town, through the Cooper River watershed, past Goose Creek to Monk's Corner to Eutaw Springs, past the Santee Indian Mound near I-95. The path they discovered continues northwest, across the sand hills of the middle state into the more rolling foothills of the South Carolina up-country. Dennis points out with delight the genius of a trail that managed to skirt several major river systems without having to ford any of them. Throughout this story, I have included sections entitled "Trail Journal" that share some of my personal experiences in my pilgrimage along this trail.

If we were able to travel back in time to walk the Keowee Trail in the 1750s, what would we discover? With Hunter's map in hand, we would follow the path from colonial Charles Town on the coast, across the colony and into the Lower Towns of the Cherokee Nation, which stretched across the northwest corner of South Carolina. You will find the map included in this volume. Using Hunter's map as our main guide, we will walk the Keowee Trail together. But first, I need to describe to you where this journey began in earnest for me.

1

Five Centuries of Indigenous Resistance to the European Conquest of North America

My grandfather planted the seed of a love of history in me and a pride in our ancestors' stories. But my early fascination with family history seemed to be little more than the sort of avocation that hits some in later life. Over the years my curiosity about my ancestors waxed and waned, and even fell dormant, as I pursued my education and career as a Presbyterian minister. But through all those years I never lost the persistent dream that I would some day write my family's story. The love of history my grandfather had planted deeply in my soul was always there, growing, until finally in 1992, during the five hundredth anniversary of Columbus's "discovery" of America, it sprouted and came to fruition.

I found myself in Washington, DC, with the opportunity to pursue a new vocational role somewhat like my grandfather's: as a self-appointed public historian not credentialed by any academic institution but committed to doing popular education about American history. My faith, my passion for justice, and my love of history converged and unleashed in me a sense of being called to a new purpose. During the Columbus quincentenary in 1992, many in our country wanted to celebrate one version of American history that allegedly began with Columbus "discovering" America, bringing civilization to a great wilderness and Christianity to savage peoples. To the theologian Ched Myers, it seemed in this moment that America was a "nation of amnesiacs"[1] who had willfully forgotten so much of our history. Many of us felt a moral compulsion to challenge this

1. Myers, *Who Will Roll Away*, 113.

forgetting, to remember what has happened in our nation's history and how it shapes our present reality in harmful ways.

What we envisioned for the quincentenary would be more like the Truth and Reconciliation Commissions established in countries like South Africa and Guatemala, where governments had inflicted widespread violence, even genocide, on people living on the margins of power. The truth and reconciliation process provided opportunities to reckon with the past, allowing the victims and witnesses of violence to tell the truth of what had happened, and forcing the perpetuators to experience some measure of public accountability. But a truth and reconciliation commission was the furthest thing from the minds of those officials planning the Columbus quincentenary. The premise of the celebration, we believed, totally erased the view from the shore: the perspective of countless Indigenous peoples who were devastated by the European invasion. The quincentenary festivities also ignored the agony of African peoples who were kidnapped and enslaved to provide labor for European colonization in the Americas.

A few historians like Howard Zinn inspired a generation of historians to write from the perspective of a "Peoples' History." We were a small movement of popular educators who sought to use the quincentenary to reinterpret American history from the perspective of its impact on Native Americans and African Americans. It offered an opportunity to pull back the great veil of denial that lay over the story of the American nation, a collective moment ripe for calling the attention of the nation to the enslavement and dispossession that have been integral to the story of this country. It was a chance to begin the work of naming the enormous wounds to the human family that had not yet been examined, learned from, mourned over, atoned for, or healed.

THE DOCTRINE OF DISCOVERY

As we plunged into this history, we learned that greed alone does not fully explain the driving force behind the European conquest of the Native peoples of the Americas or the enslavement of Africans. In the fourteenth and fifteenth centuries, various popes of the Roman Catholic Church, exercising their authority over the nation states of Europe, issued a series of decrees establishing the legal framework for the laws of nations. These decrees provided a veneer of legality for European rulers to claim all unoccupied lands their emissaries discovered around the globe. With supreme authority, the church established the right of European states to seize, explore, and occupy lands not already claimed by other European states.

The church directed these earliest pronouncements eastward toward the Muslim world to provide the rationale for the Crusades and the subjugation and enslavement of the Muslim "Saracens" as enemies of the church. Awful as they were, the centuries-long Crusades launched against the Middle East amounted to a dress rehearsal for the westward expansion of Europeans into the Americas. These decrees also applied to peoples of the continent of Africa who, according to church law, were legally nonpersons, rightfully enslaved by European Christians.

All this laid the foundation for the Doctrine of Discovery—the theological rationale and ideological foundation for the African slave trade and for the conquest of Native peoples in the Americas. As nonpersons in European terms, Africans and Native Americans had no legal standing or rights that needed to be respected. Their labor, their freedom, and their lands were Europe's for the taking. The Doctrine of Discovery underlies the cultural assumptions that prevail when white Americans speak of Columbus "discovering" America. But this misperception is simply the tip of the iceberg. The Doctrine of Discovery continues to function even today as the legal foundation that defines the shape of international law, making it difficult, if not impossible, for Indigenous people to uphold their rights.[2]

---

2. The Presbyterian Church renounced the Doctrine of Discovery. In 2016, the General Assembly of the Presbyterian Church (the national decision-making body that convenes every two years) adopted a faith statement repudiating the Doctrine of Discovery. The statement reviewed the history of the Doctrine and its descent from Catholic Church teaching into international secular law.

This resolution adopted by the Presbyterian General Assembly calls for a basic spiritual practice for all gatherings of Presbyterians to simply acknowledge whose land this once was. The resolution called for an educational strategy about the Doctrine of Discovery within the overall anti-racism mission and programs of the PCUSA (Presbyterian Church of the USA).

As I write this, Pope Francis, whom I greatly admire and respect, has just completed what he has called a "penitential pilgrimage" to Canada in order to dialogue with Indigenous peoples there about the cultural genocide that forced thousands of Native children into Catholic boarding schools, where they were systematically abused. During this papal visit, numerous Indigenous leaders called for the pope to renounce the Doctrine of Discovery, asking him if he understood how it helped justify the genocide of Native Americans. When asked if he would formally repudiate the Doctrine, he replied, shockingly, that he needed the phrase explained. In the wake of his visit, there was disappointment that he had not rejected the Doctrine clearly and forcefully.

As we pursued these historical reorientations, one of the most helpful resources we found was a controversial exhibit and publication the Smithsonian Institution produced called *The West as America*.[3] It catalogs and interprets countless American paintings, including those in our Capitol Rotunda, which taken together construct a version of the history of the United States that must be carefully deconstructed if we are to overcome the erasure of Native peoples from our history. The five paintings in the Rotunda that I want to focus on here include *The Departure of Columbus*, painted by Emmanuel Leutze in 1855; John Vanderlyn's *The Landing of Columbus* (1836); *The Baptism of Pocahontas at Jamestown, Virginia* by John Gadsby Chapman (1840); *The Embarkation of the Pilgrims* by Robert Weir (1843); and *Discovery of the Mississippi* by William H. Powell (1853).

The Departure of Columbus[4]

The *National Catholic Reporter* decried the failure of the pope's advisors to adequately brief him on the concerns and issues he was likely to face in conversation with Canadian Indigenous leaders. Months later the Vatican did in fact repudiate the Doctrine of Discovery.

3. We can well understand why *The West as America* provoked controversy, but efforts to present these images as windows into the American story offered highly effective educational consciousness-raising. I commend to you the publication *The West as America*, which is still available, and encourage all visual learners like me to look up some of these paintings and reflect on what they tell us about Native Americans and white civilization.

4. *The Departure of Columbus*, by Emmanuel Leutze, 1855; https://philaprintshop.

Discovery of the Mississippi[5]

American Progress[6]

com/products/vanderlyn-john-the-landing-of-columbus-from-the-original-painting-in-the-rotunda--the-capitol-washington-d-c.

5. *Discovery of the Mississippi*, by William H. Powell, 1853. https://www.aoc.gov/explore-capitol-campus/art/discovery-mississippi-de-soto.

6. *American Progress*, by John Gast, 1872.

THE CAPITOL ROTUNDA: THE TEMPLE OF THE NATION

The National Picture Gallery, viewed by some three million visitors to the Capitol each year, depicts the dominant national story. Four portray Washington and the American Revolution. The other five suggest in equally formative ways the emerging identity of a nation. In *The Departure of Columbus*, painted by Leutze in 1855, the brave, heroic posture of the explorer, pointing westward beyond the ocean, conveys his Christ-like willingness to sacrifice himself as a martyr to the great end of discovering America. Next is Vanderlyn's *Landing of Columbus*, which projects the explorer's right to discover and conquer the New World. The *Discovery of the Mississippi* by William H. Powell (1853) depicts the brutal conquistador De Soto on horseback, parading through a village of awestruck Indians. De Soto's supporting cast of priests and soldiers suggest that if conversion to Christianity falters, military might will prevail. The *Embarkation of the Pilgrims* by Robert Weir (1843) and finally the *Baptism of Pocahontas at Jamestown, Virginia* by John Gadsby Chapman (1840) are less concerned with conquest and more focused on the divine will at work behind the creation of our nation and the construction of a national civic religion.

Other famous paintings in the exhibit include one by George Caleb Bingham (1851) portraying Daniel Boone leading a group of settlers through the Cumberland Gap, the gateway to progress, like a Moses leading the Israelites out of Egypt. Another genre summarized in a section of the exhibit called "American Expansion, Indian Doom" is epitomized in Tompkins H. Matteson's melancholy painting *The Last of His Race* (1847): a tribal elder at the center "surrounded by his family, stands at land's end, contemplating the ominous procession of clouds on the horizon"[7] that suggest his inevitable demise. The disappearance of Indians is the preordained predicate for the advance of white civilization.

Perhaps the message of all these paintings is best captured in one painting by John Gast (1872) entitled *American Progress*. A beautiful woman, floating through the air, bears on her forehead the "Star of Empire." She carries a book in one hand, perhaps representing the Bible or knowledge or both. In the crook of her arm is a ring of telegraph wire that descends to the land below, adorning a line of telegraph poles that will one day connect the American coasts. Alongside the poles are wagon trains, stagecoaches, and several railroads advancing westward bathed in

---

7. Truettner, *West as America*, 169.

the light of dawn. In the foreground, groups of settlers, both farmers and miners, advance westward beneath the "Spirit of Progress." But not all will share in the bounty of advancing civilization. Fleeing the light of dawn in the east into the still shrouded darkness of the west are Indians and wildlife, the vestiges of a savage past. Let's take a closer look at the historical truth that lies behind these paintings by examining the career of the first European to "discover" the southeast: Hernando de Soto.

THE SPANISH CONQUISTADOR DE SOTO

Forty-seven years after the first voyage of Columbus to the Americas, the Spanish conquistador Hernando de Soto came to the Southeast. Before landing in North America in 1539, he had led the conquest of Native peoples in Panama and Nicaragua and then, in the expeditions under Pizarro, participated in the conquest of the Incan Empire in the Andean highlands of South America. It boggles the imagination that the career of one conquistador could distribute such widespread suffering across the hemisphere of the Americas. When De Soto finally brought his gold-greed and war-making expertise to the North American southeast, he deployed a tried-and-true method of conquest: extortion. Repeatedly, he and his expedition would march aggressively into a village and take its leaders hostage, releasing them only in exchange for massive tribute and subjugation.

Queen Cofitalchiqui, Hernando De Soto, and the Depredations of Conquest

This is exactly the tactic De Soto used on May 1, 1540, when he approached the Indigenous people near what is today Camden, South Carolina. Their sovereign queen was called Cofitalchiqui, a name interchangeable with the identity of the people as a tribe. Indigenous women in the history of the Americas have always occupied a highly vulnerable space, situated at the contested boundary between colonial conquest and Native resistance. This has been a pattern of conquest since Cortez invaded Tenochtitlan and kidnapped Malinche, the Aztec noble who became his interpreter and consort—or sexual slave. Malinche is seen in Mexican history as a tragic figure who seemingly betrayed her people and facilitated their conquest by aiding Cortez—though her agency in that situation of subjugation was obviously constricted. The same might be said of Cofitalchiqui.

Hearing of the approaching Spanish expedition, Cofitalchiqui sent messengers to De Soto with gifts and assurances of welcome. Crossing a river in a royal canoe to meet them, she was, according to Spanish accounts, a beautiful and gracious monarch. She presented De Soto with long strings of pearls, which she placed around his neck, inviting him to come to join her as her guest in her primary town, with its temple mounds and impressive palace. (I was able to climb one such ceremonial mound from this period that still stands on the Santee River just off I-95. In an instance of the very colonization we are considering, this site is known today as the Fort Watson Historical Landmark because the British built a fort on top of the mound during the Revolutionary War.)

As the Spaniards explored the area searching for treasure, they were struck by outlying settlements situated in fertile agricultural fields that had been abandoned. Epidemics had already cut a wide swath through Indigenous populations on the Atlantic Seaboard. The queen herself told De Soto of this attrition, apologizing that her people were unable to provide more substantial provisions because population loss had diminished their farming capacity. Disappointed by the lack of gold and treasure, De Soto set off again on his savage quest. Though the queen had been remarkably generous in her dealings with the Spanish, "providing them food from the meager stores available in her plague-ridden country and even acquiescing when they asked to ransack her nation's temples in search of pearls,"[8] De Soto showed his gratitude by taking her captive and placing her under armed guard. She remained a prisoner for weeks until finally escaping near the western border of her domain in the French Broad watershed of western North Carolina, near today's Asheville. According to Spanish chroniclers, her escape was assisted by the enslaved Native who the Spanish believed had become her lover.

De Soto's Route through the Southeast

Historians and archeologists have for decades sought to determine the precise route De Soto took through the Carolinas. Early on, some speculated that he went directly through the Cherokee Nation by way of Keowee. Subsequent research has debunked that theory, suggesting a

---

8. Duncan, *Savage Quest*, 343.

more easterly route that may have carried his expedition northward to present day Hickory, North Carolina, and then westward toward present day Asheville. If this was indeed the route, it would have been less impactful for the ancestors of the Cherokee. De Soto would have passed around their mountain homeland, skirting the Overhill Towns in what is now eastern Tennessee. However, the Spanish expeditionary force, driving herds of pig and cattle as sources of food, undoubtedly introduced disease to the areas where they traveled.

De Soto descended into the Deep South, spreading disease and devastation as he went, until he eventually reached the Mississippi and met his own death at the hands of Native warriors. It would be another twenty-six years before another Spanish conquistador, Juan Pardo, would return to this land. A Spanish helmet found in a cornfield in Spartanburg County, South Carolina, was believed to be left behind by this expedition. In 1936, the so-called Pardo Stone was also found in a field in Spartanburg, inscribed with the date 1567. Juan Pardo would crisscross the Piedmont and mountains of the Carolinas until finally building a fort, Presidio San Juan, near what is now Morganton, North Carolina. After a couple of years of what was surely a tenuous coexistence, local tribes wearied of Spanish presence, attacked the fort, and wiped out the garrison. But Juan Pardo during his travels across South Carolina would encounter no great cities populated by the people of Cofitalchiqui. This civilization had already disappeared.[9]

Europe for centuries had been a breeding ground for epidemic disease as the continent experienced plague after plague that wiped out vast numbers of people. Over time, Europeans had developed, if not herd immunity, at least a functional resistance to these diseases. Native Americans had none. Estimates of the Indigenous population in North America prior to contact with Europeans range widely. James Mooney was the first to offer a population estimate of 1.15 million Native people in North America, and because of his reputation, others venturing estimates cleaved closely to his. Population estimates since Mooney have risen dramatically, approaching ten million in North America. After the ravages of epidemic disease introduced by Europeans, the mortality rate for Native populations could have been as high as 90 percent. The scale of the depopulation of Native peoples on the Atlantic Seaboard even prior to established European settlements and initial contact with explorers

---

9. Duncan, *Savage Quest*, 340.

and traders is easier to imagine today than it has ever been as we have coped with a global pandemic that has killed millions and remains an ever-present threat. Turn with me now from this broad introduction to zoom in on my family history and their migration journey from the British Isles to North America.

2

Celtic Origins and the Migration Journey of My Scots Irish Ancestors

WE ENTER AN ANCIENT story with no clear beginning and no end yet in sight. It is the year 100 CE. A Roman sentry, shivering in the cold, is looking out from a fortified wall beyond the boundaries of the Roman Empire. He is gazing toward the wild hinterlands of unconquered territory that centuries later would be called Scotland. The sentry, having come from a warm Mediterranean climate to this freezing frontier, feels the cold keenly. The wall he stands on was raised by the command of the emperor Hadrian. Approximately ten feet wide and twenty feet high, it would stretch seventy-three miles across the Island of the Angles—today's England. The wall was part of an imperial defense system that reached not just across this island but across continental Europe, marking and fortifying the outermost frontier that separated the empire from the many peoples the Romans considered "barbarian hordes." Beyond the wall roamed the wild, violent savages the Romans called *Scoti* (raiders). Hidden in forests, on craggy mountains, in impenetrable marshes and swamps, these were the fierce, indomitable people that the Roman legions, with all their brutal military power, could not conquer. And so, they built this wall, a testament both to the capacity of Roman imperial power and, ironically, to its limits.

On the southern side of the wall, in what would later be known as England, the Roman Empire had accomplished its conquest of Celtic people and Roman order had begun to shape, ineluctably, the lives and culture of the conquered. On the other side of the wall, the Celtic people continued in their wildness with traditions and customs utterly alien to Rome.

The sentry spots activity on the horizon. The Scoti are on the move. He shivers now, not so much from the cold but from his own fear of this warrior people with their strange tattoos, their wild hair, their blood-curdling battle cries. He sounds the alarm, a trumpet blast that will summon the legion in pursuit. And in wild defiance, the Scoti respond with their own war music: a single beat on a goat skin drum. *Boom, boom, boom* sounds the war beat between two clashing cultures—the Roman Imperium, bent on domination, and the Scoti, determined to resist. *Boom boom*—a drum beat echoing down through the ages.

CELTIC LANDLINES

When I submitted my DNA to Ancestry.com, as so many have done, my genetic history corresponded with the path of Celtic migration across Europe. Who were these Celtic people? A loosely related group of tribes and cultures, they originally occupied a homeland that spanned the whole of middle Europe, extending from Turkey to the Atlantic coast of Spain. One driver of their gradual migration across the continent of Europe was the aggressive expansion of the Roman Empire, which pushed them into the continent's periphery and eventually to the very fringe of Roman civilization: the British Isles. The seven areas of the so-called Celtic homeland that remain today are Ireland, Scotland, Wales, the Isle of Mann, Cornwall, the area called Brittany in France, and Galatia in Spain. Not unlike Appalachia, to which so many Celts would eventually migrate, the Celtic homeland in both Scotland and Ireland is an arduous terrain of water barriers, sharp mountains, deep hollows, soggy bogs and isolated moors, rough pastures, and thin, uncultivable soil blanketing wide reaches of granite.

Seeking to penetrate Scotland's interior, Roman armies became bogged down, even lost. Again, not unlike the history of Appalachia, a central government like the Roman Empire intent on imposing its will on the tough, combative folk who dwelled back in the hollows would be guaranteed a hostile reception. The ancient Celts established no great cities but lived in smaller settlements—loose confederations of families intensely loyal to their clan and its chief. The human settlements of ancient Scotland grew haphazardly and emphasized a rugged form of survival that had few links to the urban, commercial culture developing across the European world. The Celts were a warrior people, "born to fight," as former Senator Jim Webb has described them in his book about the Scots

Irish. Others have suggested that the Scots' propensity for violence owed more to the times they lived in and the adversaries they confronted. They could be hospitable and festive, given to celebration and to drink, but also quick to anger if crossed. Any insult or injury to one clan member was an insult or injury to all.

CELTIC SONG LINES

The Celts were a people of paradox, deeply attached to the land of their origins and yet strangely restless and on the move. They remembered and honored their ancestors in tales and ballads. Most of all, they loved their music—so much that wandering musicians (minstrels) could make a living traveling from clan to clan, playing a fiddle or harp or flute for any occasion. One of the sources for this migration story is Fiona Richie and Doug Orr's wonderful book *Wayfaring Strangers: The Musical Voyage from Scotland and Ulster to Appalachia*. Long before Christianity ever came to the British Isles, the Celtic people sang. All human experience found its way into their songs: romance, momentous events, supernatural phenomena, comedy, tragedy, crimes and violence, adventurous exploits of heroes and outlaws. The minstrels sang about royal families and the lives of the poor, about the daily joys and sufferings of ordinary folk. And when Christianity came to the British Isles, the Celtic converts sang about God.

The love of music ran deep in the life of the Celtic people. And like a great carrying stream, they brought their music with them to new lands. That music expressed their love of both their old homeland and the unfamiliar places to which they would journey. It expressed their lamentations and joys, their hopes and fears, their virtues and failings, and their faith in the God who they believed accompanied them on this journey. As this brief narrative suggests, we might read the stories of a people as song lines, which are simultaneously vessels of family history, traces of migrations, and maps of spiritual connections. This is true whether our ancestors came from Europe, from Africa or Asia, from Australia, or from the Americas, like the Indigenous peoples who arrived on this continent millennia before Europeans.

In addition to their songs, many of these families carried with them a Bible passed down from generation to generation. That old family Bible was cherished because it was the primary repository for genealogical information: births, baptisms, marriages, deaths, political affiliations, and sometimes even migration journeys. It is as if a deep intuition once led our ancestors to preserve their family stories within the covers of the Bible, the sacred story. This story—of faith, of calling—is central to the culture of the Carolinas, of the Presbyterian Church, and of many who claim Scots Irish ancestry.

I try to imagine what it was like for my Celtic ancestors as they left home, crossed the Atlantic, and came down the Great Wagon Road in wagon trains, fanning out to settle along the way by rivers and streams in America. I want to better understand the forces that compelled my ancestors to uproot themselves from all they held dear and leave behind family, communities, and the land itself to undertake a perilous journey to an unknown country. What turned a people rooted in their native land and culture into immigrants, starting over in a new and foreign place?

Historical evidence strongly suggests that there were significant forces of poverty, exploitation, and displacement pushing the migration of the Scots Irish. The most infamous cause of Scots migration was what historians call the Highland Clearances: the forced displacement, during the eighteenth and nineteenth centuries, of multitudes of Scottish people who, as tenants on large land estates, had practiced small scale subsistence agriculture for generations. Because of the global economy of that day, the hereditary aristocratic owners of these large estates, driven by the profit motive, evicted these farming people and converted the land to large sheep raising operations for export. With subsistence agriculture undermined, the landless poor grew ever more vulnerable to famine. The Clearances were particularly notorious because of the abruptness and brutality of these evictions. Their cumulative effect, and the large-scale emigrations that resulted, devastated the cultural landscape of Scotland.

This enforced displacement intertwined with another. While King James I, the Protestant sovereign over the British Isles, was establishing a colony in Jamestown, Virginia, he was also establishing a colony of English-speaking Presbyterians in Ulster, Northern Ireland. In the ongoing conflicts across Europe between Protestants and Catholics, James devised an ethnic cleansing strategy to suppress and control Irish Catholics. Beginning in the 1600s, England declared that over 500,000 acres in Northern Ireland were open to settlement.[1] Thousands of Scots, encouraged by the English crown, migrated from Scotland to Northern Ireland. These folk, who came to be known as the Scots Irish, became pawns in the British scheme to colonize Ireland.

---

1. Dunbar-Ortiz, *Not "A Nation of Immigrants,"* 122.

Motivated by the demands of survival, the Scots Irish were in no position to question, resist, or even fully comprehend the political aims of the British Crown. They came to Ireland as landless tenant farmers, again working the fields of English landlords. This dispossession would be a central part of England's strategy to suppress Ireland. Entire Irish clans were evicted from lands they had worked for generations. Irish Catholic families were crushed under the weight of debt and increasing hunger. The English banned expressions of Irish culture, including music and songs that reflected pride in Irish identity.

Even Scottish religion became part of this process: by 1641, a quarter million Scots Presbyterians would occupy Ulster alongside one and a half million Irish Catholics. They were the foot soldiers in a larger English strategy to suppress Ireland.[2] This British colonial strategy in Northern Ireland would become a template for British colonies on the Atlantic Seaboard of America, where Great Britain continued to use the Scots Irish as foot soldiers for building their empire in the "New World."

In this context, coexistence between English, Scottish, and Irish in Northern Ireland inevitably led to conflicts. (The reverberations of these imperial strategies continue to this day, echoing in the painful and often violent coexistence of Protestant and Catholic in Northern Ireland.) After a promising migration, the Scots Irish began to experience the downside of their unfortunate partnership with the English. In Ulster, they found themselves just as repressed as their new Irish neighbors had been. Mounting religious and economic discrimination discouraged and further alienated the Ulster Scots. The British Parliament had long since decreed the Church of England to be the official religion of the land. Now in Ulster, Anglican authorities punished Scots Presbyterians along with Irish Catholics for being dissenters from the official religion. And much to their chagrin, they were taxed by England to support a church to which they did not belong.

Other economic practices further marginalized these Scottish immigrants. English proprietors raised the rent while decreasing the length of land leases. Between landlord and priest, one Scots Irish settler lamented, "The very marrow is being squeezed out of our bones."[3] Recurring crop failures along with declining market prices for their products further undermined their viability in Northern Ireland.

---

2. Dunbar-Ortiz, *Not "A Nation of Immigrants,"* 123.
3. Ritchie and Orr, *Wayfaring Strangers*, 92.

A SCOTS IRISH EXODUS

> Uprootedness is by far the most dangerous malady to which human societies are exposed, for it is a self-propagating one. For people who are really uprooted there remain only two possible sorts of behavior: either to fall into a spiritual lethargy resembling death, like the majority of slaves in the days of the Roman Empire, or to hurl themselves into some form of activity necessarily designed to uproot, often by the most violent methods, those who are not yet uprooted.[4]

As more waves of new Scottish immigrants descended on the country, there was simply less and less land available. All these social forces pressed in on the Scots Irish in Northern Ireland. And so, this restless people, chafing under multiplying irritants and threats, were pushed to continue their migration, abandoning their roots in Ireland to strike out for the British colonies in America. Small groups of Scots Irish immigrants began to arrive as early as 1685, scattering from New Hampshire to South Carolina. But after 1715 the numbers swelled rapidly. These were not the scattered small-scale migrations of the past but the exodus and relocation of an entire people—one of the largest immigrant explosions in American history. From the early years of the eighteenth century to the eve of the American Revolution, historians estimate that some 200,000 Scots Irish migrated from Ulster to the American colonies. Following the American Revolution and well into the nineteenth century even more, by the tens of thousands, came. In many ways this rising tide marks the beginning of the story of the Presbyterian Church in America.

Imagining this trans-Atlantic voyage, I think of the many families who had to say goodbye to loved ones who they knew they would never see again. No wonder they gradually developed a ritual of leave-taking they called a living wake. The farewell ritual began at least a week before departure. As with an actual wake, tears of sorrow and prayers of lamentation mingled with drinking and storytelling and singing of beloved songs. The departing travelers would hear admonitions never to forget the homeland. Write frequently, send back money, come home again. In the aching hearts of these families there was little difference between dying and going to America, never to be seen again.

Traveling to one of the coastal harbor towns of Scotland or Ireland, whole families would be looking for the best passage. Those who lacked

---

4. Myers and Enns, *Healing Haunted Histories*, 53, quoting Simone Weil.

the capital could pay their fare by promising to work for five to seven years as indentured servants in the colonies. Among ports along the Atlantic Seaboard, Philadelphia was a popular choice because of Pennsylvania's culture of religious liberty. This was especially attractive to the Scots Irish, who had experienced repression by the official religion of England.

Just before departure, a convoy of family members and neighbors would escort the voyager to the edge of the community. A bridge in one Scottish community became known as the Bridge of Sighs because it was there that many said final goodbyes. The wrenching moment finally came when the departing immigrant, standing on the ship's deck, saw the homeland slip out of sight. And out of that sadness came songs like the ballad "Farewell to Scotland": "my foot is on the ocean; my heart is on dry land, I come here brokenhearted on deck as I stand."

A DANGEROUS OCEAN VOYAGE

In those first few days of their voyage, I imagine that these immigrant ancestors might have had occasion to wonder about the reliability of the vessel, its captain, or its crew. Surely, they would have worried about the stories they had heard of the dangers of the transatlantic crossing itself, over three thousand miles, taking a minimum of six to ten weeks. Anything could happen—turbulent storms could wash over you with waves higher than ships. Passengers could be tossed overboard. Shipwrecks occurred. And even supposing that none of these disasters happened, the journey itself held many challenges. The holds of the ships were stacked with bunks eerily like those we see in photos of concentration camp barracks. Sleeping space was a bare straw bed or a hammock in a large communal area.

The daily fare included a monotonous round of potatoes, salted beef, and hardtack. Beer was the standard drink because the water became contaminated. And there was illness: sea sickness was bad enough, but ships became actual pest houses of rampant diseases like dysentery, typhus, smallpox, and cholera. While these voyages were not so deadly as those of the slave ships in the infamous Middle Passage, which killed millions of enslaved Africans, or those of the vessels called "coffin ships" that crossed during the potato famine in Ireland, when Irish immigrants already weakened by chronic hunger died in droves during the passage to America, they were nevertheless perilous enough. Many of the Scots Irish did die in crossing. And many an immigrant family suffered the trauma of watching a loved one's burial at sea.

Nevertheless, there were consolations. I imagine myself among all the immigrants gathered on the deck of the ship once a day for fresh air and exercise. And I listen for the fiddler—sometimes hired by ship's captains for the voyage—as he takes up his fiddle for music and dancing. As he starts a tune we all know, soon we are joining our voices in the refrain, "I am bound for the promised land." And I wonder: listening to this music, are they buoyed with hope that this difficult journey will lead them to a better life?

Philadelphia Wagon Road

THE JOURNEY CONTINUES

At last they disembark onto dry land. Their destination is Philadelphia, the largest city in the American colonies. As their ship comes into harbor and they brace themselves for the challenge of the new, perhaps they sigh again for all the familiar things they have left behind. And as their feet once again touch dry land, they give thanks at having made it safely thus far. For they know that others have not survived the ocean voyage. Towing all their possessions down the gangplank, they walk along Market

Street in Philadelphia, engulfed by the sounds, sights, and smells of a thriving coastal city larger than anything they have ever seen.

Market Street in Philadelphia is the beginning of the Great Wagon Road that they have heard so much about. This road will carry them farther along to where they do not yet know. They search out a Presbyterian church where they can worship among their compatriots, who welcome them like long lost brothers and sisters. Chances are they would have listened to a preacher with a thick Scottish brogue, opening the scriptures to them much as preachers did in Scotland. Every word this preacher proclaimed would have seemed to circle back to the idea that God has called them to be here. Philadelphia is where the Presbyterian Church in America began. Instilled deeply into its worldview was the Calvinist idea of divine election, of a chosen people who have made a covenant with the God of history who is leading them into the promised land.

CONESTOGA WAGONS: MOBILE HOMES

The task before the new arrivals would be to locate a leader to guide them on the next leg of the journey. Like the captain who piloted their ship across the Atlantic, a waggoneer in whom they can place their trust would lead them along the way to their eventual destination. He would take them one day's travel west toward Lancaster County, Pennsylvania, where they could buy a fine wagon made to bear the long journey ahead. In Lancaster, their waggoneer would have made inquiries about buying a wagon in the Conestoga Township—already well known for its wagons made by skilled German settlers. These Conestoga wagons, towed by horses, mules, or teams of oxen, could carry tons of cargo. They were sturdy in fording streams and rivers but known to leak. Conestoga wagons would later be strongly identified with the wagon trains that led to the settlement of the West. But long before they traveled west in the nineteenth century, they would travel south in the eighteenth century, carrying families and extended clans of Scots Irish down the Great Wagon Road.

After procuring wagons and teams along with several other families, the immigrants follow a path that becomes a little more like a road with each passing wagon. Each wagon became a temporary home on wheels until the journey carried them to a place where they might find land to build a proper home. Thoughts about their eventual destination give way to the immediacy of where they would spend the night. Around a bend they come to an inn and tavern with an adjoining field to park their wagons and graze their animals. They are offered food and shelter and maybe even a chance to bathe in a stream close by. After a bath, a good meal, and drink their spirits lift even more when the music begins with songs from the old homeland. Around the campfire that night several families that came over together on the boat across the ocean gather to discuss their plans. Some share their intention of moving west toward the frontier of Pennsylvania. But the disastrous defeat of the British army under General Braddock in the battle for Fort Duquesne in April of 1755 has left many anxious and uncertain about the outcome of the yet undecided French and Indian War. The western frontier of Pennsylvania and other northern colonies remain vulnerable and exposed to attack. They too have heard the stories of bloody conflicts with the Indians who are hardly willing to give up their lands to these waves of settlers. Who could blame them?

WHERE TO FROM HERE?

Their hopes and fears hang in the balance. Some Scots Irish were bold enough to run the risk of settling on the Pennsylvania frontier, not afraid to fight for a place no matter how dangerous it might be. Other families, having heard of land recently opened in the Carolinas after a fierce war with the Cherokee, were more inclined to migrate farther south. Around the campfire that night amid their wagons, they decide to travel south through the great Appalachian valley. They have heard of land, good land, available in Carolina, near Pilot Mountain in the Yadkin River valley and beyond to the foothills of South Carolina. They followed an ancient pathway long used by the Cherokee and other Indigenous peoples traveling from northern points of origin southward toward the Carolinas—a trail that in fact led to Keowee. On they go to see what they might find. Since their wagons could travel about five miles a day, they calculate that it would take them at least two more months to make this journey.

Of course, everything depended on whether there was severe weather or flooded rivers. There was also the risk of a disabled wagon or, even worse, being robbed by bandits. And Indian attack was still a danger. They travel day after day, week after week, passing through Maryland, an already well-established agricultural colony with a growing Catholic presence. They enter Virginia. The valley and nearby mountains must have seemed overwhelming in their vastness, frightening and beautiful at the same time. They stop again for the night, circle the wagons, make a fire. They find fresh water and prepare food. And then a fiddler pulls out her fiddle. Music was the flowing stream that carried them, and they learned new songs or variations of old songs and passed them on. Again, their thoughts must have gone back to the land of their origins and forward to the land of their dreams.

And so, they flowed down the wagon road and all around them they gazed upon a labyrinth of steep mountains, plunging into remote hollows, sharp ridges, meandering streams, and treeless pastures alternating with old growth forest, a vast decoupage of blue hills receding into blue hills. Names of these mountains and rivers spoke of the Indigenous inhabitants: the Appalachian Mountains and the Potomac, Rappahannock, and Appomattox Rivers. Some landmarks had been renamed by settlers before them—echoes of European points of origin. Perhaps as they gazed at these vistas, they felt that this new land they were discovering was reminiscent of the old one they had left behind.

HOSPITALITY ALONG THE WAY

Their wagon train consisted of several families from different clans. Here and there a family or a small group of families peeled off the Wagon Road and onto side trails or up rivers, farther removed from towns and settlements. One group of wagons continued deeper into Virginia, to the little settlement of Lexington. There they encountered a Presbyterian church, founded by other Scots Irish who had come before them. They were warmly welcomed, offered hospitality, supplies, and wise counsel from their Presbyterian brothers and sisters. Wherever the Scots Irish settled they founded a church and a school and eventually, given enough time, a hospital. The pastor of the church often doubled as the teacher of the newly founded school. Schools established by congregations evolved into public schools and academies. Some even grew to become colleges, such as Washington (and Lee) College in Lexington, Virginia, or Davidson College in North Carolina.

Initially Presbyterianism thrived on the frontier because Presbyterian clergy were willing to go where Anglican clergy of the lowlands were less inclined to venture. The frontier was far from the reach of the ecclesiastical authority of bishops, so the more democratic populism of the Presbyterian Church was a pragmatic alternative. At this moment in our nation's history, being Presbyterian seemed to be the right fit for the American frontier, focused as it was on lay leadership and impatient with any scent of hierarchy or distinctions of class. Nevertheless, the tension and conflict that these Presbyterians had experienced with the Church of England in Great Britain persisted in the American colonies. As Scots Irish Presbyterians migrated south through the colony of Virginia, they again encountered the political power of an entrenched Anglican church, supported officially by the colony. They chafed once again against what they considered to be hierarchical power that restricted their religious freedom.

PILOT MOUNTAIN

They finally came to a fork in the road on the plateau of the Blue Ridge Mountains near the present-day intersection in Virginia of I-77/I-81. If they traveled west, they would be entering the homeland and hunting grounds of the Cherokee in what today is Tennessee, Kentucky, and beyond. They have heard reports of the recent war with the Cherokee and how the colonial frontier of the Carolinas has been pushed forward, opening new land for settlers. At this juncture, their wagon train turned south and proceeded down Fancy Gap, where they caught sight of the Pilot Mountain that told them that they had finally reached Carolina. (Pilot Mountain is the most distinctive landmark of Surry County, where I live today.) Among the foothills flowed a river called the Yadkin. This, at last, was the land they had hoped for. There was water. There was forest. There was pasture. There was abundant game. All that would be needed for a new life. They gave thanks to God because they were God's chosen people and here was the land that had been promised to them—or so they wished to believe.

Several families settled there. Others pushed on to South Carolina, where they intended to build a new life. And so they did, these Scots Irish Presbyterians: gritty, determined, proud, and fiercely protective of individual rights and freedoms, hard-working, sentimental, impetuous, hotheaded, sociable, adaptable, restless. There are multiple strands and currents that make up American history, but many historians see the migration story of the Scots Irish as right at the heart of who we are as a nation, a core narrative of American history and culture. It was this migration story that brought my people here.

CELTIC BLOODLINES: THE ANDERSON ANCESTORS

The up-country of South Carolina in the decades leading up to the Revolution was still a backwater removed from the main currents of the society that had been established in the low country in and around Charles Town. Presbyterian settlers were attracted to the frontier of the back country, distantly removed from the authority of any state-supported church. The settled low country closer to Charles Town held a ruling class of a predominantly Anglican hierarchy that the Scots Irish preferred to avoid. My Anderson ancestors, along with a cluster of other Scots Irish families, settled in what is now Spartanburg County in the Piedmont of South Carolina. They founded Nazareth Presbyterian Church, a vibrant congregation in an emerging network of Presbyterian churches near the frontier, building a prosperous farming community.

Like all human stories, the "immigration" stories of my ancestors are socially complex and morally ambiguous. I do not wish to demonize them in self-righteous hindsight, but neither am I willing to simply write off their lives as products of time and place. Rather, I seek a necessary middle path. As Elaine Enns and Ched Myers point out: "Righteous distancing from our ancestors is simply the opposite swing of the pendulum from romanticizing them."[5]

> The original trauma of European immigrants lay in their disconnection from their roots. Only a people severed from their own land and culture could turn around and so systematically disinherit Indigenous peoples from theirs. We must inquire into these primal traumas and their relationship to the conquest of this continent if we want to break their power over us.[6]

In *My Grandmother's Hands*, an in-depth exploration of racialized trauma, Resmaa Menakem sensitively probes the generational trauma that the ancestors of white European North Americans may have carried with them when they immigrated to the United States. For thousands of years, European history was characterized by brutal white-on-white violence practiced in a myriad of forms, producing victims who were deeply traumatized. Many of these Europeans fled this violence by immigrating to North America—and brought their trauma with them. Unhealed, this generational trauma continued to be passed on not just in violence waged by white bodies against white bodies but increasingly by white

---

5. Myers and Enns, *Healing Haunted Histories*, 52.
6. Myers and Enns, *Healing Haunted Histories*, 90.

bodies against red, black, and brown bodies. Menakem discusses how, for America to heal itself of white supremacy and racial violence, white bodies not only need to imagine what red, black, and brown bodies had to endure but do the same with the bodies of their own ancestors.[7]

A NATION OF IMMIGRANTS?

This migration story of my ancestors is part of my story: it has brought me to this very place, this very time. Reliving the story of Scots Irish migration reminds us of the oft-phrased affirmation that the United States is a "nation of immigrants." That affirmation has been for many of us a kind of patriotic creed, pointing to a vision of diversity and inclusion that we rightly aspire to as a country. In wrestling with the migration story of my ancestors, I am indebted to Roxanne Dunbar-Ortiz's provocative thesis in *Not "A Nation of Immigrants": Settler Colonialism, White Supremacy, and a History of Erasure and Exclusion*: that true immigrants join a culture and polity to which they adapt and into which, to some degree, they assimilate. In contrast, settlers are those who arrive and supplant the culture and polity of those already there with a new culture and polity of their own making.[8] By this definition my ancestors were not technically immigrants, but settlers. Even as this distinction offers greater clarity, the question remains: Has the United States ever been a nation of immigrants? Are we now?

Through the stories we have passed down about our "immigrant" ancestors coming to America, we have avoided seeing how the history of the US is the history of settler colonialism with the explicit purpose of driving Indigenous peoples from their lands to make them available to white European settlers and most often for the extension of slavery and the plantation economy.[9] This is not to make one's ancestors into villains, though villainy was widespread and commonplace. Those settler ancestors who originated in Europe were carried by historical waves of social, economic, and political forces beyond their ability to control. But to simply call the United States of America a nation of immigrants without understanding settler colonialism is to continue to perpetuate the erasure of Indigenous people from American history and their continued exclusion from white society today.

7. Menakem, *My Grandmother's Hands*, 65.
8. Dunbar-Ortiz, *Not "A Nation of Immigrants,"* 50.
9. Dunbar-Ortiz, *Not "A Nation of Immigrants,"* 23.

HOW DID WE GET HERE?

Part of our work here is to dig a little deeper into the mythology that surrounds our migration stories. How each of us feels about being a citizen of the United States is largely shaped by the experience of our own ancestors in coming here. Were our ancestors among the very first Americans who migrated from Eurasia down the Pacific Coast or north from Mesoamerica? Were our ancestors passengers on the Mayflower? Or were they kidnapped in their native land and brought here against their will in the hold of a slave ship? Did our ancestors arrive as refugees at Ellis Island having fled war or persecution in Europe? Or did our family cross the desert of the US-Mexico border on a more recent journey from violence and poverty in Central America? My location in the American story is determined more than I know by how my ancestors arrived on the continent.

There is more work that white America must do to make real this vision of a multiracial democracy. Indigenous voices are declaring ever more insistently the truth that the United States is in fact not a nation of immigrants but a country that was founded on land theft and genocide. Until white Americans grapple with our settler colonialism that resulted in the displacement and dispossession of countless Indian nations from their lands, the trope of a nation of immigrants is a whitewashing of history and a weak foundation for building a genuine and equitable multiracial society.

I am indebted to the work of the theologian Ched Myers and the educator Elaine Enns for their book *Healing Haunted History*. They wrote it as a kind of toolbox for folks like me doing this work of historical reclamation. They provide a structure for the kinds of inquiry I undertake in my own book—bloodlines (family history), landlines (migration journeys), and song lines—that name larger movements and stories of exceptional individuals who embody hopeful alternatives. These diverse but intertwining lines are the bones and sinew of my narrative and will be discussed at greater length in chapter 14: "Doing History."

It is at this point in the migration journey of my Scots Irish Presbyterian ancestors that I must pause, turn, and look back up the Great Wagon Road and for a moment lead us to retrace our steps to the point of departure in Lancaster, Pennsylvania, and specifically the Conestoga Township where the great wagons were constructed that carried the settlers south. It was not until very late in my own research that I discovered a reference to the Conestoga massacre. This discovery proved indisputably that after all

I have learned of our history, I can still be shocked. The excellent history *The Massacre of the Conestogas*, written by the journalist Jack Brubaker, explores the incident like a reporter investigating a horrific crime.

In 1763, a group of Scots Irish Presbyterians associated with the Paxton Presbyterian Church went on a rampage of settler violence. They were a Scots Irish frontier militia group, known as the Paxton Boys under the command of their Presbyterian pastor, the Reverend John Elder. Reverend Elder was the famous "fighting parson" who brought a rifle with him into the pulpit on a Sunday morning. In his sermons, Elder invoked the God of Joshua (who students of the Old Testament can recall as the warrior leader who led Israel in the conquest of Canaan, making a place for the Israelites in the promised land). Uplifted by such a spurious use of Scripture, some fifty of the Paxton Boys rode to the Conestoga Indian settlement outside Lancaster that was inhabited by approximately twenty Indian men, women, and children. In the cover of darkness, they entered the settlement and brutally murdered seven members of the community they found there and then burned their dwellings.[10]

The remaining members of the Conestoga Settlement who were not there escaped destruction—for the time being. In the aftermath of the initial assault, authorities moved quickly to relocate the survivors to Lancaster where they could be protected in the workhouse of the local jail. Rumors were circulating that the Paxton Boys were not done. A larger paramilitary group estimated to be over 150 marched on Lancaster. They stormed the workhouse where the survivors had temporary refuge. Within ten minutes the remaining twenty Conestoga Indian women, men, and children were massacred and their bodies mutilated. But the Paxton Boys were still not done.[11]

---

10. Brubaker, *Massacre of the Conestogas*.

11. In 1764, the Paxton Boys rose up yet again, this time with some 250 recruited from a wider area of Pennsylvania counties, which marched on Philadelphia threatening to exterminate more Christian Indians associated with the Moravian Church. Philadelphia, believing itself to be insulated from frontier violence, had no ready militia to defend the city against an insurrection. Governor Penn hastily recruited a force, and they were put to work, throwing up defensive barricades against the invading Presbyterians. Learning of the city's preparedness, the Paxton Boys stopped short of Philadelphia and called for negotiations.

The colonial government sent Benjamin Franklin as the head of a team of negotiators to quell the crisis. A list of demands was proffered. Reverend Elder communicated to the government that he had tried to stop militia, but it was simply impossible to restrain indignant settlers from this violent reaction, given what they had suffered. None of their demands were ultimately granted, but the Paxton Boys did not come away from the conflict empty-handed. The colonial government soon after decreed a bounty for

I share this story of the Conestoga massacre for several reasons. Pennsylvania was the birthplace of Presbyterianism in America. This area was the cradle of my family history. This was the place from which my Scots Irish ancestors migrated. My Anderson family history makes much of this, even comparing the similar architecture of the Presbyterian churches in Pennsylvania with those in Carolina. These Presbyterian ancestors, whether in Pennsylvania or Carolina, originated from the same places in the Old Country. When they gathered in their meeting houses, they prayed the same prayers, sang the same psalms, heard the same sermons and stories from Scripture. This was the political, social, and theological milieu that formed them. Not every Presbyterian of this time and place would participate in or support such violence. And I do hope my ancestors didn't. But this was their worldview they carried with them from the frontier of Pennsylvania to the frontier of Carolina. The frontier of both places became a zone of vicious racial violence.

The Conestoga Settlement was believed to be inhabited by a surviving remnant of the once mighty nation of the Susquehannock Tribe, decimated by war and epidemic disease. But there is evidence that this

---

every scalp of an Indian man, woman, or child, meaning that it was "open season" on the Indigenous population. And no real effort was ever made to investigate the massacre or to bring any of the perpetrators to justice. It was a joint failure of both church and state. William Penn's "Peaceable Kingdom" became a zone of racial violence.

Furious public debate ensued across the colony. Opposing sides published pamphlets, generating the very first political cartoons, snapshots of a colonial culture war. Presbyterians denounced the "hypocrisy" of the Quakers and their nonviolence, who would take up arms against their white neighbors while protecting Indians. Quakers ridiculed the Presbyterians ("Piss-brutarians"), accusing them of acting as barbarian savages.

Benjamin Franklin, who played such a critical role in resolving the immediate crisis, published a tract, entitled *Narrative of the Late Massacres in Lancaster County of A Number of Indians, Friends of this Province, By Persons Unknown*. In it he described the people murdered as individuals, known to their neighbors, innocent of any wrongdoing. Then Franklin went on the attack, questioning why any settler who has ever been hurt or wronged by an Indian could justify attacking another Indian in retaliation. Franklin exposed the racism behind the violence ("the only crime of these poor wretches seems to have been, that they had a reddish Skin and black Hair"). And then Franklin, after denouncing the sacrilege of distorting Holy Scripture to justify violence, drew his prophetic message to this final charge: "All good people everywhere detest your actions. You have imbued your hands in innocent blood; how will you make them clean? The dying shrieks and groans of the murdered will often sound in your ears; their specters will sometimes attend you and affright your innocent children! Fly where you will, your consciences will go with you!" Franklin predicted that the spirits of those innocent Indians they had massacred would haunt the murderers (Brubaker, *Massacre of the Conestogas*, 70–72).

area had also been a destination for Native refugees from various tribes, displaced from other areas, perhaps as far away as South Carolina. With the Quaker anti-war influence and William Penn's policy of racial tolerance in Pennsylvania, these Indian refugees had at last found a sanctuary in Pennsylvania. By treaty they were under the protection of the colonial government in Philadelphia.

It is as difficult to understand this explosion of violence that is the Conestoga massacre as it is to explain the actions of any lynch mob. But to understand the massacre, we have to reckon with the wider geopolitics of this moment. Following the end of the French and Indian War, the Native rebellion, led by the great chief Pontiac, pushed back against waves of settler encroachment on Native land. Pontiac's uprising forced the British Crown to create a boundary between colonial settlers east of the Appalachian Range from the Indian nations west of the mountains.

The Proclamation boundary line established in 1763 made the settlements of some Scots Irish Presbyterians in this area of Pennsylvania illegal, and they were ordered off their land claims. Furthermore, the Scots Irish Presbyterians inhabiting the Pennsylvania frontier were indignant that the colonial authorities in Philadelphia were protecting friendly Indians who in their view were nothing more than enemies, spies who provided information to warring tribes. Reverend John Elder vehemently declared that no real distinction could be made between a peaceful Indian and an enemy Indian and demanded their removal. Furthermore, the Scots Irish Presbyterians on the frontier of Pennsylvania were disgruntled at the colonial government so influenced by Quaker anti-war values, who had done little in their eyes to support the frontier settlements or provide for their defense. The situation in Pennsylvania was replicated all along the colonial frontier marked by the Proclamation of 1763 and demarcated by the Appalachian mountain range.

Historian have different opinions about when settler violence became racialized. Some believe it began with the Conestoga massacre. All Native people were no longer members of this tribe or that nation but were all "Indian savages." And all settlers no matter from whence they came in the Old World, England, France, Scotland, Ireland, Germany, or elsewhere, were "Whites." I think the racialization of settler violence began even earlier in colonial American history, from the time of King Philip's War in 1675–1678 across New England. You might argue that it began from the moment of first contact. But each new chapter in American history seemed to build on the previous one, reinforcing white supremacy and inciting racial violence.

3

The Cherokee Nation Encounters the Colony of South Carolina

JOURNEY UP THE KEOWEE TRAIL

WE NOW SHIFT OUR focus from the Great Wagon Road that brought my ancestors to Carolina, to the Keowee Trail, connecting Charles Town and the Carolina low country with the Lower Towns of the Cherokee Nation. I try to imagine what it might be like if I were a Scots Irish trader who followed the Keowee Trail into the Cherokee Nation to barter for furs. A trader with a copy of Hunter's map of the Keowee Trail in hand would depart the commercial district along King Street in Charles Town and proceed up the Cooper River watershed until it intersected with another trail that descended from Virginia via the Cape Fear watershed.

A couple of landmarks are identified on Hunter's map near this intersection. One is the plantation called Rice Hope. It was one among numerous others scattered throughout the Cooper River watershed, many owned by the extended Ball family.[1] A couple of my ancestors from other lines of descent also owned plantations in this area. One, by the name of Benjamin French Hard, was my grandfather Taylor's great-grandfather, who, in addition to a plantation, owned a shipping business that provided transport up and down the river. Alongside Rice Hope on Hunter's map is Strawberry plantation, which marks a ford across the Cooper River.

---

1. The story of the Balls and their enslaved workers is documented in Edward Ball's book *Slaves in the Family*.

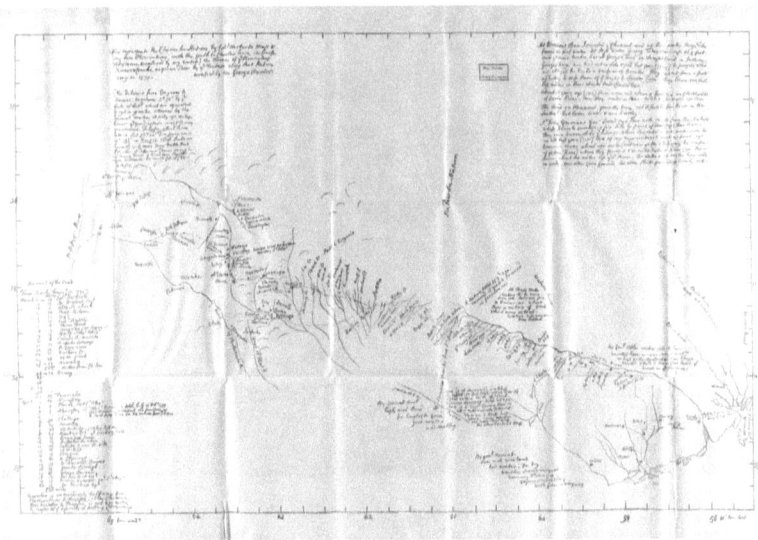

Hunter's Map of the Cherokee Path (1730)[2]

TRAIL JOURNAL: LIFE ALONG THE COOPER RIVER

A few miles from Strawberry is Mepkin Abbey, a Cistercian monastery that now occupies what was once one of the largest plantations on the Cooper River, which belonged to Henry Laurens and his wife, Eleanor Ball Laurens. I have been a guest retreatant at Mepkin Abbey many times and have enjoyed strolling around its beautiful low country gardens shaded by oak trees hundreds of years old. Among these oaks and palmettoes is the ancient cemetery of the Laurens family and the graves of Henry and Eleanor. Keeping my eyes open for the alligators that are everywhere, I have walked along more rugged trails atop what were once dikes that enclosed the huge rice fields of Lauren's plantation. Rice, called Carolina Gold, and long staple cotton were the chief cash export crops that made the Laurens family and other plantation owners some of the wealthiest people in the American colonies.

2. Source: South Caroliniana Library, University of South Carolina, Columbia.

Mepkin[3]

At Mepkin, I have sat beside the Cooper River trying to imagine how the boats would come and go from Charles Town, carrying passengers, free and enslaved, hauling rice exports to Charles Town for shipment on the first leg of the journey to Europe. These same boats, returning up the Cooper River, would dock at the Strawberry ferry just downstream from Mepkin to deliver various imported goods from Europe, necessities and luxuries prized by the slave-holding families that populated the plantations. But rice and cotton were not the only source of wealth for Henry Laurens. Laurens, who would play a significant role in the future of South Carolina and the American colonies, made his primary fortune as a slave trader. He was the chief executive of a global operation of human trafficking that kidnapped hundreds of thousands of African people from their homelands and transported them to the southern shores of America. He will reappear in our story as our narrative unfolds.

The monks at Mepkin Abbey, who now reside on what was Laurens's former plantation, are aware of the layers of history there and acknowledge them with a memorial bell tower at the entrance to their chapel. When the bell tolls, it is a reminder of the Native Americans who once occupied the low country and of the enslaved African Americans who worked the rice fields of Mepkin and other plantations along the South Carolina coast. The monks are now planning another memorial as well: a memorial dedicated to truth and reconciliation. It has been a couple of

---

3. Fraser, *Charleston Sketchbook*, 35.

years since I have been to Mepkin. It is time for me to return to see this new memorial.

My spiritual retreats at Mepkin Abbey have cultivated and nurtured within me a capacity for what the monastic tradition calls contemplation. The monks, in their common life, have taught me a way of prayer that begins and ends in silent awareness of the divine. As one contemplative has written, there are "ways of seeing and sensitivities of knowing hidden in the soul, waiting to be discovered, ready to be set free."[4] Disciplined vision is the central faculty of the spiritual life. Jesus of Galilee repeatedly questioned his disciples with this query: "Do you have eyes that see?" Right seeing can be transformative because it always raises questions about what we think we see. These ways of seeing, as partial as they are in my own spiritual practice, I hope to bring to bear on this project of contemplating the truth of our history. It has taken us so long to clearly see our history and to look upon one another with regard. This is evident in our persistent unwillingness as a nation to see the full truth of our history that is right before us, around us, and within us. In the merciful presence of my Creator, I confess the sins of my church, my nation, and the world. I am seeking greater awareness of how racism has impaired my identity and wounded the human community to which I belong. I am seeking to open myself to a cleansing of the legacy of white supremacy, walking step by step a path that I hope will lead to individual and collective repentance, a constructive way forward toward justice, healing, and someday reconciliation. This journey before me is very much a spiritual pilgrimage. So let us put on our walking shoes and follow this trail.

Saluda Old Town

The Keowee Trail emerges from the low country and crosses the sand hills of the middle of the state into the more rolling foothills of the South Carolina up-country. Near the town of Saluda, the trail carries us by what was once the site of a major Indian settlement, called Saluda Old Town. The Saluda Tribe, like most tribes near the colony of South Carolina, was decimated by epidemic disease. One historian asserted that a remnant of the Saluda Tribe migrated to Pennsylvania and the Conestoga Township, the same area where my Scots Irish ancestors may have procured their Conestoga wagons.

4. Newell, *Sounds of the Eternal*, 16.

There in Saluda Old Town a major treaty was negotiated with the Cherokee in 1755. The South Carolina colonial governor James Glen brokered a treaty with the Cherokee in which they ceded most of up-country South Carolina. By means of this treaty, the Cherokee hoped that South Carolina would desist from the Indigenous slave trade which was accentuating inter-tribal conflict. They also hoped a treaty would provide more equitable exchange for the deerskin trade. The primary negotiator for the Cherokee was Attakullakulla, known as the Little Carpenter, a man very small in physical stature but respected for his diplomatic acumen. Attakullakulla was well acquainted with English ways having participated in a delegation of Cherokee leaders who crossed the Atlantic to have audience with King George at Windsor on June 22, 1730.

Under the aegis of Sir Alexander Cuming, a self-styled Scottish adventurer seeking his own fortune through grandiose schemes, seven Cherokee warriors, including Attakullakulla, crossed the Atlantic and came to England bearing eagle feathers and enemy scalps as signs of their fealty and as gifts to be given to His Majesty. The Cherokees' tour of England was quite the cultural sensation among the English people, exciting great public curiosity. One wonders if it was from this voyage to Great Britain that Attakullakulla, having witnessed the metropolis of London and the grandeur of the Royal Court and the vast population of England, became convinced that the interests of the Cherokee Nation would always have little choice but to accommodate British power. For decades after he returned from England, Attakullakulla functioned like a secretary of state for the Cherokee, handling the complex negotiations with the European powers surrounding the Cherokee Nation and tirelessly working to preserve peace with the British colonies.

In those early years, Attakullakulla represented the beloved First Man of the Cherokee, Conocotoko, known among the English as Old Hop for the pronounced limp in his walk. At Saluda Old Town, Attakullakulla negotiated for trade concessions more favorable to the Cherokee and demanded that the English cease capturing and enslaving Cherokee people. With Governor Glen's agreement, Attakullakulla ceded to the English most of the South Carolina up-country except for the most northwest corner inhabited by the Lower Towns. One week after this treaty was signed, General Braddock's army suffered their devastating defeat in the French and Indian War, which threw the entire colonial frontier into chaos.

Ninety-Six

Let us imagine a Scots Irish fur trader as he traveled along the Keowee Trail. He could plainly see that this was a long-trod route. Centuries of Native travel back and forth from the mountains to the low country and coastal regions had carved the trail so deeply into the earth that, as he rode his horse, he could have touched the ground with his feet on either side of the trail. Proceeding north, he would note on Hunter's map a simple "96." From Saluda, the Keowee trail proceeded along a high ridge and descended at last to a trading post operated by a man named Gowdy, who encircled it in a palisade for protection. The trading post and settlement was identified on Hunter's map as Ninety-Six, indicating the number of miles yet to go to reach Keowee.

During the American Revolution, Ninety-Six would become the location of a major British "star" fort—thus called because of its distinctive shape, drawn from European fort architecture—and would be the site of much significant Revolutionary War history. Visiting this national historic landmark today, you can view the ruins of the British fort and walk along the actual Cherokee trading path that remains clearly visible. Along this path, creeks became landmarks, notated on Hunter's map simply by how many miles they were from Keowee: 23-Mile Creek, 18-Mile Creek, and so on. Today, on the state trail that commemorates the route, several of these creeks still retain those mile-marker names.

The Lower Towns of the Cherokee

A day or two north of Ninety-Six our fur trader would have reached an intersection in the trail. If he turned left and went west at the Dividing Paths, he would soon come upon two of the most prominent of the Cherokee Lower Towns: Tugaloo and Eastatoe. Tugaloo possessed a unique honor among the Cherokee as the sacred place where the Great Spirit first gifted the people with fire. Tugaloo was a border town near the Creek Nation, situated along the Tugaloo River that, together with the Keowee River, comprised the headwater tributaries of the Savannah River, which flowed to the coast.[5] This close to the boundary with the Creek Nation, the town of Tugaloo was vulnerable to periods of antagonism between the Creek and the Cherokee. History records that at Tugaloo the Cherokee

---

5. Today, most "Creek" people prefer their original tribal name, Muscogee. Creek was a name given the tribe by the British.

killed a number of Creek warriors who had come there unsuccessfully to recruit the Cherokee to join them and other tribes waging war against the South Carolina colony in 1720. There was also evidence within Tugaloo of mixed ethnicity between the Cherokee and the Creek Tribes. The site of the Tugaloo village is located along the South Carolina–Georgia border. Today, if the water level in the Hartwell Reservoir system is low, a small island in the middle of the river can be seen—probably what remains of the central mound of the Tugaloo village.

Tugaloo and Eastatoee are both indicated on Hunter's map, but other maps put Eastatoee at several other possible locations. One explanation for this variance is that because the oldest location of Eastatoee on the Tugaloo River proved too vulnerable in times of Creek-Cherokee conflict, the village was relocated to the far eastern boundary of the Lower Towns, in a beautiful valley at the foot of the Blue Ridge Mountains. In one colonial report, Eastatoee had over two hundred dwellings and was influential in larger councils of the Cherokee. The importance of the village was also reflected in the naming of a major trading path through the nation, the Eastatoee Trail, which ascended the North Carolina Mountains on to Tennessee and Virginia. *Eastatoee* means "the place of the colored bird," a haunting reference to the multicolored Carolina parakeet that went extinct in the nineteenth century. Its feathers may have been a valuable trade item for the Cherokee, as they would be for the white settlers who would later hunt the parakeets to extinction.

Keowee Town

If, at the Dividing Paths, our imagined trader turned right in a more northerly direction, the trail would bring him at last to the waters of the Keowee River. He would have entered the town of Seneca, located near today's Seneca, South Carolina, but now submerged under Lake Hartwell. Andrew Pickens—who will soon figure prominently in this narrative—would establish his plantation, Hopewell, at the edge of the Keowee River near the site of the Cherokee village of Seneca. At Hopewell, Pickens would negotiate a major treaty with the Cherokee in the year 1785. Finally, Hunter's map led our trader to the town of Keowee, Cherokee for the "place of mulberries" (The double *e* at the end of Cherokee words signifies "place.") Mulberry trees provide delicious fruit that resembles large blackberries of purplish hue. Cherokee women, who were accomplished agriculturalists, were known for their orchard keeping, and I suspect some of these mulberry plants might have been pruned to keep as bushes. But unpruned, the mulberry, with their heart-shaped leaves, can grow into lovely shade trees of forty feet and higher.

Keowee was the mother town of the Lower Cherokee settlements, perhaps the most populous of all the towns and probably the residence of some of the most influential Cherokee elders and headmen. Larger councils were convened here, and the town's proximity to a major intersection of trails assured a flow of Cherokee kin from other clans who lived in the towns farther into the Blue Ridge Mountains. Today, the Cherokee Foothills Scenic Highway (SC-11) roughly follows the major trail that connected Keowee and other Lower Towns with Virginia. It was this trail that my Scots Irish ancestors took when they came into Carolina.

Principal towns like Keowee may have been palisaded to provide protection from hostile raids. Summer dwellings were rectangular, built with pole frames, cane matting, and clay plaster, with thatch roofs. Habitations were often divided into sections for cooking, eating, and sleeping, with beds made of rush matting over wood splint frames. Animal skins served as bedding. Most Cherokee homes were one story; some were two. More compact circular winter dwellings, easily heated, were adjacent to the summer dwellings. A council house sometimes built on top of an ancient mound would be a gathering place, seating hundreds of people for ceremonial purposes and community consultations, where collective decisions were made by consensus. The sacred fire, the gift of the Great Spirit, was maintained in the council house at all times.

The Cherokee had for many years entreated the British to build a fort amid the Lower Towns. They finally did so in 1753, erecting Fort Prince George on the eastern shore of the Keowee River, opposite the town of Keowee. The fort would provide the Lower Towns of the Cherokee with some protection from raids by warring tribes and would consolidate the growing trade in deerskins with a central trading post. It was another star fort, surrounded by a trench, with walls up to fifteen feet high, and encompassing approximately two hundred square feet. In that space there was a guardhouse, a magazine, barracks for the troops, a kitchen and storehouse, and officers' quarters. By the time the fort was finished the Keowee Trail had become less like a trail and more like a road that could accommodate a colonial wagon train carrying military equipment, tools for construction, and all the necessary material, livestock, and goods to equip and sustain a frontier fort. From the British perspective, the fort's construction was a necessary step to ensure that the Cherokee remained as allies.

Sugar Town

Upstream on the Keowee River on a spur from the main trail our trader from Charles Town would come to Sugartown. Like the village of Keowee, named for the mulberry tree, Sugartown was named as the place of the honey locust tree, whose long seeds were used for sweetening food and brewing a medicinal tea. The Cherokee prized honey locust wood for making bows and game sticks for their favorite recreation of ball play, much like today's lacrosse. I read an interview with an archeologist who observed that when he saw a grove of honey locust trees it seemed to him that he could throw a rock and hit an archeological site of a Cherokee town. And his research indicated that Cherokee cultivation of the honey locust trees was the most important factor determining where they would grow in abundance. Following the trail past Sugartown would lead us to other villages like Toxaway. The approximate location of Toxaway can be seen where the Cherokee Foothills Scenic Highway crosses the Keowee River near the town of Salem, South Carolina. Beyond Toxaway, a trail advanced toward New Eastatoee and up the Eastatoee trail (near Rosman, North Carolina) to the village of Connestee (near Brevard, North Carolina) and beyond into Virginia.

Oconee Station

If our trader continued the main trail from Keowee, the next Cherokee town he would encounter would be Oconee (*Aconee*). Nearby, in 1792, South Carolina established a fort, Oconee Station, to defend the frontier from the French and their Native allies. This was one of a series of forts built along the South Carolina frontier. Other stockades and trading posts were at Tugaloo and Eastatoee, in the Oolenoy Valley near Pumpkintown, and the Blockhouse in northern Greenville County. This stone fort at Oconee was also intended to anchor and establish a trading post to facilitate the deerskin trade that was an economic mainstay of the South Carolina colony.

Oconee Station

Here a white trader would establish a "fur factory," where he supervised the processing of skins, removing hooves and snouts, and making sure the skins were properly dried to prevent mold. Skins were weighed and their quality graded, prices assigned, and records kept. Controversies arose as well. Some traders were notorious for cheating their Cherokee partners. Rum came to dominate trade transactions, even being offered as a free gift at the beginning of negotiations, making the Cherokee hunter all the more vulnerable to being swindled. Some traders even waylaid the hunters before they ever reached the trading station, attempting to get them drunk before negotiations began. The imposing brick residence of an early English trader still stands beside the fort at Oconee as a clear indication that a trader could make a fortune in this fur-skin business.

The village of Oconee was also a beloved town of the Cherokee and the hub of a trail intersection. Cherokee sovereignty over this land was the very last to be relinquished in treaties made with South Carolina in the early nineteenth century. This area today is within the boundaries of Oconee County, South Carolina. And according to Luther Lyle, the founder and director of the Cherokee Museum of South Carolina located in Oconee County, genetic research on the county's population reveals at least 15 percent of residents have Cherokee heritage. I have been most impressed by the work that Luther and his allies have accomplished as they seek to interpret the history of the Cherokee in South Carolina. They are guardians of the site of the ancient village of Oconee and hope someday to facilitate an archeological dig there. Luther attended a recent historical gathering where a state official mentioned the Cherokee Path beginning in Charleston and culminating in Keowee. Luther rose to disagree with that characterization, saying the trail did not end at Keowee but continued on to Oconee and from there ever more deeply into the Cherokee heartland. "For goodness' sakes," he said to me, "the Keowee Trail could just as easily be known as the Oconee Trail." Point well taken.

Chattooga River

The next village along the trail is Chattooga. The name of the Chattooga village has survived as the name of South Carolina's wild and scenic river in the beautiful wilderness where the borders of South and North Carolina and Georgia converge. In 2004, a 250-year-old canoe, measuring thirty-two feet long and carved from a single tree, was found in the river. The Cherokee Path crosses the Chattooga a stone's throw from today's Earl's Ford in Oconee County. Close by is a tributary named War Woman's Creek, commemorating a Cherokee woman who participated in the defense of her homeland in a forgotten conflict.

The Lower Towns of the Cherokee were in the northwestern-most tip of what is today South Carolina, due west of Greenville. These population centers grew up around a mound as a ceremonial center. A council house built on these mounds could be large enough to seat as many as four hundred people. A Cherokee village might be as populous as a principal town but would not have a mound or council house. A Cherokee hamlet might consist of a group of families sharing clan ties located anywhere along a creek or river.

There are no known Cherokee towns or village sites in Greenville and Spartanburg Counties. The area around Greenville and Spartanburg was a borderland between the Cherokee and the Catawba Indians to the southeast. My Anderson ancestors settled in this area, which they probably saw as "empty," but teeming with plentiful buffalo, deer, and other game. This assumption of territory being "empty" because uninhabited by Native communities was a cultural perception in the minds of European settlers that somehow justified their invasion and land theft. But they were wrong: as Cherokee hunting ground, this land was not free for the taking. It was Cherokee homeland, with densely inhabited areas farther west and north surrounded by vast hunting territories that were necessary to sustain the Native population.

BOUNDARIES AND BORDERS

Following farther along the Keowee Trail our Scots Irish trader would be carried deeper and deeper into the Cherokee heartland. Within the Cherokee Nation there were at least five major groupings of settlements that each enjoyed a high degree of political autonomy. Overlapping kinship united the Cherokee Nation and the separate groupings of towns. Bloodlines of distinct clans like the Bird, the Wind, and the Bear clans created a web of connection among all the settlements across the mountainous homeland. Besides the Lower Towns in South Carolina, this Cherokee confederacy included the Middle Towns spread over the Little Tennessee River watershed near present day Franklin, North Carolina.

Just northeast along the Tuckasegee River were the Out Towns, situated much closer to the bounds of the current reservation of the Eastern Band of the Cherokee. These Out Towns included the first Cherokee town, Kituwah (near today's Bryson City, North Carolina), whose cultural significance cannot be overstated: the name *Kituwah* was almost a synonym for the name of the Cherokee people, meaning "the people of Kituwah," for according to oral tradition this was where the Cherokee people first emerged from the earth. If the Cherokee had one beloved town above all others, a capital town, it was Kituwah.

Farther west along the Hiwassee River basin and into the Nantahala River Gorge were the Valley Towns surrounded by fertile agricultural fields (from Andrews to Murphy to Haysville, North Carolina). This area has been referred to as the "breadbasket" of the Cherokee Nation, with extensive corn fields under cultivation by Cherokee women. The Overhill Towns, located in what is now Eastern Tennessee, were farthest removed from Carolina and opened out on vast hunting territory farther north and west into the Ohio Valley.

IMPERIAL CARTOGRAPHY

We have used Hunter's map of the Keowee Trail to guide us into the Cherokee Nation. Other early colonial maps reflect white perceptions of the Cherokee as a formidable nation living in the vastness of mountains beyond the frontier of white civilization. One way to tell the story of colonial South Carolina in its relationship to the Cherokee Nation is to look at maps of this contested space. We are accustomed to thinking of maps as simply reflecting physical geography or transportation routes between inhabited areas, but the earliest maps of colonial South Carolina were published with a political agenda and distinct purpose: plotting the course of empire. As you can surmise, I am a lover of maps. So I was delighted to discover Max Edelson's analysis in *The New Map of Empire: How Britain Imagined Empire*, which uses early colonial maps to illustrate the competing interests for this contested space.

First, "A Map of the British and French Possessions in North America" in 1755, by John Mitchell, imagines the British Empire as horizontal lines proceeding west from the boundaries of the colonies all the way to the Mississippi. These latitudes on the map depict the land ambitions of colonial settlers, who would never be content with occupying only the Atlantic Seaboard. A contrary vision to this map was represented by two others, drawn by Captain John Stuart, who would become the British superintendent of Indian Affairs. His 1761 "Map of Cherokee Country" was derived in part from his harrowing escape from the massacre of Fort Loudoun, aided by his good friend, the Cherokee chief Attakullakulla, who led him to safety in the Virginia colony. Stuart's map offers more specific information in handwritten notations, such as the number of warriors in a particular Cherokee village or the navigability of a major river—geographical information that Stuart might very well have gathered on his flight from Fort Loudoun.

As superintendent of Indian Affairs, Stuart would draw yet another map that clearly demarcated the area of Cherokee sovereignty. This map reflected official British policy of preserving the political boundaries of the Cherokee and the other Indian nations of the southeast—a project of vital interest to the British. Ensuring the integrity of these Indian lands would preserve the Cherokee as trading partners and allies against the French. The need for such a boundary was impressed upon the British by the uprising led by the great chief Pontiac, who launched another pan-Indian confederacy against colonial expansion in 1763, shortly after the conclusion of the French and Indian War.

A MOUNTAINOUS BORDER

The defined boundaries of these different maps reveal how many of the interests of the colonists of British North America were at cross-purposes with the official policies of the British Crown. Great Britain's Colonial Board established an official boundary line that ran down the Appalachian Mountain range from Maine to Georgia, generally demarcated by whether a river flowed east to the Atlantic or west to the Gulf of Mexico. A mountain range as a visible feature of a contested frontier appealed to both Indian and British desires for clarity. This boundary line had to be negotiated locally in conferences between colonial authorities and tribal leadership and in treaties that were constantly being challenged and changed by events on the ground.

The boundary line between the Cherokee and the Colony of South Carolina ran through Greenville County, where I was born and raised. Respecting this boundary line was official British policy and seen as politically advantageous to British interests. The most important advantage was military security. If Indian nations on the other side of this border could be satisfactorily retained as allies, they would form a protective buffer between the English colonies and the French and their Indian allies farther west.

WHITE CAROLINIANS: A DOUBLE MINORITY

Outnumbering whites until the early eighteenth century, the Cherokee Nation and its thousands of warriors were greatly feared by the colony of South Carolina, whose white colonists were keenly aware of their vulnerability. In the early to mid-eighteenth century, white Carolinians were a double minority, outnumbered not only by their Indian neighbors but by the Africans they had enslaved.[6] They readily perceived their vulnerability to the twin threats of an Indian war and an insurrection of the enslaved—as happened in 1740 with the Stono Rebellion just southwest of Charles Town. First and foremost, then, remaining at peace with the Cherokee was an existential necessity for colonial South Carolina. During the Yamasee War of 1720, other South Carolina tribes fought to the very gates of Charles Town and almost wiped the colony off the map. The Creek Nation met with the Cherokee at the town of Tugaloo, seeking to recruit them to this alliance. But their appeal was violently rejected, and the Creek delegation was killed, no doubt cementing the historic enmity between the two tribes. Had the Cherokee joined this Native alliance, they might very well have succeeded in destroying the colony.

6. Hatley, *Dividing Paths*, 73.

Part of the colonial military strategy was to instigate inter-tribal conflicts. One colonial authority declared that their purpose was to assist the tribes wherever possible in cutting each other's throats while remaining friendly to the colonists.[7] Another way that the colony could weaken the tribes was by paying for the capture of Indian slaves, rewarding the Cherokee and other tribes for the captives they brought into Charles Town. These enslaved Indigenous, numbering in the thousands, were largely shipped out to the northern colonies or to the sugar plantations of the Caribbean, where all slaves, red or black, were worked to death in a matter of years if not months. The African slave trade probably operated on the same logic. The exchange of desired trade goods for slaves, the commodification of slavery, encouraged more African tribes to pursue slave raids and exacerbated inter-tribal conflict both in Africa and in America.

CHEROKEE HUNTING AND THE GLOBAL ECONOMY

The boundary line running down the Appalachian Range was important to the British not only to maintain a military alliance with the Cherokee but for a second, equally important reason: to preserve the economic opportunity of trade with the Cherokee and other Indian nations. A few white hunters began to penetrate Cherokee lands, harvesting pelts of deer and beaver. They were soon followed by traders who, in exchange for yet more furs, offered the Cherokees things they would come to value. The British colony of South Carolina began to see the Cherokee as a significant trading partner.

With hundreds if not thousands of skilled hunters among the Cherokee, they opened to the English the coveted economic resources of the wilderness in the form of fur skins: beaver, otter, fox, bear, and especially, in astounding quantities, deer. The British market had a great demand for deer skins for the many uses of its leather, from book binding to gloves to a new style of hat that was all the rage in London. Shoes, jackets, artisan aprons, coverings for boxes and trunks, military uniforms, and equipment all required the raw commodity of deerskin leather. And the Cherokee hunters were well equipped to meet this demand. Their hunting territories, vital to their economic sustainability, stretched beyond the identifiable homeland into Kentucky and the Ohio Valley.

7. Hatley, *Dividing Paths*, 29.

TRADE ON THE KEOWEE TRAIL

The Keowee Trail became a trade route on which the Cherokee would carry thousands of deerskins first on their backs and then later, as the trail was expanded, on horses and even wagons. Depots and warehouses were constructed along the trail. These Cherokee trading caravans were able to barter skins for a host of European products like iron tools, weapons, cooking pots, glass beads, textiles, and, unfortunately for the Cherokee, rum. Alcohol became a much sought-after trade item. Carolina authorities with oversight of the trade developed a precise register of prices for a range of goods and the number of skins required for each item. For example, a blanket cost three buckskins or six doe skins. A knife—one doe skin. A brass kettle—one buck or two does. A saddle—eight bucks or sixteen does. Powder and bullets—one doe. One gun—seven bucks or fourteen does. And on from there, items like shirts, shoes, magnifying glasses, earrings, caps, etc., all had their prices in skins.[8] (Going over this register you may have recognized the origin of our slang word for dollar—a buck!)

Hunting, the major vocation of Cherokee men, shifted dramatically under this market pressure. Before this time, Cherokee hunters were limited by the instruments of the hunt: their bows and arrows, spears, blowguns, and traps. But the rifle and the horse would exponentially expand their ability to hunt. Before contact with Europeans, Native hunters were driven by the requirements of subsistence, of feeding one's village and family. After contact, trade with the colonies accelerated. Cherokee hunting became harnessed to a larger market force of trade to satisfy South Carolina's seemingly inexhaustible appetite for those skins. The role of Cherokee women was similarly altered. To acquire European trade items, they became laborers in the work of preparing skins, neglecting or abandoning traditional practices like basket weaving and pottery. As Cherokee hunters spent more time on longer, wider-ranging hunts to supply this growing market demand, these new socioeconomic pressures began to change the workings of Cherokee economic life and distort long-standing traditions of the culture.

---

8. Rozema, *Cherokee Voices*, 18.

JUDACULLA: THE CHEROKEE LORD OF THE HUNT

One story line in Mooney's *Myths of the Cherokee* seems relevant to changes wrought in Cherokee society by the deerskin trade with colonial South Carolina. In conversations with the Cherokee elder Swimmer, Mooney learned of oral traditions surrounding the legend of a slant-eyed giant named Judaculla, who was for the Cherokee the larger-than-life guardian of the hunt. This story provides a significant vantage point on the cultural impact of the deerskin trade on Cherokee culture and economy. As Swimmer told Mooney, Judaculla was first known in the stories of his wooing a Cherokee maiden to be his wife and providing for her family with bounteous meat from his hunts.[9]

In the legend, Judaculla seems to personify the values that defined the way Cherokees were supposed to hunt. These sacred traditions that surrounded the Cherokee hunting economy included the formulas for song and chant and dance to be performed before and after a hunt, ritual acknowledgments of respect and gratitude for the life of animals, and the imperative to harvest only what was needed and could be used for the good of the people. In the home of Judaculla in the high mountains there was a place of judgment where the traditions of the hunt and tribal boundaries were upheld. Failure to honor these traditions displeased Judaculla, who dispensed justice from his "courthouse." Settlers, reflecting their own misunderstanding and disrespect toward Cherokee tradition, corrupted the myth of Judaculla and his place of justice by naming this spot the Devil's Courthouse. But to the Cherokee Judaculla was not evil. He was something more like the Lord of the Hunt. What settlers called the Devil's Courthouse was to the Cherokee the symbolic place where the values of balance and sustainability were overseen and enforced.

The Potawatomi author Robin Kimmerer, in her splendid book *Braiding Sweetgrass*, describes what in Native tradition is called the Honorable Harvest:

> Know the ways of the ones who take care of you, so that you may take care of them. Introduce yourself. Be accountable as the one who comes asking for life. Ask permission before taking. Abide by the answer. Never take the first. Never take the last. Take only what you need. Take only what is given. Never take more than half. Leave some for others. Harvest in a way that minimizes harm. Use it respectfully. Never waste what you have

9. Mooney, *Myths of the Cherokee*, 476–79.

taken. Share. Give thanks for what you have been given. Give a gift, in reciprocity for what you have taken. Sustain the ones who sustain you and the earth will last forever.[10]

There can be no doubt that a similar set of values governed the culture of the Cherokee in relationship to the harvest of species upon which they depended. Can we imagine how our world might be different if the industrial western nations practiced the ethic of the Honorable Harvest?

The Devil's Courthouse today is a popular destination along the Blue Ridge Parkway, at the northern end of Transylvania County. From this peak, you can find a beautiful 360-degree view of the mountainous homeland of the Cherokee. Near the courthouse are the Old Fields, a series of grassy balds that the Cherokee believed were the slant-eyed giant's farm. Judaculla would not have been pleased with the deerskin trade because it violated every value and custom that had guided Cherokee hunting for generations. The boundaries that had limited hunting of deer to the basic need of survival were bent and stretched until they were no longer in force. Hunting deer to meet market demands for skins had a destabilizing effect on these traditions that had maintained a sustainable relationship to the land and its creatures. Killing deer in these numbers for trade did more than crush the deer population. It undermined a pillar of the spiritual and economic culture of the Cherokee.

The profit motive of the European trade injected into this sense of balance an unquenchable desire for skins and a system of economic rewards that dramatically changed the culture of the Cherokee, not just how they hunted but how they farmed, how they dressed, how they cooked and ate and drank. Many would come to value European products, but others would feel deep ambivalence as they experienced changes in their culture, in traditions that had been passed down from generation to generation. Some began to resist the impact of encroaching white civilization by renouncing the products gained in trade with the English and returning to the old authentic ways of their ancestors. But the advantages procured through European products made this, too, a losing battle.

A SACRED LANDSCAPE

From his courthouse in the high mountains, it was one step for the giant over an intervening ridge line to what is now known as Judaculla Rock, near present day Cullowhee, North Carolina: a large flat boulder

10. Kimmerer, *Braiding Sweetgrass*, 183.

inscribed with many symbols and signs that puzzle archeologists to this day. In one corner of the rock there is a large marking that the Cherokee believed was the footprint of the giant as he stepped from his home in the mountains down into the valley. Though the precise meaning of each symbol in this collection of pictographs can never be known with certainty, it suggests to the eye a kind of map, perhaps a cartographic mix between spiritual reference points and physical landmarks that define a homeland. No one can know for sure. Mystery remains an important dimension of this ancient map carved in stone.

Judaculla Rock probably predates the arrival of the people we know as the Cherokee. Some scholars suggest the oldest earthen mounds characteristic of Cherokee settlements do as well. Perhaps the prevalence of mounds in Cherokee villages reflects a sacred landscape tradition that predated the Cherokee but that they carried on. On these mounds there was usually a conical town house that could accommodate hundreds of tribal members, the village gathering place for rituals, storytelling, political discussions, and tribal decision-making.

The Cherokee typically lived near rivers and streams that provided an abundance of the necessary resources for life: clean water, food, transportation, agriculture, raw clay for pottery, river cane for weaving and construction, and so on. A watershed people, the Cherokee personified the rivers beside which they lived, giving each a name as a living being, the "long man." Water was at the heart of their spiritual practice. Going to the water was a ritual of purification that prepared them for any number of meaningful activities and contributed to their health and hygiene.

Judaculla Rock[11]

11. https://www.dncr.nc.gov/blog/2016/03/27/judaculla-rock-cherokee-petroglyph-prominence.

TRAIL JOURNAL: EXPLORING MY MOUNTAIN BACKYARD

One summer a few years ago I decided it was time to continue exploring the landscape of Cherokee history. I was at my family's cabin in Cedar Mountain, North Carolina, when I learned of a talk about Native American history at the Dupont State Forest visitor center nearby. The lecture was being offered by Dr. Keith Parker, a Jungian psychoanalyst who lives in Brevard and is a respected scholar of Cherokee history and mythology. His presentation motivated me to pursue a meeting with him over coffee in Brevard. Mr. Parker knows his stuff, and I will be forever grateful for his directions to the site of the Lost Village of Connestee, halfway between Cedar Mountain and Brevard. There is a rock marker along Highway 276 that memorializes the site of Connestee but indicates only that it was nearby. With Dr. Parker's directions, I found what I think was the site, just a little over a mile down the Island Ford Road. Connestee, I am told, was one of the first, if not the first, archeological digs in North Carolina. I am puzzled that Connestee does not show up on any of the early colonial maps I have seen. Perhaps that was because of its mysterious disappearance, to which we will turn in a moment.

Dr. Parker also gave me contact information for another Parker relative who owns the farm where Judaculla Rock is located. Carrying a trail guide to Cherokee history, I set out on an exploratory journey, going first to the giant's place of judgment, known today as Devil's Courthouse. From that vantage point, I looked around 360 degrees at the Cherokee mountains all around me. I descended into the next valley, though not in one step as the giant Judaculla might have done. Finally, after getting lost on a forest service road, I reached the rock bearing his name. The other Mr. Parker graciously took me around his farm and showed me the rock, which still to my eye looks like the map of a homeland.

He also showed me a place in a creek running through his farm where some ancient etchings in the rock convinced him that this was where local Cherokee once "went to the water," the cleansing ritual so central to Cherokee spirituality. Mooney writes that the Cherokee practiced going to the water as a plunge bath in a nearby river or creek, sometimes accompanied by a shaman, who chanted from the shore. Going to water was seen as preparation for a new moon, a significant dance, or an important ball game with a rival town, perhaps before or after hunting or warfare. Going to the water was also a medical remedy, as was the sweat lodge. The fall was an optimum time because fallen leaves in the water added their medicinal qualities. But Cherokees practiced "going to the water" in all four seasons, exhibiting a tolerance for the cold to the point that they might have had to crack ice first.[12]

From the rock, I drove to Cullowhee, the site of what was once a Cherokee village and is now the campus of Western Carolina University. I had coffee with Dr. Brett Riggs, a professor at Western Carolina who was then the director of their Cherokee Studies program. He is a true gentleman and scholar and, as it turns out, an archeologist of the Eastern Band of the Cherokee. Throughout his career he has been deeply involved in the preservation and interpretation of Cherokee history. I learned more about Cherokee history in an hour and a half from Brett than in most of my prior reading. It was only after I left him that I realized he was the co-author of the *Cherokee Heritage Trails Guidebook*, my guide on this pilgrimage.

A MATRIARCHAL SOCIETY: THE CENTRALITY OF CHEROKEE WOMEN

In Cherokee culture, gender roles were clearly less hierarchical than in colonial society. Customarily, Cherokee men were largely employed in the vocational role of hunter and as warrior in defense of the boundaries of the homeland. But women sometimes accompanied men on war parties and in several instances took up the fight as warriors when their husbands were killed or wounded. Cherokee women oversaw the equally important agricultural dimension of the Cherokee economy. Colonial descriptions of Cherokee towns regularly reported extensive agricultural fields of corn, squash, and beans: the "three sisters" generally planted together in a mutually sustaining way.

Cherokee women were not simply agricultural laborers tending to this all-important source of food. They had political agency as well. They were listened to and called upon in tribal councils. Cherokee culture defined family systems as matriarchal, tracing bloodlines of households and clans from the lineage of the mother. As Hatley notes, "Cherokee women confident of their place in their own matriarchal world were largely responsible for the basic management of village life and the preservation of tribal identity."[13]

---

12. Duncan, "Going to Water," 95.
13. Hatley, *Dividing Paths*, 53–54.

Colonial white men were often confused and unsettled by the influence Cherokee women exercised in tribal life. Their social stature went far beyond what was allowed to colonial women. The prominent headman Attakullakulla once asked the governor of South Carolina why the white people did not include women in politics: "White men as well as red were born of women."[14] The unwillingness of colonial authorities to deal directly with Cherokee women was a direct attempt to undermine their status and influence within their society. Early colonial records reflect a growing ambivalence toward Cherokee women, often referring to them as "wenches," suggesting both lower status and sexual desirability. But as time went on, colonial records acknowledge a Cherokee woman only as "squaw," which today cannot be heard in any other way than as a derogatory racist slur.[15]

Under the leadership of Secretary Deb Haaland, the first Native American member of a presidential cabinet, the Department of the Interior is carrying out a process by which racist names of the nation's natural monuments, including hundreds of places named "Squaw __" are removed and the monuments renamed in more appropriate and respectful ways. As Secretary Haaland put it (in a *Washington Post* editorial),

> The word . . . squaw [is] a term so offensive that I have never used it except in issuing the order to make the name change, and beyond this sentence I will not repeat it here or anywhere. It was stolen from the word for "woman" in one specific Indigenous language, I believe Algonquian. The word was then perverted as so many Indigenous words and customs were, turning it into a broad racial slur, a caricature that removed individual identity and dignity from all women of Native American heritage.[16]

The power and influence of women in Cherokee society becomes clearer as we consider the life story of one particular woman: Nanyehi.

A BELOVED WOMAN: NANCY WARD

There are well-documented historical accounts of Cherokee women giving warning of an impending attack to white settlers. The most famous of these is Nanyehi, renamed by the English as Nancy Ward, a niece of the

---

14. Tortora, *Carolina in Crisis*, 74.
15. Hatley, *Dividing Paths*, 152.
16. Haaland, "How We Expunged," para. 3.

great chief Attakullakulla. Nanyehi accompanied her husband Kingfisher on a war party against the Creeks, and legend has it that she chewed on his bullets to increase their impact when they found their Creek target. When Kingfisher was killed, she took his place in the fight. Nanyehi became a "beloved woman" in the hearts of the Cherokee, with full voice in tribal councils, including the right to grant reprieve to captives. She granted pardon to a settler woman by the name of Lydia Bean who had been wounded and captured, taking Mrs. Bean into her home and nursing her back to health. In return, it is told, Mrs. Bean showed Nanyehi how to utilize a captured milk cow, introducing dairy products to the Cherokee diet.

Nanyehi remarried a British trader, Bryant Ward, and their daughter Elizabeth married another British trader named Joseph Martin. More than once, Nancy warned colonial settlements of impending attacks. Perhaps it was these stories of Nancy Ward/Nanyehi that gave rise to the legend of Cateechee, a young Indian woman who, learning of an imminent Cherokee attack on the white settlements in Ninety-Six, raced through the night to give warning not just to her white lover but to the whole settlement. As the case of Nanyehi/Nancy Ward suggests, Cherokee women often occupied a liminal space that was dangerous because their loyalty to either side—settler or Native—could be questioned. Despite these risks, Nancy Ward and other Cherokee women worked hard behind the scenes for a peaceful resolution to the conflicts that were destroying the Cherokee.

THE CHEROKEE APOCALYPSE

The Cherokee, because of their distance from the coast and the inaccessibility of their mountain habitations, had been largely protected from the rampant epidemic disease that had destroyed the Indigenous populations along the Atlantic Seaboard. At the same time, the Cherokees had only to look around them to see that they were the survivors in a country where their neighbors had vanished. Epidemic disease had already wiped out tribal nations from the South Carolina coast, moving like a wave northward to the up-country. Disease was delayed for the Cherokee until contact with Europeans became more frequent, but eventually plague would travel up the Keowee trading path and ravage the Cherokee people. No one can precisely estimate the population losses, but they were massive. The Cherokee population was cut by more than half, from approximately

32,000 in 1685 to roughly 12,000 in 1715.[17] Subsequent waves of disease further reduced this remnant by a third.

Connestee Marker

Mooney depicts this decimation quite graphically:

> In 1738 or 1739 smallpox, brought to Carolina by the slave ships, broke out among the Cherokee with such terrible effect that according to Adair (an early explorer who documented Native life in the Carolinas) nearly half the tribe was swept away within a year. The awful mortality was due largely to the fact that it was a new and strange disease to the Indians for which they had no immunity. As the pestilence spread unchecked from town to town, despair fell upon the nation. The priests, believing the visitation a penalty for violation of ancient ordinances, threw away their sacred paraphernalia as things which had lost their protective power. Hundreds of warriors committed suicide on beholding their frightful disfigurement. Some shot themselves,

17. Hatley, *Dividing Paths*, 8.

others cut their throats, some stabbed themselves with knives or sharp pointed canes; many threw themselves with sullen madness into the fire and there slowly expired.[18]

With the rapid spread of epidemic disease, suicide might also have been a way for infected individuals to sacrifice themselves for the good of the whole village.

The devastating impact of epidemic disease on the Cherokee is brought home most dramatically in the tragic story of Connestee. I first heard of Connestee as the name of a waterfall near our mountain cabin in Cedar Mountain, North Carolina, but the waterfall had an antecedent: halfway between Cedar Mountain and Brevard is a historical marker dedicated to the Lost Village of Connestee. It records how British troops passed through this valley in 1725 and found a thriving Cherokee settlement stretched along the banks of the French Broad River. But by 1777, other British troops would find no trace of the former people, prompting the legend of the lost village. I have long suspected that this mystery has a very real explanation.

Here is the beginning of the story as told by Swimmer to Mooney:

> Long ago, while people still lived in the old town of Kanasta on the French Broad River, two strangers, who looked in no way different from other Cherokee, came into the settlement one day and made their way into the chief's house. After the first greetings were over the chief asked them from what town they had come, thinking they were from one of the western settlements, but they said, "We are of your people and our town is close at hand, but you have never seen it. Here you have wars and sickness, with enemies on every side, and after a while a stronger enemy will come to take your country from you. We are always happy, and we have come to invite you to live with us in our town over there," and they pointed toward Pilot Knob. "We do not live forever, and do not always find game when we go for it, for the game belongs to Tsukalu (Judaculla), who lives in Tsunegunyi, but we have peace always and need not think of danger. If your people will live with us, let them fast for seven days, and we shall come then to take them." Then they went away to the west.[19]

The story of Connestee (*Kanasta*) as Swimmer relayed it to Mooney goes on to tell how the Cherokee were led to the mountain, where they

18. Mooney, *Myths of the Cherokee*, 36.
19. Mooney, *Myths of the Cherokee*, 341–42.

found a secret entrance into a hidden sanctuary, within which was a village, where they were welcomed with gracious hospitality by their kin. I had driven by this marker commemorating the Lost Village of Connestee many times in going between Brevard and Cedar Mountain and have wondered about the mystery of it. It was not until years later, as I came to understand the breadth of the devastation wrought by epidemic disease that ravaged Native American communities across the continent, that I suspected this story might be rooted in the reality of this overwhelming loss.

Now, reading the story of the Lost Village of Connestee, I imagine the Cherokee people trying to grapple with the magnitude of this loss and to find some way to assuage their grief. How does a people remain a people as they experience wave after wave of conquest coming at them like a tsunami, with disease the first crashing blow, followed by war and dispossession? This context gives new depth to their story and their faith that their people still lived—that a safe place of refuge was close by and that, like the rocks and cliffs of the mountains around them, they would be able to stand up to the waves of conquest, to resist with courage and survive.

However, the memory of this historical trauma reverberates through the telling and the meaning of the story:

> The people of the Lost settlement were never seen again, and they are still living in Tsuwatelda. Strange things happen there, so that the Cherokee know the mountain is haunted and do not like to go near it. Only a few years ago a party of hunters camped there, and as they sat around their fire at supper time they talked of the story and made rough jokes about the people of old Kanasta. That night they were aroused from sleep by a noise as of stones thrown at them from among the trees, but when they searched, they could find nobody, and were so frightened that they gathered up their guns and pouches and left the place.[20]

Whatever comfort the Cherokee might derive from the story of Connestee as they grieved their lost loved ones, no story could ever completely erase the trauma of genocide. The ghosts of the past could still trouble those who lived in the present.

The former location of Connestee is now a pleasant-looking pasture with an excellent view of *Tsuwatelda*—Pilot Knob, as it is known

---

20. Mooney, *Myths of the Cherokee*, 341–42.

today—situated a few miles north of Brevard. This is the mountain where the hidden village was found. The story of the Lost Village also alludes to other habitations of the invisible people, perhaps an allusion to the Shining Rock Wilderness area not far from the Courthouse of Judaculla on the Blue Ridge Parkway. In Cherokee mythology there are other stories of a similar hidden village within the mountain and of the shining rocks as a kind of gateway into it. Cold Mountain, made famous in Charles Frazier's novel, lies just beyond the Shining Rocks.

Amitav Ghosh, the author of *The Nutmeg's Curse: Parables for a Planet in Crisis*, has pushed me much further in my thinking on the "great dying," the catastrophic impact of epidemic disease on the Indigenous of the Americas with massive population decline as high as 90 percent. He reminds us of the most recent theorizing about this with the plausible theory of virgin territory, in which Native populations were highly vulnerable to epidemic tidal waves because, never having been exposed to these diseases, they had no immune system defenses—certainly true to a degree. Taking note of the correspondence found by the nineteenth-century historian Francis Parkman, between Sir Jeffery Amherst, commander in chief of the British forces in North America in the early 1760s, and Col. Henry Bouquet, a subordinate on the western frontier during the French and Indian War, discussing the use of smallpox as a biological weapon against the Shawnee, Ghosh suggests that biological warfare was a well-tried weapon in the arsenal of white colonial military strategy, providing more documentation suggesting this was not a historical anomaly.

Beyond even this, he makes the persuasive case that history cannot separate out so neatly the Indigenous deaths brought about by disease from those brought about by direct conflict with European settlers, as some historians have tried to do, somehow exonerating settler colonialism from a genocidal event that was biologically driven, simply an unavoidable act of nature. More recent historical work confirms that any human population is more susceptible to epidemic disease if it is already experiencing hunger, dislocation, the loss of land, slavery, and crushing labor. More intangible but no less real was the loss of the will to live or to reproduce as families. Furthermore, actual warfare waged against Native populations did not happen in a historical vacuum. Colonial military strategy was enmeshed in all these other material factors, emerging in calculations of opportunity to use overpowering force against Native communities that were increasingly vulnerable because of population loss.[21]

21. Ghosh, *Nutmeg's Curse*, 57–59.

CHEROKEE INDEBTEDNESS AND COLONIAL LAND GRABBING

It was inevitable that, under the pressure of the fur trade with England, the deer population of the Carolinas would crash. Cherokee and white hunters would have to travel farther and farther away to find deer skins. I remember hearing that the numbers of deer in up-country South Carolina did not rebound to the population of pre-contact days before the fur trade until well into the 1970s. The widespread disappearance of deer meant for the Cherokee that their primary food system, based on hunting, was out of balance. What had been a sustainable subsistence system was now harnessed to the consumption and greed of European economies. Providing meat for their village was becoming increasingly difficult for hunters. And yet the desire for those goods that Europeans had to offer, including alcohol, was not sated.

Corrupt practices of colonial traders engendered disagreements with the Cherokee, and negotiations over prices often turned hostile. A trader might hold an entire village accountable for the debts of one hunter. As trading exchanges continued, debt mounted on the Cherokee side of the ledger. How were they to pay the growing debt to colonial traders? What could they provide the colonists if they could not find deerskins? The Cherokee had land. The concept of private property was still quite foreign to their culture, but cessions of land became their way to resolve indebtedness with colonial traders.

At first these land sales amounted only to the granting of land to a trader who may have been residing near the Cherokee village, or perhaps had even married a Cherokee woman and had children of mixed blood. Debt owed to that trader for European goods could be settled for a land grant. The relationship the Cherokee had with individual traders depended largely on the moral character of the trader. James Beamer, the Scots Irish trader married to a Cherokee woman and associated with the Cherokee town of Eastatoee, appeared to enjoy the people's respect and trust because of his honorable dealings with them. But corrupt traders who cheated the Cherokee were a source of great mischief and discord, supplying only rum and extending credit only to seize the land as payment.

However, it is likely that the Cherokee could see the benefit of having a few trusted white or mixed-race people who could translate English, serve as go-betweens with colonial authorities, interpret changes in colonial behavior and policy, and, in the best case, help solve problems that arose from commercial transactions. Land grants were made to mixed-blood trading families that could form a protective buffer along the Cherokee–South Carolina border, blocking further white settler encroachment. The Cherokee increasingly saw these *metis*, or mixed blood individuals and families, as useful for controlling the illegal immigration of the colonists.

RICHARD PEARIS, THE TRADER WHO FOUNDED MY HOMETOWN

This was certainly the case in what is today Greenville County. Richard Pearis was one of the first white traders to settle in Cherokee territory. He married a Cherokee woman and, with a mixed-race family, was able to accumulate large landholdings through grants and land sales from the Cherokee. He owned well over a hundred thousand acres in what today is the area of Greenville. Paris Mountain, a landmark and state park just outside the city, is named for him. Pearis was able for a time to maneuver around English law prohibiting land sales to whites from Natives because his mixed-race son, as a Cherokee, was legally entitled to make these transactions. The son bought parcel after parcel along the Reedy River (about thirty miles east of Keowee) and deeded them back to his father. The Cherokee allowed all this, hoping that granting land to allies like Pearis could serve as a stopgap against other settlers coming in.[22] Pearis maintained this precarious position as an intermediary between South Carolina and the Cherokee until the American Revolution forced him to declare his loyalty to the British Crown and the Cherokee instead of the colony.

THE SHIFTING BALANCE OF POWER

As the balance of power between the Cherokee and colonial South Carolina shifted, pressure was growing from the numbers of white settlers pushing past boundaries that had been negotiated in treaties. Violent conflicts were erupting between encroaching settlers and Cherokee determined to defend their territory. The power dynamics in the South Carolina–Cherokee relationship began to shift. For many years the colonists

---

22. Hatley, *Dividing Paths*, 90.

had thought it necessary to keep the Cherokee as military allies against the French and Spanish and their Indian allies. And the deerskin trade had been one of the pillars of the Carolina colonial economy. But as more settlers poured into Carolina, the acquisition of land became the colony's overriding concern. In 1760, this fundamental conflict would lead to an all-out war between South Carolina and the Cherokee. In historical hindsight, war might appear to have been inevitable. But a different narrative could have been written if only the worldview of white colonialism had included a willingness to respect the Cherokee as a people with a sovereign right to their homeland.

A PRESBYTERIAN MISSIONARY AMONG THE CHEROKEE

The growing tension between colonial South Carolina and the Cherokee Nation was readily apparent to a Presbyterian missionary living among the Cherokee in the Overhill Towns. The Reverend William Richardson had been commissioned by the Waxhaws Presbyterian Church in the South Carolina up-country to evangelize among the Cherokee. His predecessor, a Reverend Martin, had given up in frustration. The Cherokee had summarized Reverend Martin's preaching thus: "We do good, we go up. If bad, down. That he could say no more; that he had long plagued them with what they no ways understood, and they desire him to depart the country."[23] The Cherokee, having wearied of hearing the same message over and over, invited Martin to conclude his ministry in their midst. Nevertheless, Reverend Richardson was determined to try himself. But what he found when he took up residence in the Overhill Towns was that he was banned from preaching to their inhabitants. No matter how often he pleaded with Chief Attakullakulla, the answer was always the same: a firm no thank you. Reverend Richardson's ministries were limited to the British soldiers who garrisoned Fort Loudoun, the colonial outpost in the Overhill Towns.

Nevertheless, Richardson, though his assignment would be brief—only three months—was well-positioned to monitor the mood of the Cherokee all around him. As rumors drifted in about incidents in which they had been abused and mistreated, the missionary perceived a growing hostility in town councils. Attakullakulla's niece Nancy Ward, a friend

23. King, *Memoirs of Timberlake*, 34.

of the English, would advocate for peace in these councils. But the voices of Attakullakulla's son, Dragging Canoe, and other young warriors would carry the day. Finally, Reverend Richardson, sensing the growing danger of war, decided it was time to leave. He made his way back to the Scots Irish Presbyterian settlement of the Waxhaws, where his evangelistic skills were put to good use. Richardson is generally acknowledged to be a founder of several Presbyterian congregations in the up-country. Because his ministry was so widely celebrated, the circumstances of his death seemed especially shocking.[24] In 1771, his wife and a Presbyterian elder found him dead in his study, in a kneeling position, with a bridle around his neck, an apparent suicide.

The death of Rev. William Richardson gives much insight into the backwoods area and the superstitions of many of the people who lived there. The man was buried, but many in the community had suspicions about the death, believing that there was some type of witchcraft or evil doings involved in the death. About a year later, a group from the community exhumed and opened the coffin of Reverend Richardson. His remains were exposed, and the hand of his widow, Agnes Nancy Richardson, was forcibly held against the skull of her long-deceased husband. An old Scottish belief was that blood would flow from the fingers of a murderer. No blood was seen, and the widow was not prosecuted for murder. This rite was called the Ordeal of Touch, and it is believed that this was the last time it was ever used in the United States. Pastor Richardson has been buried at the Old Waxhaw church three times.[25]

The Waxhaws Presbyterian Church will surface again and again in our story so this might be an opportune moment to get a sense of its culture and influence over so many, including Andrew Jackson, who was born in 1767 and baptized in this congregation. In his biography of Andrew Jackson, the historian Jon Meacham describes the kind of services that the Jacksons attended at Waxhaws. Worship likely started midmorning:

> A psalm was sung—but without organ music, for Presbyterians were austere not only in their theology but in their liturgy—and a prayer said. Church historians suspect such prayers could stretch beyond twenty minutes in length. Then came a lesson from scripture—the selection could range from an entire chapter of a book of the Bible to a shorter reading followed by an

---

24. Howe, *History*, 290.
25. Waxhaw's History, "Ordeal of Touch."

explication—followed by the centerpiece of the morning: the minister's sermon, an address that could range in length from thirty minutes to an hour. Another psalm or hymn closed the morning, which had by now consumed two hours of the day. There was a break for lunch, then an afternoon version of the same service, which everyone attended as well. From his babyhood, then, Andrew Jackson probably spent between three and four hours near every Sunday for about fourteen years worshiping in this Presbyterian mode.[26]

Meacham displays an uncanny grasp of the theological content of the sermons that were preached from the pulpit at Waxhaws to young Jackson or for that matter to any of the members of Presbyterian congregations in the up-country. "Jackson would have been transported to imaginative realms where good and evil were at war, where kings and prophets on the side of the Lord struggled against the darker powers, where man's path through a confusing world was lit by a peculiar intermingling of Christian mercy and might. God may well plan on exalting the humble and meek, but Jackson also heard the call of Gideon's trumpet[27]—the call to, as Saint Paul put it, fight the good fight."[28]

TRAIL JOURNAL: TRACING THE CHEROKEE PATH TODAY

In 2022, Dennis Chastain, South Carolina's award-winning naturalist and historian, generously offered to guide me on a circuit of some Cherokee sites among the Lower Towns. Several members of my family, game for an adventure, decided to come along. Early one morning in April, we made our way from Greenville to meet Dennis and his wife Jane at the intersection of Highway 178 and Highway 11, the Cherokee Foothills Scenic Highway.

---

26. Meacham, *American Lion*, 17.

27. Gideon's trumpet is a reference to an obscure biblical event, recorded in the book of Judges, that occurred during the conquest of Canaan. Gideon had summoned an army of Israelite warriors to do battle with the Midianites. Their God, concerned that this army would consider the victory about to be given them, a result of their own power, spoke to Gideon instructing him to send away most of his army. Facing overwhelming numerical odds, the Israelites under Gideon went into battle with trumpets and torches concealed in pots. At the moment of attack, just before dawn, their light and sound were unleashed, convincing their enemies that a much larger army was arrayed against them.

28. Meacham, *American Lion*, 17.

Our first stop was a stone's throw away: an old church graveyard on a bluff. As we gazed across the valley to the mountain horizon, Jane told us that they knew most of the people in the graves around us. At an altitude just shy of 3,500 feet, Pinnacle Mountain stood shoulder to shoulder with other peaks along the ridge. Dennis pointed out an outcropping of rocks where he and a now deceased archeologist had discovered a cluster of circular petroglyphs, a percentage of the three thousand of which have been identified in the Carolinas—reminders of the Indigenous past.

The main lesson Dennis wanted to convey here was geographic. Contemplating the mountain range rising before us, the traveler from times past would have been wondering how to get through it. Well-disguised gaps allow passage into the interior of the Blue Ridge Mountains, and Dennis and Jane were about to lead us through one. We set out along what is today Highway 178, called one of the more dangerous roads in the state for its winding path up into the mountains until it crosses the North Carolina border. This mountain road revealed some of the last remaining pockets of old time Appalachia, ever more squeezed by encroaching development like the high-end subdivisions being built along Highway 11. Through this gap we entered an earlier epoch of Appalachian history, for this valley was the location of the Eastatoee village, one of the more prominent of the Lower Towns of the Cherokee.

Eastatoee got its name as the place of the multi-colored bird known later as the Carolina parakeet. Though these birds had been abundant in the southern Appalachian Mountain range, the species flourished so here that their presence was the distinguishing feature of the valley. Another possible explanation occurred to me: the Eastatoee Trail, a major north-south trading path, passed through this valley. Perhaps it was the birds' colored feathers, so valued for their beauty, that were among the goods exchanged between Indigenous people passing through this area. Carolina parakeets were hunted to extinction in the mid-nineteenth century. Thinking of that disappearance, I still feel a pang of loss; I have Audubon's portrait of them on my wall. We pulled off the side of the road and gazed around this beautiful valley. Seeing the looks of appreciation on our faces, Dennis exclaimed, "It's a bit of heaven on earth!" Nearby was a mountain called Wadakoe where, according to Dennis, nine different species of the wildflower trillium could be found, together with another species of flower that until recently had never been documented by science. Heaven on earth indeed.

Memories of an Earlier Visit to Eastatoe

The last time I was in the Eastatoe Valley was so long ago that I cannot remember the year. But I have never forgotten the experience. I don't know if I was looking for the valley intentionally or if I stumbled upon it. I told Dennis how I came upon a handsome old farmhouse much longer than it was wide, with a front porch that ran the length of it. As I parked and approached the house, I saw an old gentleman sitting on the porch in a rocking chair. Identifying myself, I inquired if I might ask him a few questions about the area. "Come on up," Mr. Paul Bowie responded graciously. Sometimes even conversation with a loved one can be awkward, and so it is especially surprising when conversation with a total stranger flows as easily as a mountain stream. Such was my conversation with Mr. Bowie as we sat on that porch for a little more than an hour.

I learned from him about his family's roots in the valley and how as a young man his first job off the farm was as a schoolteacher in a one room schoolhouse located much higher in the mountains, to which he walked and where he stayed during the school week. My questions for Mr. Bowie on the porch that day concerned the Cherokee presence in the valley. He said that as a boy he found many arrowheads at the location of the battle that took place here when colonial troops invaded and ultimately destroyed Eastatoe. It grew late in the afternoon and, knowing that I needed to return home myself, I thanked him for his time and left. I would not return until this trip with Dennis, over thirty-five years later. He said he knew the Bowie family—though of course, Mr. Paul Bowie had been dead for many years—and promised as we drove through the valley to point out the old farmhouse where Mr. Bowie's son and his family still lived.

James Beamer's Trading Post

A few miles farther, Dennis also showed us the place where Eastatoe had been, centered around a council house, numerous habitations, and maybe a defensive palisade. He noted that the devastating force of epidemic diseases like smallpox decentralized many of the Cherokee towns, causing people to spread out to escape infection. Finally, we pulled off the road at a South Carolina historic marker. The text, which Dennis had authored, explained a little about Eastatoe. Now he chuckled over the challenge of condensing this history into the constricted space of a small sign.

The marker was located at the site of the trading post run by the Scots Irish trader James Beamer, who married a Cherokee woman and carried on trade with the people of Eastatoee for over sixty years. He could not have enjoyed that longevity without the trust and goodwill of the Cherokee. Dennis said that it had been Beamer who strongly urged the colonial governor, James Glen, to build the fort at Keowee. If South Carolina did not build the fort, Beamer had predicted, French influence would increase, and the British would lose its most important Indigenous ally. Governor Glen did not really need to be convinced of this; he understood the value of the alliance with the Cherokee. But the Charles Town planters and merchants who composed his government did need convincing that more taxes were warranted to build the distant fort.

Before we departed for our next destination, the town of Keowee, Dennis shared some information that he had only recently learned. The Cherokee Nation had seven principal towns with council houses. Keowee was certainly one of those, as was Nikwasi, for the Middle Towns, Kituwah for the Out Towns, and Chota for the Overhill Towns. Dennis now believed that Eastatoee, like Keowee, also held the status of beloved town. Keowee and Eastatoee were about the same size, perhaps two hundred dwellings, and the headmen from both towns had great influence. The only substantial difference between the two was that Keowee was at the intersection of many trails, a nexus of trade, transportation, and diplomacy.

On to Keowee

On the drive to Keowee we pulled over a few more times along the way so that Dennis could point out what appeared to our eyes to be a ditch. Overgrown and completely unremarkable, it was in fact a trace of the historic Cherokee Path, hidden in plain sight. We finally reached Keowee landing, a boat launch on Lake Keowee that looks out on the site of what was once was the mother town of Keowee and Fort Prince George, now underneath hundreds of feet of water. What were once ridges towering over the Keowee valley are now shorefront lots occupied by luxurious lake homes. A closed, overgrown service road nearby is the only link to the location of an old granite marker identifying this historic site: "Keowee Town, Capital of the Lower Cherokee Indian Settlements. Visited by De Soto in 1540. Destroyed in 1760. Erected by the Tamassee Chapter

THE CHEROKEE NATION ENCOUNTERS SOUTH CAROLINA

of the Daughters of the American Revolution [DAR] in 1935. Relocated in 1972." In the 1930s the prevailing opinion was that De Soto's route carried him through Keowee, but more recent historical research has not confirmed that view.

The DAR was a formidable organization in its day, having founded a boarding school nearby around the time the monument was erected. We drove briefly through its campus, impressed by the numerous granite buildings. In 1972, when Duke Power created Lake Hartwell/Keowee, the DAR marker to Keowee was relocated from its proximate location to the village. It occurred to me that this marker's dedication in 1935 must have been the occasion of my grandfather's address on Keowee. I made a mental note for when I got back home to go through my family history archives and find his address. I also vowed to return and find that granite marker that Dennis said was a couple of hundred yards back in the woods. From the Keowee landing we went on to Oconee Station, where we all shared a picnic lunch. Agreeing that another road trip in the future would be appropriate, we parted after a most satisfying day.

Once back home, I went straight to the family history archives to find my grandfather's address at Keowee in 1935: "Unveiling of Memorial Tablet on the Site of the Ancient Cherokee Village of Keowee. By John S. Taylor. July 31st, 1935."

> Madam Regent, Ladies and Gentlemen: I esteem it a genuine pleasure and a privilege to be present on this occasion, and I count it an honor to have a part in this program. May I, at the outset, express my personal appreciation to you the Regent and Wizard of Tamassee Chapter of the DAR, and to your splendid chapter for the valuable contribution that you are here making in the marking of this Historic Indian Site. I feel that I express not only the gratitude and appreciation of those present, but also the citizens of this state for the work you are doing in preserving and perpetuating the history of this commonwealth. It is to be hoped that your good work shall continue and that eventually the lawmakers of our State may be encouraged by your precept and example to make an adequate annual appropriation that this work may be carried on. Throughout the whole length and breadth of South Carolina from the ramparts of Caesar's Head to the walls of Fort Sumter, our State is a veritable treasure house of Historic Shrines which should be permanently marked for posterity.

John S. Taylor Dedicating Keowee Marker

Keowee Marker

He goes on to list a series of encounters at Keowee between the British colony and the Cherokee Nation, including several I have not mentioned at all in my history. He noted that Chief Attakullakulla, who went to England in 1730, received an audience with King George and had his portrait painted in London. He described the Indian trade at Keowee and the construction of Fort Prince George. Recounting the Cherokee War of 1760 that destroyed Keowee, my grandfather acknowledged that the English bore a measure of responsibility for bringing about the conflict. Then, after quoting the poetic passage from *Bartram's Travels* as the famous botanist, leaving the Keowee Valley, looked back on its lush beauty, he ended his address with a tribute to Cherokee leaders:

> In conclusion, may I again thank and commend you for the placing of this memorial. In the future it shall remind us of Attakullakulla, the firm friend of the English whose loyalty never wavered; of Oconostota, the great war chief; and of many others, both red and white race, who lived here and came here, playing their parts in the great pageant of South Carolina history. May it be a reminder to us and to our children's children, of the days and deeds of the past, keeping before us the recollection of this phase of our country's history, that its memory may not perish from the earth!

Three weeks later I drove out to Keowee Landing and parked my car to the side of the road, hoping to find the granite marker my grandfather had dedicated. Just as Dennis suggested, I had only to walk a couple of hundred yards back into the woods to find the marker, off the beaten path and forgotten, overlooking Lake Keowee and the approximate site of Keowee. It was an uncanny feeling to stand there and think of the words my grandfather had delivered, as if I were almost channeling him. With that old Kodak photo of him giving the address, it was easy to visualize that moment. I am impressed by his eloquence, and I appreciate the value he put on remembering the past. Our interpretations of this history may differ significantly, but in my own way I am trying to continue a conversation with him about its meaning.

4

A Vicious Cycle of Violence: The Cherokee War of 1760–61

IRONICALLY, THE LONG SLIDE into conflict began as the Cherokee were returning from the French and Indian War, where they had fought as allies to the British colonies. While colonial military commanders valued the contribution of their Indigenous allies, the Cherokee themselves felt unappreciated and uncompensated for their sacrifices. With the British military effort stalled in defeat, the Cherokee warriors were all too aware that the hunting season was closing and, along with it, the capacity to feed their families and villages through a long winter. Accustomed to their freedom to fight or not as they saw fit, they left the war to return home.

Led by pro-British chiefs like Attakullakulla, the Cherokee had gone to war as valuable allies of the British colonies in a global conflict fought between the European powers on the American continent. But to white English-speaking colonists on the frontier, for whom conflict between Natives and white colonials was becoming increasingly racialized, these Cherokee allies were no longer differentiated as a particular people or community. They were seen as part of the racial other, indistinguishable from Native enemies: red people, bloody Indians, dangerous savages, permanent adversaries.

Thus Cherokee war parties, returning home through the Shenandoah Valley, experienced aggression from Virginians the Cherokee had thought were allies. Near the present town of Winchester, Virginia, one war party, having been forced by near starvation to kill and eat their own horses, captured other horses in open pasture to replace those mounts lost. In fact, both sides "stole" horses. But the Cherokee's acquisitions in this instance led to a bloody retaliation by white settlers, with the scalping and mutilation of several of their warriors whose remains were paraded in white settlements in Virginia. The great head man Attakullakulla himself, the faithful friend of the British since his transatlantic voyage to England in 1730 to meet with the king, was accosted and disarmed by settlers in Virginia. This humiliating blow to his status as head man must have strained his loyalty to the British.

In all, thirty-seven warriors lost their lives in the journey home from the French and Indian War.[1] The Cherokee regarded these deaths as an outrage, inexplicable and deeply injurious. As groups of Cherokee warriors progressed farther south into the Carolinas, they exacted revenge on frontier communities along the way. Blood vengeance was a code of justice that to our conscious sensibilities seems raw and violent even as it shapes international relations today more than we would like to think. Blood vengeance as it was exercised within Cherokee culture was not just revenge for the aggrieved but a restoring of balance, which was itself a kind of justice. Even in Judaic law of the Old Testament, the admonition of an "eye for an eye" was intended to limit retribution to a commensurate measure. Sometimes prisoners taken in war by the Cherokee were subject to those Cherokee families that had suffered losses. It was the prerogative of these grieving families to decide the fate of captives, either for mercy and perhaps adoption into the clan, or sometimes for harsh torture and execution.

In response to the depredations committed against them in Virginia, the Cherokee went on the warpath with attacks against Moravian settlements at Bethabara and Bethania in the Yadkin River watershed (near today's Winston-Salem, North Carolina). When other communities along the Yadkin, like the Bryan Settlement, fell under attack, some of the settlers, including the extended Boone family, removed to Fort Dobbs, which had been built in 1755 for protection (near today's Statesville, North Carolina).[2] Tension was extremely high in the South Carolina up-country as well. The Cherokee attacked the Tyger River settlements and killed nine people.[3] Many Scots Irish Presbyterians retreated to

---

1. Tortora, *Carolina in Crisis*, 33.
2. Tortora, *Carolina in Crisis*, 22.
3. Tortora, *Carolina in Crisis*, 107.

Waxhaws and other points lower in the colony. Others hunkered down in their frontier stockades.[4]

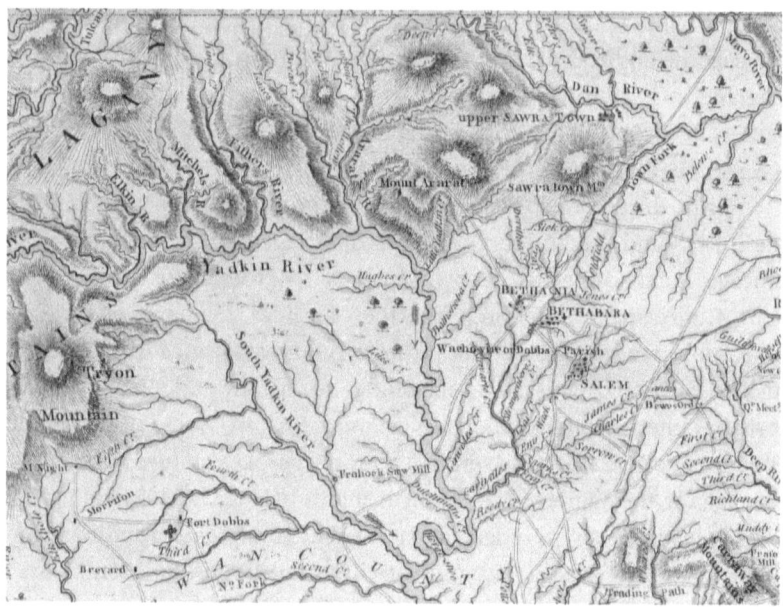

Forks of Yadkin

From Keowee, a high-level delegation of Cherokee elders went to Charles Town to enter complex negotiations, believing that these talks with the colony would lead to peace. It was a necessary political act of foreign policy that the Cherokee would have to repeat many times and would learn well through bitter experience. The Cherokee expected that their coming would offer an opportunity to express their grievances and address specific difficulties, to discuss how to adjudicate justice in these outbreaks of frontier violence. A successful peace negotiation could involve apologies and mutual professions of respect and goodwill, gift giving, and symbolic acts and rituals. This was not what they experienced in Charles Town. Governor Lyttleton of South Carolina had replaced Governor Glen in 1756 and had none of his predecessor's political acumen. Lyttleton received the Cherokee peace delegation with great hostility. Having already committed the colony to war, he took the Cherokee

---

4. Tortora, *Carolina in Crisis*, 113.

peace delegation prisoner and placed them under armed guard. His troops assembled in Charles Town, boarded boats to be transported up the Cooper River to Strawberry, near Mepkin, where they disembarked to march up the Keowee Trail toward the up-country and the Cherokee mother town of Keowee and Fort Prince George.

As noted earlier, the erection of Fort Prince George in 1753 had marked the beginning of Britain's effort to defend the colony's western border from French influence. South Carolina also reckoned that the presence of an English fort would serve as a proper deterrent to Cherokee antagonism. The sly Attakullakulla had suggested the actual site for the fort, across the river from Keowee and surrounded by rolling hills on all sides. Soldiers inside its walls soon realized that a Cherokee marksman could see the buckle on a shoe from a nearby ridge line.

The current tension between South Carolina and the Cherokee Nation was no doubt exacerbated by the fact that weeks before, soldiers from Fort Prince George had raped several Cherokee women in Keowee—women who could well have been the wives of Cherokee warriors fighting for the British far away from the village. Lyttleton ordered an attack on the village of Keowee, which had already been largely abandoned upon their approach. He locked the twenty-two Cherokee elders from the delegation in a small cell, large enough for only a handful of prisoners, within the Fort Prince George stockade.

When smallpox broke out among his troops Lyttleton decided to proclaim a military triumph and beat a hasty retreat. Lieutenant Cotymore, the commanding officer of Fort Prince George situated near Keowee, viewed the epidemic as his ally: "I can't help being so inhuman," he wrote, "as to wish it may spread through the whole nation."[5] This outbreak of smallpox spread first among the Lower Towns and ultimately reached the Valley and Middle Towns as well, further devastating Cherokee society. The Overhill Towns were spared because of their strict adherence to a quarantine, refusing to allow any Cherokee from other places to have contact. Governor Lyttleton would carry the smallpox back to Charles Town with his troops' return, igniting another outbreak there among the city's population.

Before he left Keowee, Lyttleton declared that the Cherokee peace delegation would remain in prison until such time as the tribe turned

---

5. Tortora, *Carolina in Crisis*, 83.

over every warrior who had killed a white settler. Attakullakulla finally prevailed upon Lyttleton to release him and two other head men, Oconostota, who was a war chief, and a third, only known as the Warrior of Eastatoee. Governor Lyttleton had no sooner returned to Charles Town as conquering hero, eager to receive the accolades of an adoring public, than the whole South Carolina frontier erupted in war.

After the departure of Lyttleton and his troops, the warriors of the Cherokee Lower Towns regrouped. Because those Cherokee elders held as prisoners in Fort Prince George were beloved men with deep clan ties among all the Cherokee settlements, warriors from the Middle and Valley Towns willingly joined the Lower Towns in a major offensive. Together they laid siege to Fort Prince George and initiated attacks on settler communities across the up-country, including killing nine Scots Irish settlers on the Tyger River, the area settled by my Anderson ancestors. The Overhill Towns attacked the settlements along the Yadkin River in North Carolina.[6] It is quite easy for me to imagine the terror these settlers must have felt as they congregated in frontier forts, awaiting a possible attack from Cherokee war parties.

SCOTS IRISH PRESBYTERIANS IN LONG CANE

Cherokee war parties drove frightened settlers into the safety of rude residential forts dotted across the up-country landscape. One such settlement, composed of Scots Irish Presbyterians, had been established since the early 1750s near the Cherokee boundary in the area called Long Cane (in present day Abbeville County). As the uppermost colonial communities along the trail to Keowee, the Long Cane Settlement and nearby settlements on the Saluda River offer a case study of cultural encounters and tension that finally led to a traumatic explosion of violence.[7] Long Cane was named after the canebrakes in river bottom land that flourished across the up-country and whose height was a measure of the soil's fertility. It was located about sixty miles southeast of Keowee, near the junction of the two forks of the Keowee Trail, dividing paths that were separate routes deeper into Cherokee territory.

6. Tortora, *Carolina in Crisis*, 107–8.
7. Hatley, *Dividing Paths*, 85–86.

It was a region filled with deer, woodland buffalo, and other game, and though Cherokee no longer lived there, they still considered it their hunting territory. The colonists who settled at Long Cane were Presbyterians, among them the Calhoun family, ancestors of John C. Calhoun. Essentially, they were squatters on Cherokee land, in violation of the 1746 Carolina-Cherokee treaty. To make matters worse, they also hunted thirty or forty miles farther into Cherokee territory. They placed dams on several creeks and fished them heavily. As Daniel Tortora notes, "They raised cattle at salt licks used not long before by deer and buffalo. They also peddled liquor and household goods as unlicensed traders."[8]

Finally, deciding that the danger of war with the Cherokee was simply too great, the Long Cane settlers left their stockade and began a perilous retreat toward Augusta. It was at this moment of heightened vulnerability, as their wagon train was bogged down crossing a creek, that they were attacked by the Cherokee. A few days later this report appeared in the Charles Town newspaper, the *South Carolina Gazette*:

> Yesterday the whole of the Long Cane Settlers, to the number of 150 souls, moved off with most of their effects in wagons; to go towards Augusta in Georgia, and in a few hours after their setting off, were surprised and attacked by about 100 Cherokee on horseback, while they were getting their wagons out of a boggy place; they had amongst them forty gunmen, who might have made a very good defense, but unfortunately their guns were in the wagons; the few that recovered theirs, fought the Indians half an hour, and were at last obliged to fly; in the action they lost seven wagons, and some forty of their people killed or taken (including women and children) the rest got to Augusta.[9]

---

8. Tortora, *Carolina in Crisis*, 104.
9. From the February 2–9 issue, 1760.

Long Canes Massacre Headstone

Some of the children were later found hiding or left for dead. Among those killed was John C. Calhoun's grandmother. Her son Patrick "returned to the site days later [and] found bodies 'most inhumanely butchered,' lying among empty wagons in a burnt clearing." As a young boy, Patrick's son, John C. Calhoun, would have heard the story of his grandmother's death from his father and seen the rough stone marker that Patrick erected to her memory, inscribed "Mrs. Catherine Calhoun Aged 76 Years Who with 22 Others Was Here Murdered by the Indians First of Feb. 1760."[10] The monument to his mother still stands today.

While the Cherokee launched other attacks against frontier outposts across the up-country, Fort Prince George was surrounded by Cherokee warriors demanding the release of the twenty-two Cherokee headmen held hostage within the stockade. Oconostota, the Cherokee war chief, approached the fort and called out for a meeting with the despised fort commander, Lieutenant Cotymore. When Cotymore came through the gate, Oconostota gave a signal to warriors hidden nearby who opened fire

10. Elder, *Calhoun*, 12–13.

on Cotymore and fatally wounded him. The ambush of Cotymore could be interpreted as an example of Native duplicity, but from the Cherokee perspective it was the colonists who were duplicitous: Governor Lyttleton had summoned a delegation of Cherokee elders to Charles Town to negotiate peace and now held them in chains inside the fort. The Cherokee may also have believed that Lieutenant Cotymore was one of the soldiers who had raped Cherokee women inside the fort—apparently not an isolated event. Cotymore was brought back into the stockade. When he died later that day, the soldiers of the garrison fell upon the imprisoned Cherokee elders and massacred them all. Now all-out war with the Cherokee commenced.

A SECOND INVASION REACHES DEEPER INTO THE CHEROKEE NATION

A second military expedition from Charles Town was launched, this time under the command of a British officer, Colonel Montgomery. They reached Keowee and the Lower Towns of the Cherokee and burned and destroyed their homes, their food stocks, and their agricultural fields. Lower Towns like Tugaloo, Seneca, Oconee, and Eastatoee, a settlement of over two hundred dwellings and hundreds of acres of corn, were also destroyed.

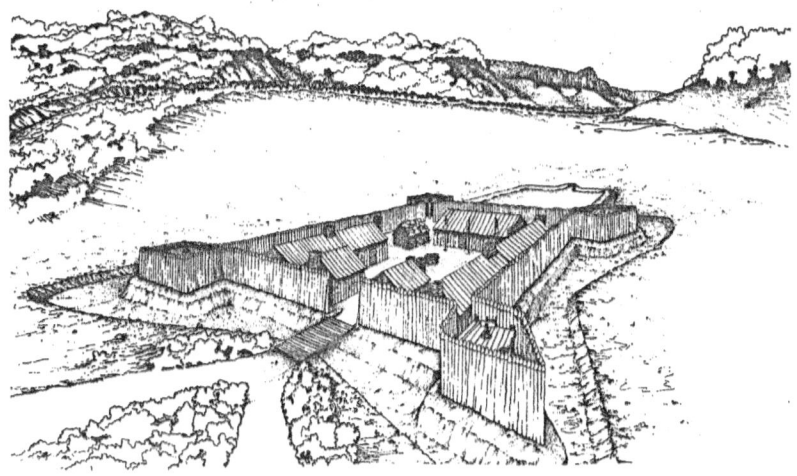

Fort Prince George[11]

11. https://southcarolinagenealogy.com/edgefield/building-fort-keowee-fort-prince-george.htm.

Proceeding beyond the Lower Towns, Montgomery and his troops advanced on the sacred village of Nikwasi, one of the principal towns of the Middle Settlements along the headwaters of the Little Tennessee in what is today Franklin, North Carolina. Like every other Cherokee town the colonial troops encountered, Nikwasi was burned to the ground, its fields and orchards destroyed. The only structure spared was the council house atop the central mound, which Montgomery utilized before and after his campaign. But the Cherokee were not yet defeated.

Just beyond Nikwasi was a narrow mountain gorge where the Cherokee forces amassed to resist the invasion. Using the topography of that gorge to full advantage, they attacked the colonial column from mountain ridges above and from dense cane thickets along the river. Using this pincer strategy, the warriors inflicted severe losses on the colonial forces. They also harassed the long train of supply wagons and pack mules behind the advancing colonial army. Montgomery, who defined military courage as the discipline required to stand in a column and return fire, as was the custom in European warfare, derided the cowardice of militiamen for returning fire from the cover of trees and rocks. The battle was a decisive Cherokee victory because it spared the rest of the Cherokee Nation from the scorched earth tactics the colonial forces inflicted on the Lower Towns.

Montgomery, like Lyttleton before him, was eager to claim a triumph so that he could return to Charles Town a hero, having saved the colony. He withdrew his colonial forces to Nikwasi and used the council house on the mound as a field hospital for his wounded.[12] In the aftermath of this attack many Cherokee inhabitants of the Lower Towns became refugees, fleeing into the mountains with no food or possessions and nothing for shelter as they faced what would be a brutal winter. More than a few must have starved to death in the mountains. Others were able to find refuge in Cherokee towns higher in the mountains. Eventually the Cherokee in the Lower Towns abandoned some of their villages and tried to rebuild others. A refugee town sprang up called Little Keowee. Other refugees from the Lower Towns moved to what is now northeast Georgia.

RETRIBUTION AT FORT LOUDOUN

Montgomery's retreat would be a prelude to yet another escalation in the Cherokee War. Part of his mission had been to bring relief to the

12. Tortora, *Carolina in Crisis*, 151.

besieged colonial garrison posted at Fort Loudoun, built in 1756 as part of a military partnership between the Cherokee and the Carolina and Virginia colonies. The fort was located about ninety miles northwest of Fort Prince George, among the Cherokees' Overhill Settlements. The Cherokee siege had left the British garrison hopelessly surrounded and almost at the point of starvation. The siege had been prolonged because some Cherokee women who had married members of the garrison were secretly supplying them with food. When Montgomery and British forces returned to Charles Town, the garrison at Fort Loudoun was forced to ask the Cherokee for terms of surrender. A negotiated solution with the Cherokee determined that the British garrison would be given safe passage from the fort and beyond Cherokee territory if they turned over the fort with all its supplies and armaments intact. Having made this agreement, the colonial forces left the fort and marched a day away to their first encampment.

What happened next has, according to one historian, been forever "shrouded in myth, controversy and conjecture."[13] Discovering that the colonial garrison had concealed and destroyed armaments inside the fort, the Cherokee regarded the negotiated agreement as abrogated. There must have been much debate among them about how to respond. Some, like the pro-British head man, Attakullakulla, probably opposed what happened next. Cherokee warriors attacked the encampment of the British garrison and massacred many soldiers—approximately the same number as the Cherokee elders who were murdered at Fort Prince George. Lieutenant Demere, the commander of the fort and hated by the Cherokee, suffered an especially torturous death.

"The Cherokees scalped him while he was still alive, forced him to dance, then chopped off his arms and legs before stuffing his mouth with dirt."[14] Our moral sensibilities are rightly horrified at the practice of torture in any time and place. But before we ascribe this murder to the savagery of Native peoples, we should remind ourselves that far worse was being done in the church's persecution of heretics and in religious wars that had wracked Europe for centuries. What from a colonial perspective might seem a vengeful "eye for an eye" would undoubtedly have seemed to the Cherokee to be justice—the just restoration of balance.

---

13. Tortora, *Carolina in Crisis*, 132.
14. Teach Tennessee History, "Fort Loudoun," para. 7.

SCORCHED EARTH: A THIRD INVASION

After the massacre at Fort Loudoun, the colonial government of South Carolina launched a third military campaign, this time under Colonel Grant, a subordinate of Montgomery's in the previous invasion. This time in another fierce battle the Grant expedition was able to push through a determined stand by the Cherokee at the gorge above Nikwasi, where they had successfully repelled Montgomery.[15] Now Grant was able to bring the scorched earth tactics of the war into the Middle Cherokee settlements of the higher mountains. His army destroyed many villages and their fields, pausing only when, running out of provisions, he decided to spare the Valley Towns—a decision for which he was much criticized back in Charles Town.[16] From 1758 to 1761, it is estimated that one-third of the Cherokee people had died from war, disease, or starvation.[17]

Grant's campaign brought about a temporary pause in the war as the Cherokee sued for peace. Max Edelson has documented another map for us made by the surveyor John Pickens (Andrew's brother) which drew a line across the streams and rivers of up-country South Carolina and recorded the marks of Cherokee headmen who had approved where the line was drawn. In the wake of the Cherokee War of 1760–1761, this new map's clearly marked fifty-mile boundary was an effort to bring clarity to a chaotic frontier. Visible in Pickens's map are the watersheds of Greenville County, the Reedy and Saluda Rivers, and areas west to Long Cane Creek, the site of the massacre.

But this was at best a fragile peace. The war between South Carolina and the Cherokee would resume ferociously at the outbreak of the American Revolution. In 1763, King George issued his own declaration, based on the Doctrine of Discovery, which established his ownership of North America but acknowledged the existence of Indigenous peoples living on unceded land. The king declared that the Crown would protect their right to own their lands.

---

15. Today there is a North Carolina historical marker commemorating these two separate battles between the Cherokee and the invasion forces of Montgomery and Grant. One side of the marker tells of Cherokee victory; the other side tells of defeat.

16. Tortora, *Carolina in Crisis*, 153.

17. Tortora, *Carolina in Crisis*, 188.

LEARNING THE ART OF WAR

The third campaign in the Cherokee War would provide several young South Carolinians their first military experience. Men like Henry Laurens, William Moultrie, Francis Marion, and Andrew Pickens—household names in South Carolina history—served as field officers in this campaign and would all become principal military leaders of South Carolina during the American Revolution. As field officers of the South Carolina militia, they would be graphically introduced to British military tactics against the Cherokee. Marion, who during the American Revolution became famous as "Swamp Fox" for his brilliant adaptation of Cherokee guerrilla tactics, would express deep regret at how the Cherokee were treated. Henry Laurens would write: "This work though necessary often makes my heart bleed. The Cherokees have totally abandoned these Towns and fled with their wretched women and children across the mountains.... They have already suffered greatly and will be reduced to extreme misery as the winter advances."[18]

Andrew Pickens would say that during this war "he learned something of British cruelty which I always abhorred."[19] Were these sentiments sincere expressions of remorse or attempts to rehabilitate their reputations as military leaders? Or perhaps both? However they felt about the military orders they carried out against the Cherokee, South Carolina troops waged a military strategy that can only be described as "irregular" and "unlimited." This kind of warfare shocked the Cherokee. They had never experienced war with other tribes as the absolute use of force to destroy a people by razing food production sources as well as the shelter of their villages and towns. For them, warfare was about the reciprocity of justice and balance. When that was accomplished, the conflict was over.

In the military vocabulary of today, irregular warfare denotes violence perpetrated by a state-sponsored army against a non-state actor seeking legitimacy and influence over a relevant population. Unlimited war is war waged against civilians and noncombatants in an effort to end resistance by undermining the will to fight among their people and their leaders. However individual soldiers of colonial America felt about their actions, their leaders waged exactly this sort of irregular and unlimited warfare against the Cherokee. European invaders had used it against Indigenous peoples from the time of Jamestown and Plymouth, and it

---

18. Andrew, *General Andrew Pickens*, 18.
19. Andrew, *General Andrew Pickens*, 18.

would continue until the Apache were finally subjugated in the 1890s in the American Southwest.

MORAL INJURY

What was the moral impact upon the soldiers who were burning Cherokee villages, destroying their food stocks, and engaging in cold-blooded murder and rape along the way? Moral injury is a concept used in recent years to describe the psychological damage that occurs when a soldier commits violence, willingly or unwillingly, during war. It is especially damaging when the soldier cannot condone his own behavior by the conventions and rules that supposedly control the waging of war. Moral injury then and now is a different kind of wound from that inflicted on the victims of violence; it is the psychic trauma internalized by those who, in perpetuating violence in war or otherwise, injure not only the other but also their own consciences. The effort to integrate what they have done as soldiers can further distort their identity, their worldview, and their relationship to the "other" they have victimized. One wonders what moral injuries afflicted the soldiers of colonial South Carolina's militia who carried out a horrific scorched earth military strategy.

I suspect that all these men who would become heroes in South Carolina Revolutionary War history wrestled with the psychic implications of moral injury brought about during the Cherokee War of 1760. Now, hundreds of years later, we might ask what moral injury scarred the soul of our young nation because of these war crimes against Indigenous people? What moral injury is done to our collective identity as a nation even now as we consider the genocide of Indigenous peoples of America in the course of our history? And can this moral wound in the soul of our nation ever find healing until it is fully and truthfully acknowledged?

5

Waves of Scots Irish Settlers Come to the Carolina Up-Country

IN THE IMMEDIATE WAKE of the Cherokee War of 1760, many European immigrants came to South Carolina to settle. They continued to arrive via the Great Wagon Road, itself a Cherokee trading path. Increasingly, European settlers arrived through Charles Town and ascended the Keowee Trail, traversing and occupying a landscape of violence, bloodshed, and trauma. Among them were my Anderson ancestors. We recall that the British Crown in Northern Ireland used Scots Irish to displace and control the "unruly" Irish. I am haunted by a related question: How were the Scots Irish used at this next stage of their migration journey to displace and control Indigenous people?

> In 1761, eight or ten families of Scotch-Irish, from Pennsylvania, settled upon branches of the Tyger River, then in Spartanburg District. Settlements certainly existed before the year 1765, for in that year the road that passes by the church between the North and Middle Tyger rivers was opened. The names of the first settlers were Barry, Moore, Anderson, Collins, Thompson, Vernon, Pearson, Jamison, Dodd, Ray, Penny, McMahon, Nicholls, and Miller. About the year 1767 or 1768 their numbers were increased by a colony which came direct from the North of Ireland, Country Antrim, through Charleston, South Carolina. They were each entitled to one hundred acres of land by a grant from his majesty, George II, and the old titles bear the date of 1768. The first colony settled upon the Tyger River, the second upon the highlands adjoining. It consisted of the families of

Coan, Snoddy, Peden, Alexander, Gaston, Morton and perhaps others. When finally settled the two colonies covered a territory nearly twenty miles square.[1]

THE BACK OF BEYOND

William and Rebecca Denny Anderson immigrated from County Antrim, Ireland, with two of their sons, John and David, in 1742, and spent several years in Bucks County, Pennsylvania, where firstborn son John permanently settled. (Perhaps they even attended Deep Run Presbyterian Church, one of the very first congregations in Bucks County, where I served as youth minister during my time at seminary.) William, Rebecca, and David eventually made their way down the Great Wagon Road through the Shenandoah Valley to their first stop in the Waxhaws community in York District, just south of the North Carolina border. This area of Waxhaws, we have already noted, was a significant stop on the Great Wagon Road where many Scots Irish Presbyterians chose to settle. Waxhaws was named for a tribe that had been virtually wiped out in the Yamasee War of 1720 and further devastated by smallpox in 1741. The first Presbyterian church was organized there around 1755, only a few years before the Cherokee War.

William and Rebecca left Waxhaws and, after a brief sojourn in Charles Town, returned to the up-country frontier and finally settled on the Tyger River near where their son David had located. Other Scots Irish Presbyterians coming behind the first settlers would push on farther to occupy lands closer to the Cherokee boundary:

> With no maps and surveys to guide them, the first settlers from the Northern colonies followed the old Indian trading paths and pushed their way in to the fertile valleys of the numerous streams. In the early grants, lands were designated as in "the Packolate settlement" or "the Tyger settlement" or "on the waters of Fairforest Creek" and so on. Tributary streams soon received names from the first settlers on them. Often agents of the landed proprietors organized and arranged for companies of immigrants. In the period of early settlement, the approach to what is now Spartanburg County was easier from the Northern colonies than from Charleston.[2]

---

1. Anderson, *History of the Anderson Family*, 15.
2. Anderson, *History of the Anderson Family*, 13.

The up-country was and is a land watered by rivers flowing down from the Blue Ridge Mountains, some retaining their Indigenous names, like the Savannah (the Shawnee), the Enoree (river of muscadines), the Saluda (river of corn) and the Tyger. There are several explanations for the name of the Tyger River. One theory suggests it was the name of one of the earliest settlers. Another is a remembered legend of a bear and a mountain lion fighting to the death. The lion (Tyger) won. I just assumed that the name Tyger was an early spelling of tiger, and this was only a reference to a mountain lion.

However, in John Lawson's *A New Voyage to Carolina*, the explorer who published the journal of his journey through the Carolinas in 1700, he was well aware of the difference between a tyger and a mountain lion or panther. "Tyger's are never met in the settlement; but are more to the westward and are not more numerous on this side of the chain of mountains. I once saw one that was larger than a panther and seemed to be a very bold creature. The Indians that hunt in those quarters, say there are seldom met withal. It seems to differ from the Tyger of Asia and Africa."[3] Could this creature described by Lawson be a jaguar? While I was living in Tucson, photographs of jaguar roaming from central Mexico to the wilderness of south Arizona were turning up regularly, suggesting that they were beginning to reclaim their ancient territory. What if the jaguar's territory in 1700, the year of Lawson's journey, included the southeast? Could the Tyger River be named for a jaguar?

"The animal called a 'Tyger' by the early settlers was a species of panther and was the most dreaded of all the wild creatures. It seemed only logical that the three branches of the Tyger River should perpetuate its name." So reads my Anderson history. Stories have been handed down of the experiences of pioneers with wild beasts:

> As Mrs. Ford sat in the doorway of her log cabin near the old Indian field on Enoree River, a panther leaped over her shoulder into the cabin and was shot on the hearth by her husband. Near Grindal Shoals on Pacolet River a pioneer hunter was kept in a tree all night by a pack of wolves. The first settlers made a practice of hunting bears in the fall, dressing the skins for robes and rugs, and salting the flesh to be used as bacon. Herds of buffalo were seen by all the early settlers in this area. The tradition handed down from them says that the herds of buffalo had regular "runs" through the forest and tall grass, that they

3. Lawson, *New Voyage to Carolina*, 124.

followed the sprouting of the young canes in spring to graze on the tender shoots and that their paths led across the fords of the streams. According to this tradition, the Indians and Indian traders took over these runs of the buffalo and developed them into paths. The settlers lived in tents, or in their covered wagons, until they could cut down trees and erect log cabins. Then fields had to be cleared and fenced; the Indian trails transformed into wagon roads; new roads laid out and put in condition for neighborhood use. The streams were not of great service for the transportation of goods because they were too swift and rocky and in places too shallow. The consequence was that horses were invaluable. An "old Indian field" on the Enoree River was the scene of annual meetings of men from the surrounding region where they "broke" colts and traded or raced horses.[4]

THE PRESBYTERIAN CHURCH ON THE CAROLINA FRONTIER

These Scots Irish settlers founded Presbyterian churches like Waxhaws in the York District, just south of the present-day border between the Carolinas. Nazareth Presbyterian in Spartanburg District, just a few miles east of Greenville district, was another of the earliest Presbyterian congregations in the up-country where the Anderson clan made their mark. The first Scots Irish Presbyterians settled on the Tyger River as early as 1761, immediately after the cessation of the Cherokee War. By 1766, they had organized a society toward the formation of Nazareth Presbyterian Church. Dr. George Howe, DD, LLD, in his *History of the Presbyterian Church of SC* says that "these first settlers were full of reverence for God's word and for the institutions of religion; and no sooner had they established their home in the forest of the New World than they made the best arrangements in their power for the public worship of the God of their fathers."[5]

Occasional visits of evangelists, sent out chiefly by the Synods of New York and Philadelphia, led to the selection of a place for a church: "This place was chosen as the site of their sanctuary because it was equidistant between what was then known as the upper and lower settlements. They were so careful to have it as near the center as possible that two of the

---

4. Anderson, *History of the Anderson Family*, 13.
5. Anderson, *History of the Anderson Family*, 13, quoting Howe.

old men stepped the distance."⁶ The first house, made of logs hewn from the surrounding forest, was built in 1765. It was in the lower part of the present graveyard, perhaps to be near the spring. Members applied to the Presbytery of the Carolinas for preaching in 1766. According to *A History of the Presbyterian Church in South Carolina*, "The first permanent settlement in what is now Spartanburg County was formed by a group of Scotch-Irish Presbyterian families who came from Pennsylvania in the late 1750s, and later were joined by Scotch-Irish families direct from Ireland."⁷ These families developed small settlements along the branches of the Tyger River. The Tyger River Congregation met for worship in homes until 1765, when the first log meetinghouse was built about two hundred yards from the existing sanctuary.

In 1772, Nazareth Presbyterian Church was formally organized. Many of the important events in the history of Spartanburg County took place at this church and in the bounds of its congregation. Every able-bodied man of Nazareth fought for the independence of this country. The church was especially active in education. In 1794, the Nazareth Philanthropic Society was organized to promote interest in learning in the country and the state by providing teachers for neighborhood schools. Nazareth cemetery is one of the oldest in upper South Carolina, dating back to the Revolutionary War. People still come from all over the United States to visit the resting place of their forebears. Nazareth is called "the mother of churches" because numerous other Presbyterian churches across upper South Carolina were formed from its membership.

Alongside founding congregations, these Presbyterians were busy organizing militia units for the common defense:

> The militia organization of South Carolina at the outbreak of the Revolution included twelve regiments. The men from the total area between the Broad and Saluda rivers were the Upper Saluda Regiment, which was under the command of Colonel Thomas Fletchall. Many of the officers and men in his regiment had fought in the French and Indian War on the Carolina frontier in 1760 and 1761. Numbers of them, no doubt, had helped to erect the string of forts along the Indian Line: Earl's Ford, The Blockhouse, Gowan's Fort, Princes' Fort (the Anderson family stockade), Jamison's Fort, Wood's Fort, Nicholl's Fort, Blackstock's Fort. There is reason to believe that the strongest of

---

6. Howe, *History*, 113.
7. Howe, *History*, 542.

these blockhouses was Fort Prince. Records of grants show that the region about it was well settled before the Revolution. The account book kept in Fort Prince shows how all these forts were operated in periods of Indian warfare. It is the only such book locally preserved, and it proves that the country was well settled and that there was already much agricultural development by the time of the Revolution.[8]

ANDREW PICKENS: THE ARCHETYPAL SCOTS IRISH SETTLER

School children in South Carolina are taught much about one of our founding fathers, Andrew Pickens, who was an early Scots Irish settler, a trader with the Cherokee, and an Indian fighter who rose to be a commander in the American Revolution. Still later, Pickens served under three presidential administrations as a diplomat who represented the new nation in its treaty negotiations with the Native nations of the Southeast. We shall return to that history, but here it must be noted that Pickens was a founding father of Presbyterian churches across the up-country frontier. He may have been one of the founders of the Waxhaws Presbyterian Church, donating the land upon which it was built. He was what the Presbyterians call a ruling elder, democratically elected by the congregation and charged with other officers to govern over their common life. Pickens was a leader within the Long Canes Presbyterian Church, organized by the Calhoun family in Abbeville District in 1769. Years later, the Hopewell Keowee Presbyterian Church—the second congregation that will occupy our interest—was organized under his leadership. He was a pillar of the Presbyterian Church of up-country South Carolina, an ordained ruling elder whose influence shaped the very character of the wider church.

It is striking how the life and career of Andrew Pickens capture the essential features of the complicated history of the colonial South Carolina up-country. Many themes interweave to create a collective tableau representative of its culture. In Pickens's life we can see the revolutionary changes that were underway and the complex, evolving relationship between the Scots Irish and the Cherokee people. Not surprisingly, his migration story is very similar to that of my Anderson ancestors. Born in Pennsylvania to a devout Presbyterian family, he journeyed with his

8. Anderson, *History of the Anderson Family*, 16.

parents down the Great Wagon Road and settled initially in Waxhaws, just south of the border between North and South Carolina.

We have already noted that at the age of twenty, Pickens volunteered to fight in the Cherokee War of 1760–1761 with the invasion forces of Colonel Grant, which unleashed devastation upon the Cherokee Lower and Middle Towns. Pickens, along with all the other soon-to-be military leaders of the Revolution in South Carolina like Laurens, Sumter, Moultrie, and Marion, gained his first experience as a soldier in this war.

Afterwards, Pickens moved to Long Canes and there began to make his fortune, not just as a farmer but as a trader of goods with the Cherokee. In 1765 he married Rebecca Calhoun, the sister of Patrick Calhoun and the grandmother of John C. Calhoun. A survivor of the Long Cane massacre, Rebecca witnessed her own grandmother scalped by the Cherokee. Andrew and Rebecca would take up residence in what was only a few years prior the old settler fort near Long Cane called the "Blockhouse." There he carried on trade with the Cherokee as he had done before the war. As Pickens's grandson remembered: "The Blockhouse in the neighborhood was a great resort for the Indians who brought their ginseng, pink root, deer and bear skins and beaver in large quantities; and he later owned a warehouse in Augusta to which he sent all those things obtained from the Indians.... He also sent droves of beef cattle to Philadelphia."[9] As the prosperity of South Carolina continued to grow, the dangerous proximity of the Cherokee was never far from heart and mind of Scots Irish settlers like Pickens and my Anderson ancestors.

A JOURNAL OF LIFE ON THE CAROLINA FRONTIER

We will return to these narratives shortly, but first I want to share the story of another faith leader, Rev. Charles Woodmason, an Anglican priest who made his mark on colonial South Carolina history and who was not at all fond of Presbyterians. His journal offers a fascinating portrait of life in the Carolina backcountry just after the Cherokee War of 1760.[10] Woodmason was something more and something less than an accurate and detached observer of life in colonial South Carolina. He had strong opinions about just about everything and expressed them with a peculiar irascible intensity.

9. Hatley, *Dividing Paths*, 174.
10. Woodmason, *Carolina Backcountry*.

He started out first as a planter and slave owner trying to make his fortune in South Carolina, but the death of his wife in England precipitated his return there. During that time he made a dramatic career shift and was ordained as a priest in the Church of England. He returned to South Carolina to become something of an Anglican missionary, one of the few priests who were willing to venture into the backcountry. Wherever he went as an Anglican priest he seemed to encounter hostile groups of Presbyterians, "gangs of ruffians" he called them, who made his life difficult. And these Presbyterian mobs, sometimes drunken, gave him just cause for ire. They staged dog fights outside the building where he was preaching, hid the church keys where he was to lead worship services, posted false notices canceling his meetings. And when Woodmason was able to preach, they often showed up shouting and whooping outside the church door.

As these instances suggest, the rancor Woodmason felt toward and from Presbyterians was intense. There was one exception, though: the Reverend William Richardson, who had been a missionary among the Cherokee until, fearing for his safety, he fled the Overhill Towns just before war broke out in 1760. When Richardson invited him to preach to his Waxhaws Presbyterian Church congregation, Woodmason took to the pulpit and preached a sermon on ecumenical tolerance with a twist, suggesting that Presbyterians and Anglicans should be more tolerant of one another because of their common enemies. Who were those enemies that should unite them? Woodmason identified three: Indians, slaves, and Baptists—the axis of evil in his eyes.

It was not only theological differences between Anglicans and Presbyterians that provoked such rancor between them. Woodmason was not just an itinerant preacher but an official messenger of the unpopular colonial government, delivering its official communications to the up-country. That government, centered in Charles Town, was dominated by the political interests of low country planters and merchants who were largely Anglican. Up-country Presbyterians and non-Presbyterians alike believed that it was entirely unresponsive to their needs.

Woodmason at first was very critical of some twenty Presbyterian preachers itinerating across the up-country, instilling their "democratical, commonwealth principles embittering them against the very name of bishops, laying deep their republican principles especially that they owe no subjection to Great Britain."[11] What Reverend Woodmason could not fully appreciate was that Presbyterians had a sober estimate of human

11. Woodmason, *Carolina Backcountry*, 240.

nature. Believing human nature sinful, they were constitutionally uncomfortable with too much power being in the hands of any one person, whether bishop, king, or colonial governor.

But Woodmason's political views were evolving. The South Carolina up-country in the wake of the Cherokee War of 1760 was a lawless and chaotic frontier. As Woodmason knew full well, violent gangs of thieves and murderers were pillaging, raping, and plundering farms and homesteads across the up-country. This violence and theft were directed not only at white settlers but at Cherokee people as well, continuing a long history of grievances that kept Cherokee-white relations in a near constant state of agitation. Not only was the colonial government unwilling or unable to control this lawlessness, they were also resistant to establishing any court system beyond what was already in existence along the coast. Any up-country settler seeking to resolve a legal question or grievance was forced to make the long and arduous journey to Charles Town to have his case reviewed by judge and jurors whom he did not know and who were less likely to comprehend his reality.

This was just one in a long list of grievances held by the frontier settlements of the up-country against the powerful interests that ruled the colony from Charles Town. This power vacuum in the up-country gave rise to the so-called Regulator movement across the Carolinas. In the absence of law and order and even the semblance of a functioning judicial system, up-country citizens—Presbyterians prominent among them—took the law into their own hands, applying vigilante justice against outlaw gangs.

These developments brought about an interesting twist in Woodmason's life: he seemed to switch sides. Maybe it was the moment when the colonial government he represented finally took action in the name of law and order that only added insult to injury. A man by the name of Coffell was a notorious rogue and the primary ringleader of the lawless bands that threatened the up-country. Coffell did more than anyone to provoke the Regulator movement. Yet the colonial government gave him a judicial commission to preserve public peace and arrest troublemakers. This was the final insult and perhaps what turned Woodmason from an up-country messenger for the colonial government to its harsh critic.

Woodmason became something of a secretary and voice for the Regulator movement, an apologist for the necessity of Regulator action, and a proponent of their larger political agenda in relation to the colonial government. He would point out acerbically that the low country

South Carolina political and economic elites who were so critical of the king and Great Britain, who were urgently pressing the Patriot protest against "taxation without representation," were guilty of the same kind of oppression toward their fellow citizens in the up-country. Woodmason denounced this hypocrisy, saying citizens of the up-country were being treated like slaves, their essential human freedoms violated. Over and over, he criticized the colonial government of South Carolina with this refrain: "Is it not slavery when . . . ." followed by a list of each grievance committed against the up-country settlements. Yet even as Reverend Woodmason could see the hypocrisy in the Patriot Revolutionaries of the low country, he remained entirely oblivious to the contradiction of decrying slavery while practicing it against African men and women.

How could he clearly denounce slavery as inhumane and practice it at the same time? It is the moral contradiction at the heart of the Declaration of Independence and of American history, then and now. It is a sad commentary that the colonial government of South Carolina and the leaders of the Regulator movement were finally able to come to some workable cooperation after the Regulators returned many African people who had escaped slavery in the low country. Low country planters began to realize that they needed and could utilize the up-country settlers. Not only could settlers on the frontier provide a secure perimeter as a defense against Indian attack, they could also provide an effective blockade against the escape of enslaved workers. (The Scots Irish were employed again in a role familiar to them since Ulster—as instruments of British policy.)

Woodmason was somewhat correct in his power analysis. White people could always overcome their differences and find unity against those they perceived as their common enemies. Tension between the low country colonial government dominated by Anglicans and the up-country settlements, many led by Presbyterians, continued to simmer. Having portrayed the perspective of these up-country settlers, let's look at this reality from the perspective of the low country. No one was more representative of the power establishment in low country South Carolina than Henry Laurens. So let us weave his story back into the narrative.

HENRY LAURENS AND THE SLAVE TRADE

Just after the Cherokee War of 1760, Col. Henry Laurens had amassed enough wealth to purchase the Mepkin plantation on the Cooper River, near the Keowee Trail. As we learn from Edward Ball's *Slaves in the Family*, Laurens's parents had sent him as a young man to study the import-export business in London, where he was mentored by the English financier Richard Oswald. Returning to Charles Town, Laurens leveraged his London business connections to become junior partner in a Charles Town slave trading business along with the senior partner, George Austin. Within a few short years Austin and Laurens would dominate the slave trading business in Charles Town, and Laurens would begin to amass the fortune that would make him one of the richest men in the British American colonies.

Working with Oswald, Laurens concentrated their purchase of human beings around what would one day become the African nation of Sierra Leone. Bunce Island, situated at the juncture of the Sierra Leone River and the Atlantic Coast, was the staging ground for the slave trade, and Oswald had already acquired rights to do business there. Cargos of enslaved men, women, and children were brought downriver from the African interior and imprisoned on the island. Enslaved workers from the area of the Sierra Leone River were highly prized by South Carolina planters, who valued their ability and experience in the cultivation of rice, the colony's chief agricultural export crop. Austin and Laurens received the first slave ship from Bunce Island to Charles Town in 1756, followed by countless others. Before Laurens was thirty-five, he had become the largest slave trader and one of the richest men in the American colonies.

Laurens was greatly advantaged by his place within the nexus of an emerging global economy: from Charles Town his ships carried deerskins, rice, cotton, and indigo to unload to markets in England; then, with their holds filled with British manufactured goods like textiles, weapons, tools, and wine, these ships might head back to North American ports or to the Caribbean. But most sailed straight to the west coast of Africa, where they traded their cargo of manufactured goods to African warlords in exchange for other Africans those warlords had captured and brought to the coast to be sold. Loaded with these captives packed like sardines in a can, the ships then set off for Charles Town; its harbor filled with Lauren's masted schooners ready to be reloaded with the raw materials western Europe craved, and the triangle trade would begin all over again. Calculating in his ledgers the number of slaves that would likely perish in the Middle Passage, Laurens still made a huge profit.

Initially, it was the deerskin trade that made Charles Town an export powerhouse, eclipsing other southern harbors in the sheer tonnage and number of its ships. When the deerskin supply finally waned and collapsed, Laurens, ever financially nimble, shifted focus. Now he would use his shipping business to import European settlers who could develop the agricultural economy of the South Carolina frontier. The promise of free land and a moratorium on most taxes encouraged these settlers, if they possessed slaves, to migrate to the up-country. As Scots Irish continued to arrive by way of Virginia and the Great Wagon Road, many other settlers with their enslaved workers migrated from Charles Town up the Keowee Trail into the Carolina backcountry.

"RIGHTS OF THE BACK COUNTRY"

In 1767 the inhabitants of the up-country listed in provincial records as the "Parish of St. Marks" sent to the government at Charles Town a lengthy petition for recognition of the "rights of the Back Country." One demand was that lines of all counties be run to the Cherokee boundary so that inhabitants need "no longer wander in the mazes of supposition." So remote seemed the backcountry as late as 1770, that Lieutenant Governor Bull, making a tour over the state in his coach, did not penetrate beyond what he described as the "uncivilized settlements" above the junction of the Broad and the Saluda Rivers. Bull, reporting on his tour, wrote to the home government that at this time there were more than five thousand men living in the upper part of South Carolina "beyond a moral possibility of being represented in assembly while elections are held in the parish church."[12]

Although the Circuit Court Act of 1769 provided for the redistricting of the state and the erection of a courthouse in each district, at which courts should be held twice yearly, not until November 1772 could the provisions of the act go into effect. In that year the inhabitants of what is now Spartanburg were first able to transact legal business at their own district courthouse in Ninety-Six. The judges and lawyers who made the first circuit returned to Charles Town amazed and delighted with their experience. They said the backcountry men would, with proper advantage, make as fine a population as any on earth.[13]

In the decade following the Cherokee War and the ensuing conflicts between Regulators of the South Carolina frontier with the low country

12. Anderson, *History of the Anderson Family*, 17.
13. Anderson, *History of the Anderson Family*, 17–18.

power establishment, many white settlers in the up-country had ample motivation to migrate even farther away from Charles Town's control. They moved ever west into the mountains, settling in Cherokee territory, bringing about more tension with the Cherokee Tribe. In 1772, the Watauga Settlement was founded near the Overhill Towns in what is now East Tennessee. The Watauga Settlement, led by Col. Sevier, was the most glaring example of settler encroachment on Cherokee lands that violated treaty agreements with Great Britain. But the Watauga Settlement led by John Sevier, the future governor of Tennessee, was only the vanguard of settler ambition.

Daniel Boone Escorting Settlers through the Cumberland Gap[14]

In 1775, Richard Henderson of the Transylvania Land Company, guided by none other than Daniel Boone, crossed the southern Appalachians in the midst of a brutal winter, bearing gifts for the Overhill Cherokee. The Cherokee chiefs who received them were led by Attakullakulla. In these negotiations held at Sycamore Shoals (Elizabethton, Tennessee), Attakullakulla ceded not just the lands of the Watauga Settlement nearby that had been a thorn in the side of the Cherokee Nation for

---

14. https://www.artchive.com/artwork/daniel-boone-escorting-settlers-through-the-cumberland-gap-1851-52-by-george-caleb-bingham/.

years. Attakullakulla, in exchange for provisions and promises, ceded all of the territory then known as Kentucky, explored by Boone. After several years of drought and in the midst of an extreme winter, Attakullakulla may have believed that his people, already hungry, had little choice but to agree. Attakullakulla, getting older, was war weary and could not ever forget the vast power of Great Britain.

His sons, Dragging Canoe and Badger, vehemently disagreed and passionately denounced the treaty as invalid.[15] The British authorities would have agreed with Dragging Canoe that this transaction was illegal. It was in this explosive moment that Dragging Canoe allegedly said to Henderson and Boone, "You have bought a fair land, but you will find its settlement dark and bloody." Of course this "dark and bloody ground" has been associated with Kentucky since its inception and its meaning widely debated. It was construed by land speculators at the time to mean that various tribes had waged war over this contested land (so was there for the taking). Dragging Canoe's words sound unambiguous to me. Dragging Canoe promised to resist the settlement of these vast and much-loved hunting grounds, refusing to surrender any of it without a cost exacted in blood. And what Dragging Canoe promised, he delivered during the American Revolution and in the years beyond. The Cherokee would be drawn inexorably into the American Revolution, casting their lot as allies of the British in armed opposition to the land hungry American colonists.

---

15. Dragging Canoe supposedly received his name as a young boy. When a group of Cherokee warriors were boarding canoes to wage war against their enemies, Attakullakulla's son, too young to be a warrior, disobeyed his father's orders to stay behind. Attempting to drag a canoe so that he might accompany them, he received his name. Later in life, Dragging Canoe would be afflicted with smallpox that left his face scarred in the characteristic way of that dreaded disease. His fame as a warrior was recognized among Indigenous nations and Europeans alike. Colonials called him the "savage Napoleon."

6

Bartram's Travels on the Keowee Trail

IN 1775, ON THE very eve of the American Revolution, the botanist and adventurer William Bartram would explore southern Appalachia, documenting everything he saw. His vivid account of these explorations—published in 1791 as *Travels through North and South Carolina, Georgia, East and West Florida, the Cherokee Country, the Extensive Territories of the Muscogulges or Creek Confederacy, and the Country of the Choctaws, Containing an Account of the Soil and Natural Productions of Those Regions; Together with Observations on the Manners of the Indians*—would become a classic work of American literature, known by its shortened title: *Bartram's Travels.*

Up-country South Carolina was still a wild and inaccessible place—a land of rolling foothills that over eons had been carved by rivers and streams flowing down from the Blue Ridge Mountains. The up-country was a veritable paradise of rich topsoil, carpeted with open pastures of thick grass and tall cane brakes of Indigenous bamboo. Old growth forest of chestnut, hickory, pine, poplar, walnut, cedar, and sycamore canopied the land. Rivers flowed down the Blue Ridge escarpment and watered the valleys. Time and time again, Bartram was awestruck with wonder at a land teeming with flora and fauna never seen by Europeans. He explored a wilderness inhabited by buffalo, wolves, deer, bear, beaver, panther, and otter. He marveled underneath skies filled with a multitude of birds, including the now extinct passenger pigeon in swarms so massive they would darken a sunny day and the Carolina parakeet with its tropical, multicolored plumage.

Bartram is famous for his poetic descriptions of the natural world, but he could not avoid seeing as well the evidence of bloody history as he explored what he often called the Cherokee Mountains. He first visited the South with his then more famous botanist father, John Bartram, in 1765—only four years after the Cherokee War of 1760–1761. Since he intended to return and continue his explorations, he needed to know more about the aftermath of the war and the current situation between the colonies and the Cherokee settlements. No one was better positioned to educate him than John Stuart, the royal superintendent of Indian Affairs in the Southern Department.[1] Stuart, a Scotsman born in Inverness in 1718, has surfaced in our story already when, because of his friendship with Attakullakulla, he was able to make his escape from the doomed garrison of Fort Loudoun to find safety in Virginia.

In 1765, Bartram visited Stuart's home south of Bay Street in Charles Town. Stuart's vast experience would have made him keenly aware of the dangers Bartram might encounter on his journey. From Stuart, Bartram learned that during the Cherokee War of 1760, the Keowee Trail, the long-standing trading path connecting colonial South Carolina with the Cherokee Nation, had become a warpath for Cherokee warriors descending south to push back white settlements and defend the boundaries of their homeland. The trail had also become a military highway for colonial forces proceeding north as they invaded the Cherokee Nation.

Finally, in 1775, Bartram returned to the southern colonies to make his long-contemplated journey. Following the trail, Bartram approached the Keowee Valley and saw a pleasing vista: the village of Seneca (which he spelled as Sinica), located on both sides of the Keowee River amid many acres of cultivated cornfields.

> The Cherokee town of Sinica is a very respectable settlement, situated on the East Bank of the Keowee River, though the greatest number of Indian habitations are on the opposite shore, where likewise stands the council-house, in a lofty plain, betwixt the river and the range of beautiful lofty hills which rise magnificently, and seem to bend over the green plains and the river; but the chief's house with those of the traders, and some Indian dwellings, are seated on the ascent of the heights on the opposite shore. This situation ... overlooks the whole settlement, the extensive fruitful plains on the river above and below, and the

---

1. Cashin, *William Bartram*, 14.

plantations of the inhabitants . . . Sinica is a new town rebuilt since the late Indian War, when the Cherokee were vanquished.[2]

The Cherokee had rebuilt and reinhabited Seneca after the war of 1760. Bartram noted in his journal that the village was surrounded by lovely foothills. But those hills could provide no protection for Seneca. Scarcely a year after Bartram was there, another more devastating invasion occurred. A military force of American Patriots, fighting the British in 1776 under South Carolina Patriot commander Williamson, would descend on Seneca, burning the town to the ground and destroying thousands of bushels of corn.

THE RUINS OF ONCE-PROUD KEOWEE

As Bartram approached Keowee Town farther upstream, he continued to observe with glowing detail the wonders of the natural landscape, "Next day I left Sinica [sic] alone, and after riding sixteen miles, chiefly through high forests of excellent land at a little distance from the river, arrived in the evening at Fort Prince George (and) Keowee." He noted that Fort Prince George no longer served as a fort but only as a trading station, and he surveyed what he called "a most charming situation": "The evening still and calm, all quiet and peaceable, a vivifying gentle breeze continually wafted from the fragrant strawberry fields . . . . How the groves and hills ring with the shrill perpetual voice of the whip-poor-will!" But he also registered a growing apprehension and anxiety.[3]

"Abandoned as my situation now was . . . all alone in a wild Indian country, a thousand miles from my Native land, and a vast distance from any settlement of white people . . . yet thank heaven many objects met together at this time and conspired to conciliate, and in some degree compose my mind." A brutal murder had been committed just as his journey had begun: a Scots Irish settler named Collins, upon returning to his cabin and finding two young Cherokee men sitting at his table at the invitation of his wife, had savagely killed both of them. Events like these were common across the South Carolina frontier and naturally enough incensed the Cherokee against the settlers. Bartram doesn't mention

---

2. Cashin, *William Bartram*, 139.
3. Van Dorn, *Travels of William Bartram*, 269.

events like these in his *Travels* but in other ways we will explore later, he reveals his sympathy for the Indians.[4]

Bartram must have been apprehensive about how he might be treated as a white man entering Cherokee territory. As he approached Keowee, he described with appreciation the steeper hills enclosing the faster flowing river and noted the abundant flora adorning the valley floor. But his musings about the beautiful landscape mingled with anxiety and a sense of foreboding as he encountered the ruins of the "once proud Keowee," the mother town of the Lower Settlements, destroyed by successive colonial invasions: "This fertile vale within the remembrance of some old traders with whom I conversed, was one continued settlement, the swelling sides of the adjoining hills were then covered with habitations, and the rich level grounds beneath lying on the river, were cultivated and planted, which now exhibit a very different spectacle, humiliating indeed to the present generation, the posterity and feeble remains of the once potent and renowned Cherokee."[5]

Bartram thought that he would remain in Keowee until a Cherokee guide could be secured to take him farther into the mountains, but after only three days, he decided to continue up the trail alone. His journey carried him past the Tamassee Knob at the head of the Keowee Valley, where in a year Andrew Pickens would fight the Cherokee in a sharp engagement during the American Revolution. It is an impressive site and has a beautiful view to this day. From there, he continued toward Chattooga town on the wild and scenic Chattooga River and crossed what is today the Georgia state line near Warwoman Creek, named for a Cherokee woman who fought the Creek Indians there.

Entering the watershed of the Little Tennessee and the beginning of the Cherokee Middle Towns, Bartram passed by Nikwasi, a beloved town that had been destroyed but not rebuilt after the Cherokee War. Noting only the ruins of the village and the sacred mound of Nikwasi, he moved on upstream through a gorge that had been a fateful battleground for the Cherokee. It was there in June of 1760 that the Cherokee defeated and turned back Montgomery's invading forces, but it was also nearby that Grant had found a way to force his way through in 1761 to carry out the scorched earth devastation of the Middle Towns. Bartram noticed with a degree of melancholy the numerous stacks of stones along the river

---

4. Cashin, *William Bartram*, 67.
5. Cashin, *William Bartram*, 138–42.

gorge, marking the graves of Cherokee warriors who had fallen in those two battles.

CHEROKEE HOSPITALITY

Finally reaching the populated Cherokee town of Watauga, Bartram was as impressed as I was by this beautiful panorama. *Watauga*, meaning the "place of goldfinches," is an expansive plain beside the Little Tennessee River, encircled by mountains. As Bartram gazed upon this valley and Watauga town, he must have wondered how he would be received by the Cherokee. He was deeply pleased and relieved to be treated as an honored guest, well fed, and invited into the chief's private chamber for a smoke. When he continued the next day, the chief personally escorted him up the trail and sent him on his way.

Reaching Cowee, the principal town of the Middle Settlements, Bartram found it enclosed in a semicircle created between two great mountain ranges. *Cowee* is difficult to translate but may have meant, according to Mooney, "the place of the deer clan."[6] The village sat on both sides of the fast-flowing Little Tennessee River. "Bartram considered the prospect 'one of the most charming natural mountainous landscapes perhaps anywhere to be seen.'"[7] (A famous story from Mooney's *Myths of the Cherokee* attests to the beauty of Cowee. A Shawnee warrior who had been a prisoner there had escaped to return to his people up north and, after peace between the two tribes was established, wandered back to the neighborhood on a hunting trip. While standing on a hill overlooking the valley, he saw several Cherokee on an opposite hill, and called out to them, "Do you still own Cowee?" They shouted back: "Yes, we own it yet!" The Shawnee, wanting to encourage them not to sell any more of their lands, responded, "Well it's the best town of the Cherokee. It's a good country; hold on to it."[8])

In the plaza that spread out before the townhouse on top of Cowee's mound, Bartram was treated to the ceremonial gathering that preceded a stick ball game with another Cherokee town to be held the next day, which Bartram describes:

---

6. Mooney, *Myths of the Cherokee*, 375–78.
7. Cashin, *William Bartram*, 148.
8. Cashin, *William Bartram*, 378.

The people being assembled and seated in order, and the musicians having taken their station, the ball opens, first with a long oration, spoken by an aged chief, in commendation of the manly exercise of the ball-play, recounting the many and brilliant victories Cowee had gained over the other towns in the nation, not forgetting or neglecting to recite his own exploits, together with those of other aged men, now present . . . This prologue being at an end, the musicians began, both vocal and instrumental; when presently a company of girls, hand in hand, dressed in clean white robes and ornamented with beads, bracelets, and a profusion of gay ribands, entering the door, immediately began to sing their responses in a gentle, low, and sweet voice, and formed themselves in a semi-circular file or line, in two ranks, back to back, facing the spectators and musicians, moving slowly round and round. This continued for about a quarter of an hour, when we were surprised by a sudden very loud and shrill whoop, uttered at once by a company of young fellows, who came in briskly after one another with rackets and hurls in one hand.[9]

A FIERCE DETERMINATION TO REMAIN

In the Cherokee War of 1760–1761, Cowee was occupied by Colonel Grant and his forces, who used it as a base camp for destroying other towns in the area before burning Cowee itself. After the war the Cherokee inhabitants, refusing to abandon their home, rebuilt the town. In 1776, at the beginning of the American Revolution, Cowee was burned again by General Rutherford and his North Carolina troops, and in 1783 militia from Tennessee once more destroyed it. Each time Cherokee survivors demonstrated their determination to remain and rebuilt their beloved town.

I wonder what became of those Cherokee girls who danced together, those Cherokee boys who played stick ball. What would it be like to grow up in a village that was to their eyes the most beautiful in all the world, only to have it invaded and destroyed, not once, not twice, but three times by the white man? And what must it have meant to these Cherokee families who, no matter what, would rebuild and remain there? It was only years later, in 1819, when the Cherokee were finally forced to give up all claim to their ancestral lands, that they finally surrendered

---

9. Rozema, *Cherokee Voices*, 55.

Cowee. But in 2007, the Eastern Band of the Cherokee Nation purchased seventy acres of land encompassing the site, finally returning the beloved town to Cherokee sovereignty.

A few days later Bartram's travel brought him to a scene that surpassed every wonder he had yet encountered: "A field of flowers and fruitful strawberry beds; flocks of turkey strolling about them; herds of deer prancing on the meads or bounding over the hills; companies of young, innocent Cherokee virgins, some busily gathering the rich fragrant fruit, others [lying] reclined under the shade of fragrant Native bowers." This scene stirred the young adventurer so deeply that "with nature prevailing over reason," he rushed forward incautiously. "The older matrons gave the alarm and attempted to gather the girls around them."[10] But a few of the bolder ones came forward and with cheerful smiles offered some of their strawberries. Bartram's journal leaves it there, and as captivating as this scene is to imagine, I will as well.

BARTRAM MEETS ATTAKULLAKULLA

This was not the only significant encounter Bartram would have. In the Nantahala Valley, he met an entourage of Cherokee accompanying a chief. "The Cherokee Chief approaches the botanist with a smile on his face and, clapping his right hand on his own breast and then extending the same hand to the white man, announces his name: I am Attakullakulla. The red man is pleased when Bartram, who is no flatterer, tells him that he knows who he is: the great Attakullakulla."[11] In introducing himself, Bartram was quick to add that he was from Pennsylvania, the Quaker colony distinguished from others for its peaceful intentions toward Native peoples.

Attakullakulla asked Bartram if he had news of the chief's good friend John Stuart, the British superintendent of Indian Affairs, whom Attakullakulla had rescued from the Fort Loudoun massacre. It is plausible that Bartram readily acknowledged his own friendship with Stuart. But did he share or withhold information about Stuart's status? A conspiracy theory was circulating around South Carolina that Stuart, a British agent, was trying to incite an Indian war against the rebellious colonies. Keenly aware of his vulnerability in those tumultuous times,

10. Cashin, *William Bartram*, 153.
11. Dallmeyer, *Bartram's Living Legacy*, 456.

Stuart had fled his home in Charles Town and was on the lam. It was a brief encounter between Bartram and Attakullakulla, who would continue his diplomatic mission to Charles Town. There the Cherokee diplomat, a longtime friend of the English and advocate for peace, would discover for himself the deepening crisis of the American Revolution and ponder its implications for the Cherokee Nation.

Strangely, just as Bartram was about to reach the long-sought Cherokee Overhill Towns, he decided to turn around and return to Charles Town. He was entranced by the beauty of the mountains and as a botanist had discovered numerous new species of flora which would make news in Europe. And he certainly had been welcomed and treated with gracious hospitality by those Cherokee he had met. But perhaps all he had seen—the ruins of destroyed villages, the graves of warriors killed, the grim evidence of past wars fought and the storm clouds on the horizon of a war yet to be waged—had stirred in him a deep foreboding, and convinced this perpetual wanderer that this was the journey's end. It was time to turn around. If so, Bartram was fortunate that he listened to that voice within. War would soon erupt.

BARTRAM'S DEEP MAP

Commenting on the significance of *Bartram's Travels*, Mark Sturges writes, "While most eighteenth-century accounts of the American South depicted the land as a smorgasbord of commodities and looked forward to its economic development, the *Travels* looked back to the natural and cultural history of the region, constructing a 'deep map' of place that was sensitive to its ecology, its evolution through time, and its Indigenous inhabitants."[12] For example, Bartram displayed great fascination with the history of Native peoples in the South, documenting mounds, ruins, and their own migration stories eastward from western points of origin. Sturges suggests that in relaying these stories of the Cherokee and Creek migration eastward from the west, Bartram displaced and decentered the geographical and historical trajectory of the European American narrative of civilization moving west across the continent from the Eastern Seaboard (the West as America). America is not just the story of English-speaking people moving west. It is also a story of multiple people who have migrated in many different directions.

12. Sturges, "Deep Map of the South," 46.

Bartram's deep map of the American South articulated a more pluralistic vision of American history, and in turn bolstered his argument for a more diplomatic approach between the United States and the Indian nations, all of whom shared a common colonial history.... Connecting nature and culture, he rewrote the past as a narrative of ecological relationships between human communities and the natural world.... His deep map of the South envisioned a political geography of pluralism.[13]

BARTRAM'S LEGACY

Before we turn to the American Revolution let's take a parting glance at our traveling companion. William Bartram's father, John, a good Quaker, was the leading light of the colonial scientific community. He had a renowned garden and home in Philadelphia that was the gathering place for the intelligentsia of his day. John Bartram had emancipated his slaves long before. He had taught them to read and write and shared meals with them. As an old man, William Bartram would return to the Quaker principles of his father. In the collections of the Pennsylvania Historical Society is a document written in Bartram's own hand around 1787, an address he proposed to deliver to Congress about slavery. It reads in part:

> Ye Chiefs of this Nation, whom the people have chosen and appointed as Watchmen . . . God is no respecter of persons. The Black, White, Red, and Yellow People are equally dear to Him and under His protection and favor . . . . Do we not continue in a woeful predicament by suffering the Black people who are fellow citizens of our Nation to be held in perpetual bondage and slavery, being dragged in chains from Africa their Native Land, man . . . of them for no crime whatsoever and none for any crime or harm they have rendered us?[14]

There exists no record that confirms the speech was delivered.

TRAIL JOURNAL: NIKWASI INITIATIVE

The highlight for me of the National Trail of Tears Association meeting of 2022 was the second day, when participants were taken on a pilgrimage of a Cherokee heritage corridor. Leaving Cherokee after a preparatory

13. Sturges, "Deep Map of the South," 58–59.
14. Pinckney, "Zambezi Dirt," 402.

lecture by Dr. Brett Riggs, we traveled by bus first to Franklin, North Carolina, to see the Nikwasi Mound. Our hosts were a nonprofit organization called the Nikwasi Initiative. Their mission: to preserve and interpret the history and culture of the Cherokee Nation. In collaboration with the Eastern Band, they are dedicated to protecting the sacred mound of Nikwasi, which sits in the middle of downtown Franklin. And as a site sacred to the Cherokee, Nikwasi has been returned to their ownership.

Exiting our three buses parked next to the mound, we quickly found our seats inside what had been, in recent history, a large garage. The good folks of the Nikwasi Initiative and their allies in the larger community of Franklin have plans to turn this former garage into an interpretative center. The Nikwasi Initiative, as their director Elaine Eisenbraun explained to us, was born in collaborative conversation with the Eastern Band of the Cherokee and understands its mission not only as the interpretation of the Cherokee cultural heritage of the past but also as movement toward restorative actions in the present, like the creation of an Apple Orchard Trail that celebrates the Cherokee husbandry of apples.

Standing about fifteen feet tall, the mound structure today, while impressive, is much reduced from earlier epochs. In the eighteenth century, it may have been another five feet higher, and before that, in the ages of Cherokee predecessors, perhaps another five feet above that, capped still higher with a council house. The council house might have been a freestanding structure built atop the mound to accommodate the village occupants for tribal events and occasions. Or it could have been a space enclosed by an earthen roof, covered in grass indistinguishable from the mound itself, except for the entranceway, allowing passage inside through a tunnel vestibule.

Mooney recounts a wonderful legend about the mound at Nikwasi. In earlier times a fierce invading force had destroyed other towns and was threatening Nikwasi. The warriors fought valiantly but were unable to defend their town. Just then warrior spirits called the *Nunnihi* began to emerge from the mound at Nikwasi, painted for war and armed. The most curious thing about them was that they were visible to the people, but invisible to their enemies as they fought. The spirit warriors repelled the enemies and saved the town. Mooney says that the Nunnihi were not ghosts, but small spiritual beings who lived under water or mountain rock. They were seen as protectors, the very ones who invited the people of Connestee to come live with them in the safety of the mountains. But the Nunnihi could also be mischievous, embodying a trickster persona more commonly associated with Native peoples of the desert Southwest.[15]

The name *Nikwasi* means "star town" or "place of stars." Dr. Riggs explained to us that the significance of this name is only just beginning to become clear as a winter night sky. The Cherokee, like many Indigenous peoples, were keen observers of the heavens. For them, as for countless cultures from the beginning of human history, the experience of wonder was a nightly occurrence. Our earliest human ancestors from eons ago could look up and, seeing a luminous night sky, feel awe. The vision of that night sky shaped their view of life and of the world in which they lived. We may know much more about the universe now than our primordial ancestors, but at the same time, primarily because of light pollution in our technological world, the night sky has become largely lost to us.

Dr. Riggs has situated the geographical locations of the Middle Towns—including the villages of Watauga, Cowee, and Nikwasi—along the Little Tennessee Watershed. The geographical pattern of the villages is astronomically organized, a kind of star map. If you had been a Cherokee in the village of Watauga, gazing up into the sky in the season of the Snow Moon, or what Europeans call December, you would have beheld with crystal clarity the seasonal unveiling of our galaxy, the Milky Way, painted across the sky just above where you knew Nikwasi, the star town, would be.

Star Gazers in Chaco Canyon, New Mexico

Awe and wonder before a night sky have been very much a part of the human experience for countless eons. I shall never forget the winter retreat I spent many years ago camping in Chaco Canyon, the remote collection of ruins of cliff dwellings and kivas in northern New Mexico. Chaco was once the spiritual center of the Chacoan civilization—formerly referred to as Anasazi. The night sky during my retreat there, in the middle of desert wilderness, was spectacular. The Milky Way seemed to be parked just above my head. As I explored Chaco, I learned that the structures of these ancient settlements, spread across the vast canyon and separated by many miles, were perfectly aligned with the movement of sun and moon. There is in Chaco what amounts to a mountain observatory, today called Fajada Butte, in which star patterns over twenty-year time spans

---

15. Mooney, *Myths of the Cherokee*, 336.

are etched into the rocks on top of the mountain. Do we realize what it means to watch twenty-year patterns of stars and our solar system? The Chacoan people were studying the movements of the heavens for generation upon generation, gradually building up a body of knowledge that they engraved on a mountain.

On the last day of my retreat, I was exploring a side canyon and came upon the steps of a ladder chiseled into the side of the canyon wall. Given my healthy respect for heights, I did a most uncharacteristic thing: I climbed that ladder, step by step, until I reached the top of the canyon wall. There, deeply imprinted in the rock face itself, I saw several pathways heading off in different directions. In that instant, I sensed the presence of the ancient ones who climbed that ladder and used these pathways. I could almost see them coming and going, carrying their bundles. I could imagine them walking on the earth during the day and gazing at the heavens at night. I haven't yet had a similar visitation from the Cherokee ancestors, but I know they are there. I know they are there.

As modern urban people our time beneath the sky is limited. Mesmerized by the false light of our televisions, our phones, our computers, we have largely forgotten what it means to be children of the sky. But not the people of Chaco Canyon, nor apparently the people of the Cherokee Nation. Brett Riggs continues to do research on the Cherokee towns—much like the settlements of Chaco Canyon—to determine how they were aligned with the patterns of sun and moon and stars. He believes that the standing flame of the council house would have been perfectly illuminated once a year by a solstice beam of light. The Cherokee, like the people of Chaco, had a detailed understanding of astronomy and practiced a complex science that shaped their culture, geography, and architecture. And they did this not on a plain in the desert Southwest but in the mountainous and forested terrain of the Blue Ridge Mountains.

A Return to Awe

Dr. Riggs has gained his understanding of the astronomical dimension of Cherokee geography only recently. It bears much more research and documentation, which he will be pursuing. But learning about it opened another whole dimension in my experience of this magnificent people and their history. I stand alongside them in my wonder and awe at the night sky. When we look up at night, we know we are not gazing at an enclosed dome, but at a universe that contains, by our most recent estimates, upward of 125 billion galaxies. This is what scientists, and an increasing number of theologians, are calling the new cosmology. And it is truly awe-inspiring, truly humbling. And in this post-Hubble moment, with the unveiling of the new James Webb space telescope, we are feasting on photos of a universe that trace our origins ever closer to the moment of creation, the Big Bang.

In this revelation of the star-gazing people of the Cherokee, entranced and awed by the night sky, I feel a deep bond. A Cherokee standing in Watauga in the late seventeenth century, looking south toward Nikwasi on a cold winter sky, beholding our glorious galaxy spreading out above Star Town, might have felt just what I feel in the twenty-first century. And our separation by time and place is nothing between us. When we gaze together out upon our universe, the universe gazes back at us and acknowledges in beauty that we belong here and are a part of this wondrous creation.

Almost to Cowee

Our cultural pilgrimage continued from Nikwasi toward Cowee. We turned off the highway onto a narrow dirt road to navigate the last stretch. But our bus immediately fell off the side of the road, tilting into a ditch. We would not make it to Cowee. I suppose I should be glad that no one was hurt, but all I remember is my deep disappointment that this mishap forced our expedition to turn back, denying us the opportunity to see the village site. As we left along a mountain highway high above the valley, Dr. Riggs directed our gaze down the slope to show us the river curving around the village site and its mounds. I share the conviction of Bartram and the Shawnee hunter, that there is no place more beautiful. And I was determined to return someday and see it. A year later I was finally able to return to Franklin, and with the help of Elaine Eisenbraun, I got to see Cowee. The landscape did not disappoint—it is a holy place.

7

The American Revolution and Other Struggles for Freedom

THE DECLARATION OF INDEPENDENCE

"You write it, John."

"Absolutely not, there is no question but that you should write it, Thomas."

This is an abbreviated paraphrase of an imaginary argument that might have taken place between two of our Founding Fathers, Thomas Jefferson and John Adams, about who should author the most important document in our nation's history: the Declaration of Independence. Jefferson asked Adams to write the document. Adams, with unaccustomed modesty, declined: "You should write it for three reasons: Reason One: you are a Virginian and a Virginian ought to appear at the head of this business. Reason Two: I am obnoxious and unpopular, and you are not. Reason Three: You can write ten times better than I can."[1] Our nation is indebted to Adams for this realistic assessment because Jefferson was persuaded and went on to write those words that have become the sacred scripture of this nation. This truly radical vision of "all men created equal" of course did not include women, or enslaved people kidnapped from Africa, or Indigenous people already here. But the vision of human equality cast in Jefferson's Declaration was let loose in the world for its revolutionary potential, yet to be realized. A less well-known dimension of the Declaration of Independence deserves our attention.

1. Rosen and Rubenstein, "Why Did Jefferson Draft."

Resentful of the unjust authority the British Crown exercised over the American colonies, our founders set out to create a new government whose power to govern originated not in the right of the king or the military or in a feudal aristocracy, but in the consent of the people. This idea that a people could and should govern themselves was just beginning in that day to be called a democracy. If a government does not possess the consent of the governed, then it is the right of the people to abolish that government. A democracy grants each one of us as citizens the right, the responsibility, of revolution.

Knowing just how radical this idea was, Jefferson went on to say in the text of the Declaration, "Prudence dictates that governments long established not be changed for light and transient causes." What are the conditions that might justify an armed revolution? In the longest part of the Declaration, Jefferson addresses the specific abuses of power the British Crown had committed against the colonies. Few of us today are fully familiar with these specifics. From high school history class, we may remember something about "taxation without representation," but to the majority of those who lived in the colonies and to the existing nations of the world, the American Revolutionaries needed to make a case far more extensive than this, needed to demonstrate that they had suffered injustices so extreme and persistent that they warranted taking up arms.

Jeffrey Ostler in an article he wrote for the *Atlantic Monthly*, "The Shameful Final Grievance of the Declaration of Independence," quotes the well-known words that many US citizens celebrate on July Fourth: "'We hold these truths to be self-evident.' Say these words, and many Americans will be able to recite what follows: 'That all men are created equal, that they are endowed by their Creator with certain unalienable Rights, that among these are Life, Liberty and the pursuit of Happiness.'"[2] The opening words of the Declaration—easily its most memorable part—are widely celebrated as signifying the beginning of an exceptional American history, one characterized, despite setbacks, by a progressive expansion of rights. The closing words of the Declaration are far less familiar. The last of a list of twenty-seven grievances against King George III, they read as follows: "'He has excited domestic insurrections amongst us and has endeavored to bring on the inhabitants of our frontiers, the merciless Indian savages whose known rule of warfare, is an undistinguished destruction of all ages, sexes, and conditions.' These words call

---

2. Ostler, "Shameful Final Grievance," para. 1.

attention to hard truths about America's founding that have often been brushed aside."[3]

Ostler explains the realities that gave rise to this grievance. The first was the charge that the British were instigating "domestic insurrection." For example, Lord Dunmore, the colonial governor of Virginia, had decreed his own "emancipation proclamation," calling on all enslaved Africans to run away and join the British war effort and gain their freedom. These and similar gestures by British authorities were pragmatic tactics, calculated less from humanitarian regard for Africans than for military advantage. The British actively encouraged this defection of African Americans in order to undermine the economic foundation of the American colonies.[4]

Nevertheless, the conflict between the British and the American revolutionaries offered many enslaved African workers the opportunity to seize their freedom by escaping to the British side of the conflict. Tens of thousands of enslaved people would flock to the British army as it moved about and occupied the rebellious colonies, just as later, during the Civil War, the enslaved would gravitate to Sherman's army in his march across the South. Many Africans gave assistance in any way they could to the British war effort, applying whatever skill they brought with them. Black carpenters built ships, Black smiths forged tools and repaired weapons, and unskilled African workers maintained roads, and in South Carolina alone, over five thousand formerly enslaved people toiled on farms occupied by the British to supply the British army with food.[5]

Ostler observes that the racist depiction of Native Americans as "merciless Indian savages" has generated much less public discussion. In indicting the king for unleashing Indians on the "inhabitants of our frontiers," the Declaration was not referring to a specific event but rather to the recent escalation of violence caused by colonists invading Native lands west of the Appalachian Mountains.[6] In response, a confederation of Native nations, including the Cherokee, had exercised a right of self-defense and attacked the encroachment of new colonial settlements. Jefferson's language seems crafted to fan the flames of the colonists' anti-Indian racism as well as their constant anxiety about a slave insurrection.

---

3. Ostler, "Shameful Final Grievance," para. 2.
4. Ostler, "Shameful Final Grievance," para. 3.
5. Raphael, *People's History*, 332.
6. Ostler, "Shameful Final Grievance," para. 5.

In this way the twenty-seventh grievance laid the foundation for a virulent American white nationalism that has flourished to this day. On July Fourth, we continue to celebrate a freedom the colonists won from the British crown while denying that same freedom to the continent's Indigenous people and enslaved laborers.

THE FIRST SOUTH CAROLINIAN KILLED IN THE AMERICAN REVOLUTION

If the American Revolution was a crisis for the Cherokee once again forced to make strategic decisions about alliances to protect their interests, it was also a crisis for enslaved people of African descent, who saw the conflict as an opportunity to gain their freedom. Fears of a slave insurrection had long haunted the white population in the South Carolina low country, heightened by rumors that the British were encouraging this possibility. Ray Raphael, in his *A People's History of the American Revolution*, describes a free Black in Charles Town, by the name of Thomas Jeremiah, who declared that he would do all within his power to support the cause of the British when the time came. As a boat pilot familiar with the waterways of Charles Town harbor and the low country, Jeremiah was a man to be reckoned with.[7]

He came under suspicion as a British collaborator by none other than Henry Laurens, who was convinced of his guilt and decried him as a proud, insolent agitator. Jeremiah was captured, tried, convicted of sedition, and sentenced to hang on the grounds of the notorious slave prison, the Charles Town Workhouse. The British colonial governor, Lord Campbell, tried to intercede on Jeremiah's behalf but was unable to save him. Declaring his innocence until the end, Jeremiah was lynched, his body burned as further example to the enslaved of Charles Town. Thomas Jeremiah is remembered by some historians as the first South Carolinian to die in the American Revolution. Celebrating Independence Day as "our" struggle for freedom from British rule, white Americans too often forget that there were other freedom struggles woven into this history, felt no less keenly.

---

7. Raphael, *People's History*, 318–20.

THE LESS FAMOUS BATTLE ON SULLIVAN'S ISLAND

A centerpiece of South Carolina history is the famous Battle on Sullivan's Island in which the British fleet, laying siege to Charles Town, bombarded the Patriot fort under the command of General William Moultrie. British cannonballs bounced harmlessly off the palmetto logs from which the fort was constructed. This victory, South Carolina's great pride, is memorialized in our state flag. But in fact, the first fight of the Revolutionary War in South Carolina happened long before. Henry Laurens, as chair of the Council of Safety, ordered his troops to attack an encampment on Sullivan's Island of unarmed Blacks who had escaped slavery.[8] Laurens's official counterpart in the colony of Georgia, facing the same situation on an island near Savannah—a community of resistance composed of runaway slaves—indicated that he could see no other recourse than to massacre them all as a deterrent to other enslaved people. Disguising themselves as Creek Indians to enhance the terror of the act, the Georgians did just that.

Laurens responded to news of the Georgia attack with the same kind of reluctance he expressed about tactics employed against the Cherokee: "It is an awful business." Even though the law sanctioned putting fugitive slaves to death, Laurens confessed that the "prospect is horrible." After a talk with his own enslaved community at Mepkin, Laurens was most sanguine that their loyalty to him was steadfast. Only when, at the first opportunity, many of his enslaved workers ran away to the British did he realize how self-deceived he had been.[9]

THE CHEROKEE CONFRONT ANOTHER EXISTENTIAL DECISION

From the Cherokee perspective, the American Revolution of 1776 was no more than a continuation of the war of 1760–1761. The conflict between the British and the American revolutionaries would force upon Cherokee elders, who debated their nation's foreign policy, yet another existential gamble: a life and death decision of how to keep from being entangled in war. Both parties in the conflict, the British and the American Patriots,

---

8. Ball, *Slaves in the Family*, 220.
9. Raphael, *People's History*, 329.

made sure there was no neutral middle ground. Where lay the long-term interests of the Cherokee? Surely this was the subject of many town councils across the Cherokee Nation. As neutrality became increasingly impossible, should they align with the British, who continued to advocate for boundaries confining the colonies to the east of the Appalachian Mountains, or with the colonist revolutionaries who, in their voracious appetite for land, were chafing against those British-enforced boundaries?

The debate crossed all lines in the Cherokee Nation. Each cluster of towns was jealous of their autonomy. Settlements closer or farther removed from the conflict might approach the issue differently. Sometimes families and clans were divided over passionate convictions about how to proceed. The family of Attakullakulla is a perfect example. His son Dragging Canoe was a passionate advocate for armed resistance, his niece Nancy Ward, a voice for peace. But ultimately the Cherokee would be drawn inexorably into the American Revolution and would cast their lot as allies with the British. A similar conversation was taking place in the households of settler families all across the colony of South Carolina. What about the up-country settlers like my Anderson ancestors? How would they respond to this deepening crisis? Where would their loyalties lie?

"THE PRESBYTERIAN REBELLION"

The British Prime Minister Horace Walpole, on hearing of the revolt in the colonies, remarked: "Cousin America has run off with a Presbyterian parson."[10] There is a very good reason why some British officials referred to the American Revolution as the Presbyterian Rebellion. A great majority of the Scots Irish Presbyterian settlers of up-country South Carolina, like the Andersons, were ardent supporters of the Revolution. As Scots Irish long oppressed by the English, they had no great love or loyalty for the king. And as Presbyterians, they were passionately jealous of their freedom and resistant to the control of bishop or king. George Howe in 1861 gave a lecture at Nazareth Presbyterian Church, on the occasion of their centennial celebration. In his talk, he extolled the Presbyterian leaders who promoted the Patriots' cause ascribing to them almost the same stature as saints in the early church, or the apostles themselves.

10. Reed, review of *"Reformed and Evangelical,"* para. 4.

For example, the Presbyterian preacher William Tennent, the grandson of the founder of Princeton Seminary, went on a speaking tour of the up-country settlements, evangelizing for the cause of revolution. Tennent also had the authority to constitute military units of Patriot soldiers. Later, he would lead efforts to finally disestablish Anglicanism as the state-sponsored church of South Carolina.

In his history of the Presbyterian Church in South Carolina, George Howe waxes eloquently:

> This fine population of back countrymen included large numbers of Scotch-Irish Presbyterians and dissenting Baptists, both of which groups had behind them a proud record of struggle for liberty of conscience and democratic principals in government. Such were the people to whom Drayton and Tennent brought appeal from the newly formed Provincial Congress of South Carolina, a body formed in January 1775; by elected representatives of the people, and replacing, by its own action, the King's "House of Assembly." On June 4, 1775, the members of this Congress affixed their names to a document solemnly binding them "to associate in the defense of South Carolina against every foe and to hold all those persons inimical to the liberties of the colonies who shall refuse to subscribe to this Association."[11]

My Anderson ancestors, it appears, did not hesitate to cast their lot with the Patriot Revolutionaries. Many others in the up-country chose to remain loyal to the Crown. More recent settlers who had come through Charles Town and received incentives to settle in the backcountry—including land, tools, and tax breaks—were loath to defy the British government lest they lose these benefits. The German settlers in the Saxe-Gotha district were Tories. Quaker communities, some of them pacifist, did their best to stay neutral. The Scots Irish of the Waxhaws were universally disaffected with the British Crown. The area between the Broad and Saluda Rivers where my ancestors settled was evenly divided between those of Patriot and Tory sympathies.[12]

On June 14, the Congress appointed a Council of Safety "with power to do whatever the safety of the State demanded," and in July it sent its representatives into the up-country to explain the revolutionary movement to the people and appeal to them to set their signatures to the

---

11. Anderson, *Anderson Family History*, 18, quoting Howe.
12. Anderson, *Anderson Family History*, 30.

"Association."[13] The response of the population to this appeal drew the inhabitants of the backcountry into a common struggle with the rest of the state and marked an epoch in their history. Henry Laurens was the president of the Council of Safety and would soon succeed John Hancock as the president of the Continental Congress.

In 1776, as the British fleet moved down the coasts of the Carolinas preparing for an invasion of the southern colonies, the Cherokee Nation launched an attack on the frontier settlements of the up-country including those along the Tyger River. My ancestor William Anderson was killed by the Cherokee/Tory attack later in the war. But this attack in 1776 has lived on in South Carolina culture as a "day of infamy," mainly because of what another South Carolina family, much more prominent than mine, also suffered on that day. There is no family more famous in South Carolina history than the Hamptons. They first settled on the Tyger River in 1774 and would have been proximate neighbors to my Anderson ancestors. Edward and Preston Hampton, who were brothers, quickly established themselves as traders with the Cherokee. As rumors of war continued to circulate, they went into the Lower Towns to see what they could ascertain and perhaps forestall. There, their worst fears were confirmed, and they quickly returned to the Tyger River settlements to warn their neighbors of the likelihood of a Cherokee offensive.

It began the next day. Cherokee warriors approached the Hampton homestead and as the Hamptons greeted them, no doubt warily, the attack began. Anthony Hampton, the family patriarch, his wife who remains unnamed, his son Preston, and an infant grandson were all killed.

They, of course, were not the only settlers killed by the Cherokee in that war, but the memory of their deaths has been perpetuated because of the significance of the Hampton family to South Carolina history. Wade Hampton, great-grandson of Anthony, would go on to be the most distinguished South Carolinian of the Confederacy as commander of the famous Hampton Legion during the Civil War. Wade Hampton would also be elected governor of the state in the much-contested election of 1876, which through corruption, violence, and national backroom deal-making brought about the end of the period we know as Reconstruction across the Southern states.

---

13. Anderson, *Anderson Family History*, 18.

I was fortunate to hear an online lecture by Dr. Evan Nooe, professor of history at USC Lancaster, on how this incident of the Hampton massacre has been routinely deployed by successive generations of South Carolinians to tell the story of this state. Dr. Nooe makes a convincing case that begins with B. F. Perry, the Reconstruction governor of South Carolina, who also was something of a historian and a newspaper man. In the 1840s, Perry first published in his newspaper, the *Greenville Mountaineer*, a series of articles called "Revolutionary Incidents," where he described the Hamptons as exemplary settlers treacherously murdered, and the Cherokee who killed them were portrayed as fiendish, malevolent devils. Other newspapers across South Carolina, like the *Charleston Mercury*, ran the series.

Perry then published the articles as a book, and the event of the Hampton massacre was fast becoming a public memory passed down from generation to generation of how South Carolinians would remember their history. With each new rendition of the story, more salacious descriptions were advanced. The unprovoked attack against the innocent Hampton family by the "treacherous" Cherokee was ever more horrific. With each telling, the victimization of early settlers was heightened. The story does not end there of course. The Hampton men who survived went on a righteous mission of vengeance, vowing to kill Cherokee in equal measure and then some. Dr. Nooe, who will soon publish a book on this, makes a persuasive case of how the Hampton massacre became a widely accepted narrative of intergenerational trauma and a celebratory glorification of retribution in South Carolina culture.

Dr. Nooe points out some of the ways that the larger historical context has been obscured by the cultivation of the Hampton massacre as a shared public memory. For example, Nooe was unable to locate a land grant for the Hamptons, which suggested to him that no grant had been given. The Hamptons may well have been squatters occupying an area on the Tyger River, right up against the Cherokee boundary, that was intended to remain unsettled as a buffer zone, separating the Cherokee from settlers. This makes me wonder if this was true for my Anderson ancestors as well, who settled along the Tyger River some twenty-five years prior to the Hamptons. The string of fort stockades these settlers built along that boundary line, including Fort Prince associated with my Anderson ancestors, was a threatening reality for the Cherokee. The Cherokees' attack on these settlers was not so much fiendish treachery committed by savages as it was a military campaign by an Indigenous nation, determined to defend its homeland from further encroachment. The lack of settler culpability is a consistent theme in the narrative of the Hampton massacre as is the regenerative nature of violence.[14]

The memory of the Hampton massacre continued to make its way through history until 1876, on the one-hundredth anniversary of the American Revolution, and ironically of the massacre itself, Wade Hampton began his campaign for governor with a rally in Spartanburg, just a few miles from where the massacre occurred. Among the six thousand in attendance were surely citizens of Greenville who traveled past the massacre site on the way to the rally in Spartanburg. There is no existing copy of Hampton's speech, but thanks to a schoolgirl's essay many years later recounting the event, Dr. Nooe believes we can be sure that Hampton invoked the memory of this massacre at his rally. In 1896, Mary Earle Lyle wrote a student essay on the occasion that won first prize for the Daughters of the American Revolution's essay contest. Her essay quoting Hampton's speech was also picked up and run by newspapers around the state. Again, the Hampton massacre was repurposed as an anchor of settler innocence, the justification of racial violence, and a through line of white supremacy.

14. In 1933, along Highway 29 that connects my hometown of Greenville with Spartanburg, a monument was erected by the Daughters of the Confederacy, commemorating the graves of those Hamptons killed in 1776. But the marker signifies not just those whose graves were nearby, but the successive generations of Hamptons, leading up to Wade Hampton himself, Confederate general, governor, and vindicator of white supremacy. Growing up I had cause to drive from Greenville to Spartanburg because of a couple of summer jobs, and I remember seeing the monument as I passed by, but I confess I had completely forgotten its existence until the lecture by Dr. Nooe. I returned to it recently to acquire a photo of the monument. The highway itself is named Wade Hampton Boulevard and leads into Greenville, past my high school named after Wade Hampton. Our school mascot was the Confederate General. This is how public memory is formed.

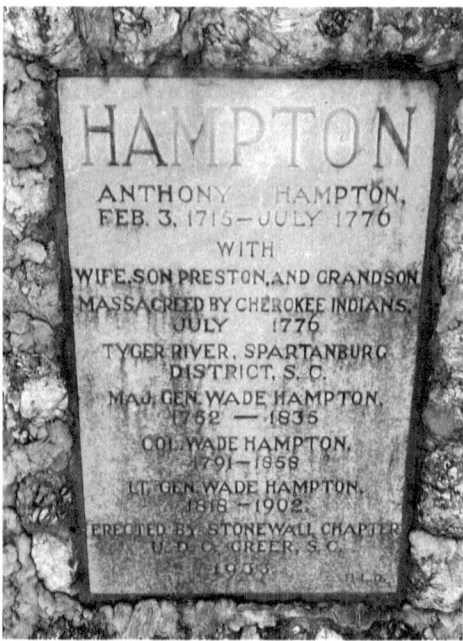

Hampton Massacre Marker

A BLOODY CIVIL WAR

Let us dig a little deeper into how the American Revolution in South Carolina affected white Scots Irish settlers like my Anderson ancestors. Their experiences during these tumultuous times testify to the extremely brutal and pervasive violence between Tories loyal to the British Crown and up-country Patriots committed to the Revolution. "Major Anderson," according to my Anderson family history, "considered his life in more danger when he was home on leave than with the army. The headquarters of the Tories was near his house, and he frequently pointed out to his children, after the war, a large oak by the river, in the thick branches of which he had lain hidden for days and from which he had watched the Tories hunting for him."[15]

His father, William, was returning home one day when he saw smoke billowing from a fire in the distance. His fears of an attack were confirmed when they came upon a burning homestead, its inhabitants all

---

15. Anderson, *Anderson Family History*, 29.

murdered. He raced to his own farm to gather his wife Rebecca, whose hip had been dislocated by a fall from her horse. Undaunted, he put her in a rocking chair and strapped her to a horse: thus they made their escape. William's luck would run out near the end of the war, however. One winter night, a band of Tories and Indians surrounded the Anderson homestead and shot William in his bed. They permitted Rebecca to escape, with nothing but her night dress to protect her from the cold as she waded two rivers, making her way to another homestead and safety six miles distant. They dragged Anderson, badly wounded, from the house, split his head open with a tomahawk, and scalped him. They then burned the house to the ground. Accounts of this attack raise a suspicion that the Tories may have dressed as Indians—perhaps a deception used either to avoid identification or to further terrorize their enemies with the threat of Indian violence.

THE CHEROKEE HOMELAND INVADED FROM EVERY DIRECTION

In 1776, Major Williamson led a militia force estimated to be around 1,100 strong on a march up the Keowee Trail. This force of troops from South Carolina would join other armies from Virginia, North Carolina, and Georgia in a simultaneous invasion of the Cherokee homeland. Virginia attacked the Overhills. North Carolina under General Rutherford targeted the Middle and Out Towns. South Carolina under Major Williamson, with Andrew Pickens as his lieutenant, attacked the Lower and Valley Towns and converged on the Overhills. Georgia troops under General Elijah Clark destroyed the settlements in the northern area of that state.

Under Williamson's command was Captain Andrew Pickens who would use his experiences fighting the Cherokee in the war of 1760 to full measure in this campaign of the American Revolution. Pickens equipped the South Carolina militia unit he commanded with short cutlasses: long, thick knives that would be ideal for close hand-to-hand combat. Williamson ordered Captain Pickens to lead a scouting expedition of some twenty-five mounted men deeper into the Cherokee homeland. Pickens and his men seemed to have stumbled upon the Cherokee town of Tamassee. In the legendary "Ring Fight," as it was remembered in South Carolina history, Cherokee warriors, estimated at around 185, surrounded

Pickens's forces in a high grass field adjacent to the Cherokee town of Tamassee. The Cherokee were literally fighting to defend their homes.

Pickens quickly arranged his riflemen in two concentric rings facing outward, one ring firing and then dropping to the ground to reload while the second ring rose and fired. Again and again they alternated this maneuver, holding off the greater number of Cherokee warriors. When Pickens set fire to a canebrake near their position, so the story is told, the river cane exploded with what sounded like the pop-bang of gunfire. The way the story is often remembered by white South Carolinians is that this sudden gun-like volley of noise deceived the Cherokee warriors to believe they were fighting a larger number of enemy soldiers. Luther Lyle, the director of the Cherokee Museum of South Carolina (in Oconee County where Tamassee and the Ring Fight are located), explains that the Cherokee were unlikely to be deceived in this way because they were very familiar with the sound of a canebrake on fire. The Cherokee had for generations used fire for controlled burns to regenerate canebrakes and would have not confused this sound with gunfire.

However, the noise of fire in the canebrake may have still played a role in the deliverance of Captain Pickens and his men. His brother Patrick Pickens, who was leading a relief column to the battle, may have been guided by all the noise and smoke generated by weapons and burning river cane alike to provide the reinforcements necessary to save his brother Andrew and win the day. It was the Ring Fight that established Pickens's reputation as a fighter both among white troops and Cherokee warriors alike. According to the American Battlefield Trust website, Pickens lost eleven of his twenty-five. Sixty-five Cherokee warriors were killed; fourteen were left wounded on the battlefield. Immediately after the battle, Pickens had his dead buried in the village itself and then set it on fire. The Cherokee village of Tamassee was burned to the ground and all the surrounding agricultural fields set aflame by Patriot soldiers.[16] Once again, the scorched earth tactics of the Cherokee War of 1760 were unleashed.

16. American Battlefield Trust, "Ring Fight."

Tamassee

If it is difficult for us to imagine now the impact that the extreme violence of this war had on actual settler families like my Anderson ancestors, it is perhaps impossible for white Americans to imagine the impact on the Cherokee who lived at Tamassee Town. But let us try. Imagine a group composed largely of women who have lost their fathers, their brothers, their sons, their husbands to war and were fleeing for their lives with their children and their elders into the mountains. There were wounded warriors to attend to as well as terrified children and elders struggling to keep up. There were women trying to keep everyone together and lead them to safety. Looking back down the valley from which they fled, they saw the smoke of their burning homes and fields all destroyed. Looking forward, they searched for a place of safety, food, and shelter. And this was the desperate plight of just one Cherokee village. The invasion continued up the Cherokee Path.

Pickens's troops continued past the Lower Towns and into the Valley Towns using their short cutlasses no doubt to great effect. Finally reaching the Overhill Towns in Eastern Tennessee, they surrounded a settlement at daybreak and attacked, slaughtering any resisters. One young warrior fled into a nearby ravine, with Pickens and about fifteen of his soldiers in pursuit. The warrior managed to escape volley after volley until one soldier charged into the ravine and killed him, cutting off his head and chopping it into pieces. Though Pickens was said to be disgusted by this display, these kinds of depredations against the living and the dead—against men, women, and children—were common as American forces from each of the states invaded the Cherokee homeland.[17]

Given the take-no-prisoners tactics Pickens himself had just encouraged, his "disgust" at the soldier who slaughtered the warrior might seem disingenuous and hypocritical. But officers like Pickens who might be genuinely appalled at such atrocities were hard pressed to use their authority to restrain it. Hatley reports that Colonel Rutherford, leading the troops from North Carolina, attempted to arrest one of his soldiers who was carrying out such egregious violations against the Cherokee, and his own troops rose up and demanded their fellow be released, which he was.[18] The desire to exact revenge and settle old scores may have motivated the American Revolutionary forces, but the recurring cycle of violence between whites and Cherokee had spiraled beyond warfare defined in any conventional sense.

What was it like to be a Cherokee woman during the turbulence of the American Revolution? The Yale historian Tiya Miles gives us a remarkable portrait of a Cherokee woman named Nancy (not the Nancy Ward previously described) whose experience may be representative of Cherokee women throughout colonial history.[19] The story takes place among the Overhill Towns of the Cherokee Nation in what is now in eastern Tennessee, but the troops Nancy encountered may well have been those from South Carolina under the command of Williamson and led by Andrew Pickens. Miles reconstructed Nancy's story, refusing to allow her narrative to be consigned to the abyss of silence. Nancy's family was encamped with other Cherokee when they were attacked by white soldiers, who terrorized and murdered Nancy's mother and took Nancy, a young girl of approximately eight years old, captive, later selling her into slavery.

Miles shows just how vulnerable Nancy and her mother were in this conflict, first as Cherokee and then as women, to the kind of sexual

17. Hatley, *Dividing Paths*, 202.
18. Hatley, *Dividing Paths*, 201.
19. Miles, "Narrative of Nancy," 59–80.

violence that often accompanies military conquest. Female war captives have always been vulnerable to sexual assault as a display of soldiers' domination. But this vulnerability was heightened when those women were also considered heathen, hence less than human. Miles notes that sexual violence against Native women in a military conflict was characterized by a "degree of hostility and brutality" that went "beyond simple sexual pleasure into torture as a purposeful expression of superiority."[20] Nancy may have witnessed her mother being sexually assaulted before she was killed. And being sold as a slave intensified her own vulnerability to sexual assault.[21]

Following this four-pronged invasion from the combined forces of the southern colonies, all Cherokee resistance collapsed except for that of a band of Cherokees led by Dragging Canoe, Attakullakulla's son. Dragging Canoe left the Overhill Towns and moved farther west to retrench and rebuild along the Chickamauga Creek (near present day Chattanooga in southeastern Tennessee). Gradually this initial band, which came to be

20. Miles, "Narrative of Nancy," 64.

21. How was it that Nancy, a Cherokee, could be enslaved when by 1777 it was illegal to enslave an Indian? One answer lies in colonial records, which describe Nancy not only as Indian but also as mixed blood, with African characteristics. Miles suggests that Nancy's father was probably Black, and that this biracial identity became the legal rationale for her continuing enslavement. Nancy became a tireless advocate with the government to gain her freedom. The legal case unfolded over a painfully long stretch of years but over that time Agent Meigs, the federal agent assigned to the Cherokee, compiled a dossier of evidence that included statements by other Cherokee and by Nancy's white enslavers.

The legal controversy of her case and the subsequent ruling of a Virginia court that enslaving Indians was illegal might have led her enslaver to sell her and her children to another slaveholder in the deeper south of Georgia. This would appear to make it even more difficult for Nancy to continue to advocate for her freedom—except that her new owner lived within the boundaries of the Cherokee Nation. Again, Meigs collected testimony from Cherokee elders substantiating Nancy's claim to being Cherokee. Colonial records first describing Nancy as Indian began to refer to Nancy as Black. When Meigs finally rendered his official decision, it was that Nancy was not a real Cherokee and could remain legally enslaved.

Somehow Nancy escaped from her enslavement and was given refuge within the Cherokee homeland. As anyone familiar with this period knows, the state of Georgia was using every legal and some illegal means to subjugate and dispossess the Cherokee from within their state boundaries. During this heightened conflict with Georgia, it was a strategically risky moment for the Cherokee to offer sanctuary to one mixed race woman and her children, and Nancy was eventually returned to her white owner. It was only at the death of this owner when his property was being legally disbursed that one of Nancy's grandsons, Moses, was purchased by a Cherokee elder and set free. As Miles reflects on Nancy's story, of thirty years enslaved and twenty years spent fighting for her freedom, the emancipation of her grandson was indeed hard won.

known as the Chickamaugas, was joined by others until over ten villages were organized. Colonial forces rarely made a distinction between Overhill and Chickamauga Cherokee. Whenever the largely non-belligerent Overhill Cherokee were attacked by whites, the Chickamauga gained new refugees and recruits. From their settlements farther southwest, Chickamauga war parties could still harass the Patriot cause and defend Cherokee independence. These Chickamauga Cherokee found allies in bands of Shawnee scattered across the Ohio Valley, who were equally concerned about protecting their homeland.

What was the strategic purpose of this multi-pronged invasion of the Cherokee homeland by Patriot forces from four of the former southern colonies? US citizens remembering the American Revolution celebrate the cause of freedom. But one of the driving forces behind the American Revolution against Britain was in fact the "freedom" to push westward past the Appalachians to seize additional space into which a new nation might expand. It was always about land. It was not just the wealthy like General Washington who were determined to acquire property west of the mountains in what would become the state of Kentucky. The Patriot soldiers under Washington's command were also promised generous grants of land taken from various tribes like the Cherokee. Scots Irish soldiers had fought for land and were now prepared to hold and defend it when at long last the impediment to westward expansion posed by British policy was removed.

FOR US OR AGAINST US

Back in South Carolina, the up-country was able to make the most of a brief respite from warfare, but not the low country. In 1780, the British laid siege to Charles Town, which surrendered in March of that year. After the British occupation of Charles Town and other major towns of the low country, many Patriots, including Pickens himself, considered the Patriot cause in the southern colonies to be hopeless. Many accepted the terms of a British parole that meant maintaining neutrality in any further conflict. At this nadir in the struggle for American independence, the British believed that they had successfully brought about the "pacification" of the southern colonies. But then they overplayed their hand in two ways that ignited a new wave of Patriot insurgency.

Dr. Melissa Walker's book *The Battles of Kings Mountain and Cowpens: The American Revolution in the Southern Backcountry* and Walter

Edgar's *Partisans and Redcoats* were indispensable sources for what follows, a sketch that is my takeaway from these two sources. First the British commander, General Clinton, changed the terms of the parole, declaring that neutrality was not sufficient: South Carolinians must actively support the British in restoring the colony to submission. In other words, to remain in the good graces of the British, they must be prepared to fight against their neighbors—perhaps even against their former comrades in arms. This led many, including Pickens himself, to renounce the terms of their parole, even under threat of death if recaptured by the British.

But the most serious British blunder was the mistaken assumption that severely punitive treatment of the people would smother the rebellion and deter further resistance. British tactics were so brutal that they caused exactly the opposite effect, provoking such outrage that many more South Carolinians took up arms. The British army not only did what most armies do in resupplying themselves through forage and plunder, they went about the up-country destroying farms and homes of those who were not sufficiently loyal.

Two of the most aggressive British officers were the Colonels Banastre Tarleton and James Weymss. Weymss was the detested British commander who called Presbyterian churches in the up-country "sedition shops" and made it a practice to burn them to the ground. As cruel as Weymss was, though, Tarleton exceeded him. In 1780, Tarleton's Green Dragoons attacked a column of Patriot soldiers under the command of General Buford near Waxhaws Presbyterian Church, refusing to give quarter to any prisoners and slaughtering nearly all. (Rebecca Jackson and her sons, Robert and Andrew, the future president of the United States, attended to the wounded survivors brought to the church.) This massacre ignited fierce determination among Patriot forces, military and civilian alike, to avenge these depredations. Patriot soldiers went into a fight with the battle cry of "Tarleton's quarter!": take no prisoners.

Andrew Jackson at the age of fourteen would experience the trauma of war. He and his brother Robert, pursued by a British cavalry unit through the night, were at last cornered in the home of a relative. As the house was being ransacked, an imperious officer demanded that Andrew shine his boots. When Andrew refused, the officer struck him with his sword, a blow to the head that was only partially deflected by his hand. The officer next threatened Andrew's brother Robert, and when he too refused, the officer again aimed a blow that better found its mark. Andrew Jackson lost both of his brothers because of the war and his mother as well, who died of smallpox while nursing sick relatives in Charles Town. I have long considered Andrew Jackson to be the incarnation of evil for what he did to the Cherokee. I still do, but another look at the trauma of his childhood humanizes him and reminds me of how the trauma of violence, if not healed, simply replicates itself in expanding repercussions, spreading far and wide.

The Patriot victory at Kings Mountain (October 1780) is much heralded in the history of the American Revolution as a turning point that led irrevocably to Yorktown and Cornwallis surrender to Washington. Commemorating this battle is the Overmountain Victory Trail, a national park that traces the routes of two separate Patriot units that marched from the mountains to the battlefield at Kings Mountain. One spur of the Overmountain Trail begins near Abingdon, Virginia, memorializing the column led by John Sevier that included other members of the Watauga Settlement, who were trespassing on Cherokee lands.

The chaplain of this Patriot column was a Presbyterian minister by the name of the Reverend Samuel Doak, who delivered a sermon and prayed to the God of Gideon that they might be granted victory. The text of his prayer survives to today:

> Let us pray. Almighty and gracious God! Thou has been the refuge and strength of Thy people in all ages. In time of sorest need we have learned to come to Thee—our Rock and our Fortress. Thou knowest the dangers and snares that surround us on march and in battle. Thou knowest the dangers that constantly threaten the humble, but well-beloved homes, which Thy servants have left behind them. O, in Thine infinite mercy, save us from the cruel hand of the savage, and of tyrant. Save the unprotected homes while fathers and husbands and sons are far away fighting for freedom and helping the oppressed. Thou, who promised to protect the sparrow in its flight, keep ceaseless watch, by day and by night, over our loved ones. The helpless woman and little children, we commit to Thy care. Thou wilt not leave them or forsake them in times of loneliness and anxiety and terror. O, God of Battle, arise in Thy might. Avenge the slaughter of Thy people. Confound those who plot for our destruction. Crown this mighty effort with victory and smite those who exalt themselves against liberty and justice and truth. Help us as good soldiers to wield the Sword of the Lord and Gideon.[22]

---

22. Log College Press, "Samuel Doak's 1780," paras. 8–15.

The other spur of the Overmountain Victory Trail begins in Elkin where I live today, and runs literally by my house, along the Yadkin River. The contingent of Patriots who marched on this section were led by Joseph Winston (from whom Winston-Salem derives its name) and Benjamin Cleveland (whose historic homeplace is just a few miles upriver on the Yadkin from my home). With Cleveland were several of my Gilreath ancestors—Scots Irish settlers who, like the Andersons, made the journey down the Great Wagon Road from Philadelphia to Carolina, settling first here in the Yadkin watershed. Later they continued their migration with Benjamin Cleveland on to South Carolina. My great-grandfather, Jefferson Davis Gilreath, married Mariah Anderson.

It is an article of faith in the Carolinas to remember Kings Mountain as the turning point in the American Revolution. I have venerated the Patriot victory at Kings Mountain since I was a young boy. I have driven past the mountain many times en route between North and South Carolina with a reverential nod. I have hiked all over the battlefield and stood in awe at the place where Cleveland and my Gilreath ancestors fought their way, "Indian style," up the slopes of the mountain to defeat the British Tories under the command of Major Patrick Fergusen. But there is a shadow that falls across the glory of this Patriot victory that turned the tide of the American Revolution. Far less often is it remembered that at the moment of victory, the Patriots exacted "Tarleton's Quarter" to Tory combatants. In the aftermath of the battle, surviving Tory prisoners were further abused. Nine were tried and hung as those who were accused of having themselves practiced violence against civilians or prisoners.

Benjamin Cleveland, the famous Patriot commander who fought at Kings Mountain, was known in the area where I live in North Carolina for his political violence. He was infamous for lynching people of Tory sympathies, so much so that an ancient oak in the nearby community of Wilkesboro was known as "Tory Oak" because of all of Cleveland's Tory victims hung from its branches.[23] It is no badge of pride for me that some of my Scots Irish ancestors (Gilreath) migrated from this area here along the Yadkin with none other than Benjamin Cleveland. So began a dark pattern to the American Revolution as it was fought in South Carolina. In their treatment of prisoners, both sides often violated the rules of war.

---

23. In his victory speech after being recently elected, my new state senator from this district proudly recounted the story of Cleveland's propensity for political violence, warning his "woke" opponents (his word) of the inspirations for which he sought office and models for how he would "govern."

Patriots were just as guilty of the torture and execution of prisoners as the British. Often, the violence of both Patriot and Tory partisans was nothing short of savage. Terrorism was a widely accepted tactic. Civilians, including women and children, often were not spared.

An exception to the rule was Andrew Pickens. This Presbyterian elder did his best to preserve discipline among his troops. For example, after Pickens renounced the terms of British parole and rejoined Patriot troops, Major Dunlap, another hated British commander, took his cavalry to Long Canes and, in the middle of a winter night, turned out Rebecca Pickens and her children, burned their home to the ground, and destroyed the Pickens's farm. The fortunes of war turning as they would, Pickens's soldiers later captured Dunlap at the Battle of Beattie's Ford. Before he could be properly handled as a prisoner of war, an enraged Patriot soldier intervened, murdered him, and made his escape. Pickens immediately put out a proclamation offering a reward for the capture of Dunlap's murderer.

Granted, this one instance might be insufficient proof that Pickens consistently subscribed to a military code of honor. But another case is equally well-documented, this time involving Pickens's efforts to protect a notorious Tory prisoner, none other than Richard Pearis, the Cherokee trader who owned what is now my hometown of Greenville and who had become one of the most militant of the Tory leaders. Pickens made sure that what happened to Dunlap would not happen to Pearis. The more I learn about Andrew Pickens, the more I feel a grudging respect for this dour Presbyterian elder. He strikes me as an honorable man, doing his best in a time of war but unable finally to control the violence it unleashed.

At the battle of Cowpens, Pickens led the South Carolina militia who lured the British regulars under Banastre Tarleton into a trap that sealed an important American victory—a military maneuver dramatized in the 2000 film *The Patriot* starring Mel Gibson, whose character seems to be a composite of South Carolina's most famous Patriot commanders: Marion, Pickens, and Sumter. During the battle, a group of women of Nazareth Presbyterian Church, thirteen miles away, were assembled at a house near the church, no doubt listening to sounds of battle and anxiously awaiting news of the outcome. In the aftermath, these same women would attend to the wounded on both sides and as always try to put life back together again in a time of war.

Pickens, along with one of my Anderson ancestors, also participated in the unsuccessful siege of the British Fort at Ninety-Six. One story about Major David Anderson during the war comes down to us from our Anderson family history. A portion of the British troops were fortified behind a brick wall of the British fort when Anderson ordered his troops to attack. Having no success in dislodging them, Anderson ordered his men to aim at the ground at the wall's base, creating the appearance that the range of their rifles was just short of the distance required. British soldiers grew more confident, daring to raise themselves above the wall to taunt their adversaries. When enough redcoats were visible, Anderson directed a volley that struck the exposed British line with significant casualties. After the war was over, he was given thirty or forty enslaved Africans as recompense for his military service. The ironies abound: land stolen from Indians and workers stolen from Africa became the rewards for white Patriots who fought for land and freedom in the Revolution.[24]

In 1780, Pickens was reunited with Francis Marion as Patriot forces rallied together at Mepkin, Henry Laurens's plantation on the Cooper River. Laurens's palatial home had been burned to the ground by General Cornwallis, the commander of British forces in the southern colonies, who brought a flotilla of troop ships up the Cooper River to disembark at the ferry at Strawberry, next door to Mepkin. The commanding general at this Patriot rendezvous was Nathaniel Greene. They marched up a route that followed the original Keowee Trail, past the ruins of Biggins Church (burned by Cornwallis) through Moncks Corner, and on to the little village at Eutaw Springs, the plantation of the third South Carolinian much heralded in the history of the American Revolution, Thomas Sumter. (Sumter received his *nom de guerre* "the Gamecock" from none other than Banastre Tarleton.) Years before, Sumter also had extensive experience with the Cherokee and had actually accompanied a delegation of Cherokee leaders to England after the Cherokee War of 1760. At Eutaw Springs, Pickens led some three hundred militia into battle and a decisive Patriot victory. He was seriously wounded by a shot to the chest, surviving only because a buckle on his sword belt deflected the bullet. He would endure pain and bear the scars of that wound for the rest of his life.

The British army under Cornwallis was unable to subdue the southern colonies. After a costly battle fought at Guilford Courthouse in North Carolina, Cornwallis capitulated and marched his army to Virginia to meet its demise at Yorktown in October 1781. Cornwallis's surrender became pivotal personally as well as politically for Henry Laurens. As president of the Continental Congress, Laurens had embarked the year

24. Anderson, *Anderson Family History*, 18.

before on a special mission to obtain a loan from the Netherlands for the war effort. Off the coast of Newfoundland he had been captured by a British frigate, taken to England, and imprisoned in the Tower of London, accused of high treason. His fortunes changed dramatically on December 31, 1781, when he was exchanged for Cornwallis in a prisoner swap.

Richard Oswald, Laurens's former business partner in the slave trade, used his influence with His Majesty's government to secure Laurens's release from prison. Laurens then went to Paris to join the team of John Adams, Benjamin Franklin, and John Jay in negotiating the final peace treaty with Great Britain that formally ended the war. On the British side of the table in these negotiations was the same Richard Oswald. As part of the Treaty of Paris, Great Britain ceded to the United States all lands from the Atlantic Seaboard to the Mississippi River, though both parties knew full well that that territory was claimed and occupied by Native peoples. The Doctrine of Discovery raised its ugly head once again. The Cherokee and other tribal allies of the British felt justifiably betrayed by Great Britain and in no way acknowledged that the sovereignty over Indigenous lands was something to be decided in a treaty between the British and the new American government.

Badly depleted from the War for Independence in blood and treasure, the new nation would have to bide its time to rebuild, as they faced a formidable array of Native peoples determined to remain on their lands. After the war, Laurens would return to Mepkin and rebuild his home. In a census from the year 1790, Laurens reported owning 298 enslaved workers at Mepkin. With the American Revolution dedicated in its founding principles to the cause of freedom for the white man, many southerners in the new nation now believed themselves to be unrestricted in their purpose to displace Indian nations from their territories and replace them with new states where they could extend the institution of slavery and the plantation economy.

MAJOR DAVID ANDERSON

When the war was over, Major Anderson returned to his homeplace, where he and his wife Miriam Mayson Anderson lived in a wagon shed until a new house could be built. And in that wagon shed my great-great-great-grandfather, Jim Anderson, was born. He was known in his lifetime and to his descendants as "Tyger" Jim for the river that ran through their land and distinguished him from his cousin "Enoree" Jim Anderson, born on the Enoree River a few miles west.[25] Up-country white families like my Anderson ancestors experienced the traumatic chaos of war. So did the families of enslaved African workers still longing for freedom, and the Cherokee people who were prepared to continue in their desperate struggle to defend their homeland.

The Anderson family history provides only a few notes of information about the impact of the Revolution on David Anderson. Before the Revolutionary War, he had worked as a surveyor, mapping public lands for the colonial government.

> When the war commenced, fearing that his house would be burnt by the Tories or the Indians he prepared a buckskin and sewed up his plats, surveys, and claims against the government and suspended them in a hollow tree in the woods, where he thought they would be secure. At the close of the war, he went to hunt for his buckskin, when, to his great surprise and mortification, he found skin and papers cut and torn into innumerable fragments lying at the root of the tree. In his great anxiety and care to secure from the Tories and Indians, he had forgotten the flying squirrels.[26]

There is an irony here that asks to be teased out. The Cherokee were always keenly concerned of the whereabouts of surveyors because they recognized that any survey done by settlers was always a prelude to future demands for land. They referred to surveyors as "land stealers." A surveyor was the instrument of private property, a concept utterly alien to Cherokee culture. Another surveyor, Patrick Calhoun, a contemporary of Anderson's, was also a Scots Irish Presbyterian who settled in the Long Canes community and father to John. C. Calhoun. Robert Elder describes Patrick Calhoun: "He would survey thousands of acres, literally laying the groundwork for the plantation economy in the backcountry of South Carolina. Surveying was a pathway to wealth in the South Carolina backcountry."[27] What was true about Calhoun was certainly true for David Anderson. Flying squirrels consuming his survey plats was only a momentary delay. He would become the owner of extensive lands in the Tyger River area of Spartanburg County as would his Anderson kinfolk for many miles around.[28]

25. Howe, *History*, 542–43.
26. Anderson, *Anderson Family History*, 28.
27. Elder, *Calhoun*, 11.
28. Anderson reunions at Nazareth often included a driving tour of these very

David Anderson had fought with Pickens in multiple engagements across the up-country. His father had been murdered; his home had been burned. Miriam, his wife, had barely escaped with her life. His infant son was born in a lean-to. Our Anderson history relates that after the American Revolution, the government gave Major Anderson a reward for his service to the Patriot cause in the form of thirty or forty enslaved Africans. In his last will and testament he bequeathed to his beloved daughter Henrietta his farm of 175 acres, his household with furniture, and the only three enslaved workers who still remained, "Tener, Frank, and Sarah together with their future increase." A notation in the Anderson family history indicates that by the time this will was drawn up (1825), most of David Anderson's estate had already been distributed to his sons, including land, livestock, and perhaps other enslaved workers.[29] We now have a better understanding of how the death of a slave-owner and the settlement of the estate was very often a crisis for enslaved families—the sale of enslaved workers and the traumatic disruption and separation of enslaved families.

David Anderson Grave

---

impressive homeplaces, and the Anderson family history included photographs of some of them.

29. Anderson, *Anderson Family History*, 30.

Major David Anderson was of course not the only Patriot officer who was awarded the largest and most select lands for their service in the American Revolution. General Benjamin Cleveland was given a large tract along the Tugaloo River, on the western boundary of the Lower Towns. Cleveland along with approximately one hundred others had journeyed from North Carolina to settle there apparently by invitation and under the auspices of the state of Georgia. My Gilreath ancestors who came to South Carolina with Cleveland were not among them, for they had chosen to leave Cleveland's band to settle on the Tyger River.

Of course, this land along the Tugaloo River was contested territory as it had been formerly inhabited by hundreds of Cherokee families, who had flourished along its banks in the towns of Tugaloo and Eastatoee. Cherokee leaders had come to Pickens to complain about Cleveland and the growing settler presence there. They weren't alone in this concern. The states of South Carolina and Georgia were also in disagreement about where the boundary between them lay. Was the Tugaloo watershed in Georgia or South Carolina? Andrew Pickens was called upon to adjudicate this controversy and warned Cleveland that until this matter was resolved legally between the states, his land claims were void. Being of a military mindset he affirmed South Carolina's territorial claim to the area in question, because of his state's "right of conquest" over the Cherokee. Georgia, in his mind, could make no such claim.

Finally, the controversy was resolved when South Carolina agreed to relinquish another disputed claim with Georgia. The Tugaloo River became the official boundary between the two states. The Cherokee claim to the land apparently had no legal merit. Cleveland, the man who exacted vigilante justice by lynching Tories throughout the American Revolution, went on to a career as a justice of the peace for the district.[30]

I wonder about Andrew and Rebecca Pickens and how they navigated the turmoil and upheaval of these times between the Cherokee War and the aftermath of the Revolution. In his biography of Pickens, Rod Andrew points out that, like her husband, Rebecca Pickens reflected something of the evolution of her generation of settlers on the South Carolina frontier. She had traveled the long wagon road from Pennsylvania to Carolina. As a girl she had witnessed in horror the scalping and murder of her grandmother at the Long Cane massacre. No doubt Rebecca carried the weight of that trauma throughout her life. She and her children had been refugees during the American Revolution. She had

30. Andrew, *General Andrew Pickens*, 184.

been turned out of her home by Tories in the dead of winter and watched them burn her house to the ground and destroy her farm. She depended on enslaved Africans for her survival. She was in effect a single parent during the long absences of her husband as a soldier during war and as a high-ranking government emissary during peace. She would later share in the postwar prosperity of a large plantation, overseeing many enslaved people. She was a Presbyterian in good standing.[31] Rebecca Pickens was a person of enduring faith. Her faith upheld her through the trauma of war. Her faith was the ultimate container of all she believed about her world, her place in history, and her relationships to her Scots Irish Presbyterian neighbors, the Cherokee they had displaced, and enslaved Africans who populated her world.

THE SOUTHERN GENTLEMAN: EVOLVING PATRIARCHY

What about Andrew Pickens, who became known as the "Fighting Elder," referring to both his office as a Presbyterian elder and to his career as a soldier? How might he have integrated within his Presbyterian soul all that he had seen in the wars against the Cherokee from 1760 through the American Revolution? Andrew and Rebecca were building a life, having children, growing crops, and making considerable wealth trading with their former enemies, the Cherokee. Yet the Indian trade would come to be perceived by the white culture of the up-country as an increasingly suspect vocation, associated with a coarser rung of society and thus unacceptable for prominent men like Pickens who aspired to become planter-patriarchs with ever larger landholdings and ever grander homeplaces—all made possible by the labor of numerous slaves.

He and Rebecca and their children and enslaved workers moved from Long Cane in 1787 to build a new home, significantly named Hopewell, that would become one of the largest plantations in the up-country. Situated on the Keowee River, it stood just opposite from where the Cherokee town of Seneca had once thrived years before. (Pickens's close friend, fellow Presbyterian, and military colleague Robert Anderson built his own plantation on the other side of the Keowee just opposite Hopewell.) Pickens and Anderson relocated to this area around Pendleton, South Carolina, in hopes of attracting other Presbyterian settlers. In the contours of Pickens's life and career, we can see clearly how the

---

31. Andrew, *General Andrew Pickens*, 309.

wars to displace Native Americans from their lands went hand in hand with the development of slavery and the plantation economy across the up-country of South Carolina.

THE HOPEWELL TREATY

Pickens emerged from the Revolution as commissioner of Indian Affairs and in that role became something of an ambassador between the Cherokees and the new nation. He was to serve as the lead negotiator of treaties with the Cherokee and was called upon as a "peacemaker" between Natives and settlers as problems arose.[32]

Two separate incidents illustrate the kinds of situations that Pickens would be called upon to engage as commissioner. One was a prisoner exchange between the Cherokee and the Watauga Settlement led by John Sevier. Pickens communicated with Sevier asking him to appear at Cowee at a certain time to transact the exchange. Pickens waited at Cowee for three days until he learned, much to his frustration, that the exchange had taken place at Hiwassee.[33] Another situation arose after a delegation of Cherokee leaders had returned from treaty negotiations with President Washington in Philadelphia bearing significant gifts and annuities. Secretary of War Knox contacted Pickens out of concern for the safety of the Cherokee delegation, fearing that they would be attacked and robbed by lawless whites on their journey home. Pickens immediately contacted Robert Anderson, who at this time was the commanding general of state militia, to cause a deployment of troops to be sent to escort the Cherokee delegation from Charles Town to Oconee Station and from there safely to their homeland. A third duty for Pickens was as a surveyor who would determine the boundary lines between Cherokee territory as these lines were agreed upon in treaty negotiations, which brings us to the first treaty the newly formed United States initiated with an Indigenous tribe.

In 1785, after nearly a decade of conflict, the Cherokee and Pickens met at Hopewell on the Keowee River at the former site of the Cherokee village of Seneca. (It appears that Pickens had purchased this land, and, in 1787, would move there from Long Canes to build a new home, the plantation called Hopewell.) Pickens and his colleagues Benjamin Hawkins of North Carolina and Joseph Martin of Virginia, all three duly

32. Hatley, *Dividing Paths*, 231.
33. Duncan, *Savage Quest*, 220.

appointed by the Washington-Knox administration, were empowered to negotiate the first official treaty of the United States with an Indigenous nation—the Cherokee.[34]

Portrait of Andrew Pickens[35]

In previous treaty negotiations, the Cherokee had no choice but to deal with the separate colonies of the Carolinas, Georgia, and Virginia. This changed somewhat when the separate states begrudgingly ceded their authority to negotiate with Native peoples within their boundaries to the Continental Congress of the new American state. Representatives from each of these states would be present because the self-interest of these states was very much at stake. Pickens also realized that the states in question had significant responsibility to honor and implement the provisions of any treaty if these were to be successful. All the treaties the United States forged with the Cherokee deserve more attention than I can provide here. But let us examine at least this one, the Hopewell treaty, in detail because of where it was negotiated, who did the negotiating, and how these negotiations would impact the relationship between the Cherokee and the United States for years to come.

On a recent visit to Hopewell where Pickens's home still stands, I stood outside and tried to imagine the place surrounded by hundreds of Cherokees—women, men, and children—gathered for this event

---

34. Andrew, *General Andrew Pickens*, 191.

35. https://www.battlefields.org/learn/biographies/andrew-pickens.

in November of 1785. Pickens understood that any treaty with Native Americans would involve the ritual of gift-giving of items of great material value like tools, textiles, guns, ammunition, and alcohol, not to mention the requirements of hospitality that any host would offer his guests. The US states who were called upon to share the financial costs of this treaty had been very slow to cough up funds for these necessary expenses. That is why Pickens invited only the head men who would represent the Cherokee. When over nine hundred arrived, he must have been somewhat dismayed, wondering how he would manage to provide for their welcome. In the course of events, the Cherokee let it be known that with the violent attacks against their villages from trespassing settlers, they had no choice but to bring their women and children with them, lest they be left in harm's way. With so many participants, the treaty-making took place outside underneath an oak tree that stood for many years thereafter and came to be known as the Treaty Oak.

In *Cherokee Voices*, Vicki Rozema provides a transcript of the Hopewell Treaty negotiations that reveals the personalities of the parties involved—both members of the treaty commission Pickens headed and Cherokee representatives. Attakullakulla and Oconostota, Cherokee headmen who had represented the Cherokee Nation in so many treaties with the British, had been long dead. By 1785, the mantle of leadership had passed to Corn Tassel, Attakullakulla's nephew, named as a boy presumably for a head of hair that stood straight up. It was Cherokee tradition that the uncle played a central role in the formation of a young man, more so than even a father. It is likely that Attakullakulla had great influence in shaping the worldview of Corn Tassel. Surely, his uncle told Corn Tassel many tales of his journey to England, recounting how the English people were "more numerous than the stars." Corn Tassel, like Attakullakulla, was a persistent voice for peace.[36]

Corn Tassel's stature as a beloved man of the Cherokee Nation was based in part on his gift of oratory, as he was called upon again and again to negotiate not only with the Americans, in defense of Cherokee sovereignty, but with the factions within the Cherokee Nation like the Chickamaugas led by Dragging Canoe, who believed that war was the only way to preserve their lands. At a previous treaty event held at the Long Island in 1781, with the states of Virginia and North Carolina, the reputation of Corn Tassel as one of the most gifted orators of the Cherokee people is confirmed in these words:

36. Rozema, *Cherokee Voices*, 73–75.

> It is a little surprising that when we entered into treaties with our brothers, the whites, their whole cry is more land! Indeed, formerly it seemed to be a matter of formality with them to demand what we durst not refuse. But on principles of which we have received assurances during the conducting of the present treaty, and in the name of free will and equality, I must reject your demand.... Let us examine the facts of your present eruption into our country, and we shall discover your pretensions on that ground. What did you do? You marched into our territories with a superior force; our vigilance gave us no timely notice of your maneuvers far exceeded us and we fled to the stronghold of our extensive woods, there to secure our women and children. Then you marched into our towns; they were left to your mercy.... Spread fire and desolation wherever you pleased and returned to your own habitations.... Again were we to inquire by what law or authority you set up a claim (for land), I answer, *none!*[37]

Corn Tassel goes on to describe the multicultural reality of Native existence alongside that of whites that is different but no less valid and sovereign.

The process of treaty-making at Hopewell was a real push and pull negotiation, expressed in speeches brimming with passionate conviction, with rhetorical nuances, and overlaid with cultural assumptions, as the participants sought to address grievances from the past and forge agreements for the future. The most critical concerns for the Cherokee recur repeatedly: abusive traders and settlers trespassing on their lands. The treaty they negotiated, forever after known as the Hopewell Treaty, would address areas of mutual concern, including the exchange of prisoners and the return of enslaved Africans who had escaped the colonies. Articles of the treaty also specified new trade regulations, sharing of intelligence, and procedures for criminal justice. The treaty declared any white settler who trespassed on Cherokee territory could no longer claim the protection of the US government and that the Cherokee had the authority to deal with any white settler as they saw fit. When subsequently the Cherokee actually exercised this provision in the treaty, granting them the prerogative to punish intruders as they saw fit, this exercise of their sovereignty would exacerbate conflicts not only with those trespassing settlers on the frontier but with the southeastern states that shared borders with them.

Above all, the treaty was about boundaries once again etched in hollow promises of perpetual peace and friendship. The Cherokee elders must

37. Nabokov, *Native American Testimony*, 122–23.

have been skeptical about these guarantees to respect new borders even as settlers were already swarming over those lines, namely the Watauga Settlement and another on the Nolichucky River. Corn Tassel addressed this concern: "The Cherokees once owned all of this land. It is but a few years since the white men came. We are willing for the white men to live here as our friends, but some have overrun our boundaries. They requested a little land and took much. Attakullakulla and Oconostota are dead. The treaties they signed did not suit all of us."[38] Corn Tassel declared that Henderson had deceived them about the extent of the land sales involving Kentucky. The commissioners replied that all the signers of that treaty were dead and gone and the treaty could not be revisited.

Corn Tassel insisted to the commissioners that genuine peace could not be achieved until the American government removed these current trespassers settling within a day's walk of their towns. The Watauga Settlement had only the year before (1784) declared its independence from the state of North Carolina and was lobbying to become the fourteenth state to be recognized by the US, as the new state of Franklin. John Sevier, of Kings Mountain fame and the leader of the Watauga Settlement, was the single most hated white man among the Cherokee for his repeated attacks against them. (In 1780, Sevier leading the Watauga militia burned seventeen Cherokee Overhill Towns along the Little Tennessee River. In 1781, he attacked and destroyed fifteen of the Middle and Out Towns, including Cowee. And in 1782, Sevier's troop laid waste to the Chickamauga Towns led by Dragging Canoe.)

The commissioners believed that what Corn Tassel asked of them would be impossible to accomplish. The new American government lacked the political will and perhaps the military capacity to evict established white settlements like Watauga in these contested areas. To attempt to do so would approach warfare being waged by whites on whites. Corn Tassel replied, "Is not Congress, which conquered the King of England, strong enough to remove these people?"[39] The answer was no. It would be several more years before the United States would finally have to address the many problems generated by the Watauga Settlement and its leader, John Sevier.

Corn Tassel was surprised that Pickens and his commissioners did not begin their negotiations with new demands for land cessions. But ultimately, the Cherokee did cede much territory within the states of South and North Carolina, Georgia, and Virginia where settlers had established

38. Dorton, *Chief Corn Tassel*, 66–67.
39. Dorton, *Chief Corn Tassel*, 66.

themselves. The Cherokee at Hopewell finally agreed to be compensated for these lands. Through Corn Tassel's steadfastness, the Cherokee preserved a heartland that for them was a nonnegotiable sanctuary for their people. But even this was too much to some white representatives of the various states, who chafed at this concession. These very same lands had been promised to veterans of the American Revolution as a reward for their service.

Beside Corn Tassel was the beloved woman Nanyehi (Nancy Ward). Joseph Martin, another member of the team negotiating for the United States, was married to Nancy Ward's daughter, Betsy. Corn Tassel realized the great effect that Nancy Ward's words had on white settlers in previous negotiations, and so she was the second speaker to address the commissioners. Over and over again she had spoken as a mother to all children, red and white, and appealed for solidarity with white women in particular. Rod Andrew in his biography of Pickens is particularly insightful as to the nature of Nancy's desire for peace when he writes, "The Warwoman was forty-seven years old when she spoke at Hopewell. She probably was not hoping for more biological children of her own, but rather envisioning a 'more encompassing conception of kinship' between whites and Indians."[40]

Under the spreading branches of the treaty oak, Nancy rose and spoke to the assembly of Cherokee and whites.

> I am glad there is now peace. I take you by hand in real friendship. I have a pipe and a little tobacco to give to the commissioner to smoke in friendship. I look on you and the red people as my children . . . you having determined on peace is most pleasant to me for I have seen much trouble during the late war. I am old, but I hope yet to bear children, who will grow up and people of our Nation, as we are now under the protection of Congress and shall have no more disturbance. The talk I have given you is from the young warriors I have raised in my town, as well as myself. They rejoice that we have peace and hope the chain of friendship will never more be broken.[41]

Nancy Ward then delivered two strings of wampum, a pipe, and some tobacco to the commissioners.[42]

40. Andrew, *General Andrew Pickens*, 201.
41. Dorton, *Chief Corn Tassel*, 67–68.
42. A provision of the Hopewell Treaty has arisen in the news just recently. In that treaty and more generally recognized in the treaty of New Echota in 1838, the United

This treaty became the blueprint for negotiations held at Hopewell between Pickens and the Choctaw and Chickasaw Nations who would soon arrive at Hopewell after long and arduous journeys from their homelands in present day Mississippi, Louisiana, and western Tennessee.

What can be said about the long-term impact of the Hopewell Treaty? The bedrock principles upon which Pickens operated in his treaty negotiations with the Cherokee were these: first, "The Indians had a right to any lands they did not willfully cede in a fair sale or honest treaty; second, the national government must have ultimate authority over the course of Indian diplomacy; federal treaties with Indians had the force of law among all American citizens; and law must trump the self-aggrandizing desires of individuals and states."[43] Unfortunately, these principles did not describe the real world in which Pickens lived.

The history of treaties between the United States and Native peoples is of course one long story of deception, greed, and broken promises of the former against the latter. Pickens would be called upon by the administrations of Washington, Adams, and Jefferson to consult on Indian affairs and to negotiate new treaties and resolve conflicts. To his credit, Pickens did not believe that every new treaty negotiation should begin with an American demand for additional land cessions. And in his own writings, there is little evidence that Pickens was all that enamored with the idea of "civilizing" the Indians into white culture. Pickens was clear-eyed about the dangers to peace posed by violent settlers trespassing treaty boundaries and stealing Native land, even if he lacked the power to do anything about it. Corn Tassel must have felt that Pickens was an honorable man of integrity because he named one of his sons Pickens.

Only a short time after the Hopewell Treaty, Corn Tassel (also known as Old Tassel as he aged) would be forced to sign yet another treaty further abrogating Cherokee sovereignty, by giving authority to US

States agreed to seat a representative of the Cherokee Nation in the US Congress, with no vote on the floor but full vote and inclusion on Congressional committees (similar to the US territories). The Cherokee Nation has recently invoked this treaty obligation, seeking to claim its right to have a representative seated in Congress. Since these treaties had already been approved by the Senate long ago, all that is required now would be a resolution in the House. The Cherokee Nation has already officially appointed their designated representative, Ms. Kimberly Teehee. I recently heard an interview with her on the PBS show *Amanpour and Company*, in which she shared her story, described why fulfilling this treaty obligation is so important to the Cherokee people, and addressed the many priorities for which she would advocate. The Cherokee continue to wait for this to happen. See Amanpour and Company, "Will Congress Follow Through."

43. Andrew, *General Andrew Pickens*, 205.

government officials to bring to justice any Cherokee involved in violence against settlers. (Prior to this, the Cherokee themselves were responsible for the administration of justice inside their territory and were empowered to deal with white intruders.) This new concession outraged many within the Cherokee Nation, who were determined to defend their lands against all intruders. In 1788, a Cherokee war party carried out a massacre against eleven of the twelve members of the John Kirk family, who were encroaching on Cherokee land, near today's Knoxville, Tennessee.

It was unlikely that Old Tassel was in any way involved in this incident; he had traveled more than once to the Chickamauga Towns to try to convince the young warriors to desist from these attacks. Nevertheless, James Hubbard, a leader of the Watauga militia and Sevier's right-hand man, coaxed Old Tassel to meet him for a peace parley under a flag of truce. When Old Tassel arrived carrying a white flag, he was led by Hubbard to a cabin for the parley. Instead of a parley, Hubbard had staged an ambush. John Kirk, the surviving member of the Kirk family, suddenly appeared with troops and murdered Tassel by tomahawk. This murder of Old Tassel under the flag of truce was denounced as an atrocity not only by the Cherokee, but by Congress, by prominent newspapers in the United States, and by an enraged Andrew Pickens, who counted Old Tassel as a friend.

Pickens contacted the governor of South Carolina and enlisted him in decrying this crime. The state legislature agreed to forward a letter of protest written by Pickens to the Congress. Pickens also convened the justices of his home district and asked them to sign a public letter denouncing the murder of Old Tassel with the intent that this letter would be sent to the settler community of Watauga. Finally, Pickens and others were able to stir Congress into some kind of response to Sevier and the treachery of Old Tassel's murder as violations of the Treaty of Hopewell and as disrespectful of the authority of the Union. North Carolina authorities eventually arrested Sevier for treason and carried him to Morganton, North Carolina, to be jailed in advance of a trial. However, there he was set free from prison by some of his Overmountain compatriots who had fought with him at Kings Mountain. Such was the checkered history of the future governor of Tennessee.

When it seemed that war with the Creek Nation and other allied tribes was about to explode across the southeast, President Washington and Secretary of War Knox approached Pickens about commanding US forces in an anticipated conflict. Pickens declined. There may have been many factors in this decision: his advancing age, the need to spend more time with his family for whom he had been absent. I have to wonder if part of the reason for this warrior, who at this time had attained the rank of brigadier general in the US army, to decline the appeal of his president to lead the US Indian wars in the South was his own conflicted conscience. Pickens believed the situation of the Cherokee was at the very least morally ambiguous. They had more than just cause behind their grievances. He did not feel the same way about the Creek Nation and saw the Choctaw and Chickasaw as potential allies.

Andrew Pickens, so like President Washington himself in stoic demeanor and strict adherence to an honor code, fully subscribed to the policies of the Washington-Knox administration regarding Indigenous peoples. Yet for all of its assumptions of white supremacy, this policy at least envisioned a space for Native peoples in the new American nation. Washington and Knox frequently consulted with Andrew Pickens about Indian affairs in the southern states and especially about the Cherokee. All indications were that they trusted Pickens's integrity and wisdom and relied on his counsel. In 1796, President Washington published an address to the Cherokee Nation, "Laying out a road map for them to follow in order to coexist with Americans."[44] In this epistle, which Washington had printed for distribution among the Cherokee, he described how the western expansion of American settlements was destroying the Indian's hunting way of life. They should learn to live as American farmers. Their women should learn to spin and weave. Washington considered that the Cherokee would serve as a role model and test case for other Indian nations.[45]

By the time of the Jefferson Administration this "civilizing" policy of gradual assimilation of Native Americans could no longer conceal the growing national intention to dispossess Indigenous peoples and displace them to west of the Mississippi River. Jefferson had expressed publicly his support for Indian removal as early as 1776. And as president he became the architect of the removal policy. Building upon the worldview created by the Doctrine of Discovery, Jefferson cast an American vision of Manifest Destiny to bring about national expansion across the continent. Jefferson applied all the legal and political tools at his disposal to fulfill this ambition. Including, of course, the Louisiana Purchase and the Lewis

---

44. Calloway, *Indian World of George Washington*, 462.
45. Calloway, *Indian World of George Washington*, 463.

and Clark Expedition. In the years of his presidency between 1801–9, Jefferson set in motion the dispossession of Native peoples that would culminate under Jackson three decades later.[46]

Recognizing that Indian removal had become national policy under the Jefferson Administration, Andrew Pickens resigned from any further involvement as a treaty commissioner. I believe it is safe to say that he imagined an American republic in which white citizens and Indigenous peoples could coexist. Pickens seems to have earned the respect of his Indian contemporaries both as a warrior and as a treaty negotiator: his Indian name, *Skyagunsta*, has been translated as "Wizard Owl." But it is hard to deny that he was a central player in the long history of fraudulent treaties made between the United States and Indigenous nations.

CHURCH PLANTING

Following the end of the American Revolution, Scots Irish Presbyterians resumed their efforts to rebuild and establish new Presbyterian congregations across the frontier. The first meeting of the newly formed Presbytery of South Carolina was held at the Waxhaws Presbyterian Church in the York District in April 1785.[47] Nazareth Presbyterian was for several years a simple log cabin situated equidistant between two settlements. It would not be able to call a pastor until 1788, when the Reverend W. C. Davis was ordained there.[48] At that time, the church had thirty to thirty-five families.[49] Reverend Davis would only stay at Nazareth for a year, but he was an outsized figure who was very prominent in the life of the Presbytery. With his prophetic voice, Davis became a powerful influence over a new generation of pastors who were increasingly troubled by the institution of slavery.

HOPEWELL KEOWEE PRESBYTERIAN CHURCH

In 1789, following the Revolution, Presbyterians between the Savannah and the Saluda Rivers met at General Pickens's home at Hopewell

46. Miller, *Native America*, 59.

47. Howe, *History*, 549.

48. A Presbytery is a regional judicatory of self-government in the polity of the Presbyterian Church; the Presbyterian churches of the low country were part of the Charles Town Presbytery.

49. Howe, *History*, 561.

to establish boundaries between the congregations of up-country South Carolina, including Hopewell Keowee (Old Stone Church), the other congregation where my ancestors are buried.[50] General Pickens and Major Robert Anderson were the founders and benefactors of the small congregation of Hopewell Keowee Presbyterian Church located not very far from the Keowee Trail. Both Pickens and Anderson were ruling elders in that congregation (elders held an elected lay position in Presbyterian polity, equal to the position of a minister). I have not yet discovered a direct link from my Anderson ancestors to this Robert Anderson, but I am still looking. One family document suggested a linkage, but it almost seemed like wishful thinking. Like Pickens himself and many other Scots Irish settlers, he came to Carolina down the Great Wagon Road from Virginia. He fought alongside Pickens in the Cherokee War, at the Revolutionary War battles of Eutaw Springs, Augusta, and Cowpens. These two founders of the Hopewell Keowee Presbyterian Church remained lifelong friends. I think I cling to the idea of my Anderson family being related to Robert Anderson as a symbol of how closely our history was tied to Pickens himself and Old Stone Church. Today, of the three upstate counties in South Carolina west of Greenville County, two are named for Anderson and Pickens and the third is Oconee, named of course for the Cherokee town.

In 1792, the Reverend Thomas Reese was called to be pastor of Hopewell Keowee. Shortly after his installation he submitted to the Presbytery this description of his congregants: the people who compose this congregation are "remarkable for the great simplicity of their manners, the plainness of their dress, and their frugal manner of living.... Clothed in homespun ... nourished by the produce of their own farms, and happily appear to have neither taste nor inclination for high and expensive living. There is a quiet degree of equality among them. None are very rich, few extremely poor. There are few slaves among them, and these are treated with great kindness and humanity."[51] This portrait may well be grounded in a measure of historical fact. But it is hard to escape the suspicion that the reverend's words are motivated by a desire to cultivate a particular self-image for his community, especially as related to the treatment of the Cherokee whose lands they had stolen and the Africans they had enslaved.

50. Howe, *History*, 457.
51. Howe, *History*, 637.

Old Stone Church[52]

Andrew Pickens Grave

52. https://en.wikipedia.org/wiki/Old_Stone_Church_and_Cemetery#/media/File:OldStoneChurchCemetery16.

THE RED HOUSE AT TAMASSEE

In 1805, Andrew Pickens made one final migration. He left his plantation at Hopewell and moved about twenty-three miles northwest to Tamassee, the site of the old Cherokee town and walking distance from the location of the famous Ring Fight where he had escaped a Cherokee attack. Tamassee was at the base of the Blue Ridge Mountains and only a few miles from the boundary separating South Carolina from Cherokee territory.[53] The house the Pickens family built was a simple and sturdy domicile, one and a half stories tall and made of hewn logs. About fifty feet long, it had ten-foot-wide porches, a rock stock chimney, and small glass windows with plain solid shutters. Pickens had the exterior painted red and the shutters green; consequently, the homeplace became known as the "Red House."[54]

The Red House was filled with children and grandchildren and up to about ten enslaved people. It was frequently visited by Indians, some of whom were Cherokee. One of the most intriguing aspects of the story of Andrew Pickens is that the Cherokee seemed not only to respect him as a former trader and strong warrior but also to regard him with genuine friendship. One story relates how a contingent of Cherokee from Tennessee, visiting the Red House at Tamassee, were playfully marching around the house while holding high in outstretched arms one of the Pickens's infant grandsons, to the great alarm of the child's mother. Pickens reassured her that there was no cause for worry.[55] Andrew Pickens seemed to relish his friendship with the Cherokee as much as they enjoyed his friendship with them.

---

53. Andrew, *General Andrew Pickens*, 287.
54. Andrew, *General Andrew Pickens*, 288.
55. Andrew, *General Andrew Pickens*, 308.

8

Slavery and the Rise and Fall of Southern Abolitionism

THE DISPLACEMENT OF THE Cherokee from their lands was the prelude to advancing the slave system into the South Carolina up-country. Slavery was progressing up the Keowee Trail. As early as 1790, the Presbytery of South Carolina was debating how it would deal with ministers who, because of their moral convictions, were inclined to preach against slavery. Every preacher with a social conscience readily recognizes this tension between the pastoral and the prophetic in ministry with a congregation, then and now. I promised you at the beginning of this book that it was not necessary to be a person of faith in order to gain insight about the role the church played in the course of American history. Perhaps here I will test your patience as I survey the persistent and sometimes heart-wrenching conflicts between clergy of conscience and conviction and the prevailing prejudices of the status quo. It is crucial to me as a Presbyterian clergyman to describe just what an opportunity to change the course of history was lost and how many lives were compromised or even ruined because the powers that dominated the Presbyterian Church in South Carolina were committed to justifying and perpetuating the institution of slavery.

Three or four examples will reveal the high-water mark of theological dissent and, sadly, how the church of this time would ultimately make an uneasy peace with the institution of slavery. George Howe's *History of the Presbyterian Church in South Carolina* records the first sign of dissent: a Reverend William Williamson was ordained and installed at the Union

Presbyterian Church in 1793 and had a "useful and esteemed" ministry until 1804, when "from a desire to manumit his servants, and for other reasons, he removed with a portion of his congregation to the State of Ohio, where he lived out his ministry to an advanced age." According to Howe, this was the first Presbyterian clergy to migrate because of ethical discomfort with the institution of slavery.[1]

Two things are of note here. First, though Reverend Williamson himself initially owned slaves, something had led him to a change of heart, a turning point—what Presbyterians would call repentance. But he could not realize this hope in the context of up-country South Carolina in 1804, for state law required that anyone who wanted to emancipate his slaves must obtain government permission to do so. Perhaps Williamson also understood that within the severely circumscribed parameters of the state, the freedom into which the formerly enslaved would be released would be no freedom at all. Their full emancipation, then, required a migration beyond the South. What could have brought Williamson to his decision to renounce slavery? One clue is the name of the colleague who preached the ordination sermon at the service where he was installed as pastor to the Union Church: William C. Davis. Davis seems to have been a significant influence behind the first and last expressions of abolitionist dissent in Carolina.

Davis had settled in the up-country of South Carolina and, after appropriate theological study, sought ordination as a Presbyterian minister. Serving in various churches, including Nazareth, where my Anderson ancestors were members, he became known around the Presbytery as an eloquent and powerful preacher, proclaiming the gospel with fiery passion. I wonder what my forebears thought of his preaching as they sat in the pews of Nazareth Church. For Davis was charismatic but also controversial, believing that the institution of slavery was a sin against God and neighbor. Davis did not stay long at Nazareth. At a Presbytery meeting at Hopewell Keowee Church in Pendleton, sixty miles west of Nazareth, he would go so far as to denounce all slaveholding as an abomination. We can only imagine how Andrew Pickens and his dear friend Robert Anderson—the founders of this church, and both ruling elders and slave owners—responded to this sermon. Having sat in the Old Stone Church—Hopewell Keowee—I find it easy to imagine, in that small

---

1. Howe, *History*, 621.

space, the visceral reaction of those in the pews. Davis must have caused a "shaking of the foundations" for the Presbytery of South Carolina.

At some point the highly regarded Reverend Reese, pastor of Hopewell Keowee, was summoned to rebut—seemingly on behalf of everyone else—the shocking challenge Davis had issued. According to George Howe's history of the Presbyterian Church in South Carolina, Reese delivered a theological response to the satisfaction of the assembly and the "mortification" of Reverend Davis. But a spirit of dissent was still very much alive, and perhaps not everyone agreed with Reverend Reese.[2]

Davis also mentored Reverend Gilleland in his preparation for ordination and ministry. There can be no doubt that the younger Gilleland was deeply influenced by Davis. After Gilleland's ordination, he supplied the pulpit of several Presbyterian communities across the up-country, including Nazareth and Hopewell Keowee. When the Bradaway Presbyterian Church sought him as pastor on a more permanent basis, grave concerns were voiced on the floor of the Presbytery about his outspoken views against slavery. The charge could not have been more serious. Many slave owning Christians equated his position with treason. But after deliberations, the Presbytery, asked to clarify its policy on Gilleland's right to preach anti-slavery sermons, advised him not to do so, restricting him to expressing his views only in private conversation. Gilleland chose, in this moment, to bide his time and submit to the ruling of his Presbytery.

The next revelation of dissent would come from Gilleland's close friend and colleague Rev. Robert Wilson. Born into a farming family between the Yadkin and Catawba Rivers in the North Carolina Piedmont, Wilson grew up just south of the boundary with South Carolina in the Waxhaws (York District) and was baptized (like his future classmate Andrew Jackson) under the ministry of Rev. Francis Cummins of the Waxhaws Presbyterian Church. Howe tells us that at the age of seventeen, having heard Reverend Cummins preach on the text from Revelation—"Behold I stand at the Door and Knock"—Robert made a confession of faith.[3] He pursued his studies in a classical tradition in a Presbyterian-created academy under the tutelage of Cummins and that other powerful mentor to so many: Rev. William C. Davis. In 1793, after his college years at Dickinson College in Carlisle, Pennsylvania, Cummins returned to South Carolina, was ordained, and began serving Upper Long Cane

---

2. Howe, *History*, 620.
3. Howe, *History*, 627.

Presbyterian Church in Abbeville District. His ministry was popular and rewarded, if not by a sufficient salary, at least by his congregants' love and admiration. His gifts as a scholar and teacher were also recognized by the College of South Carolina, which offered him their presidency. Apparently content with congregational ministry, he declined.

But all was not well with Reverend Wilson. When the US Congress joined Great Britain in banning the cruel and barbaric Atlantic slave trade in 1807, taking effect a year later in 1808, only South Carolina of all the states refused to go along, allowing the slave trade to continue supplying the state with enslaved labor. And with the action of the Jefferson Administration and the Louisiana Purchase, slaveholders anticipated a great expansion of the market for slaves in the new territory. South Carolina Governor Henry Middleton estimated that during this period thousands upon thousands of enslaved people were smuggled into South Carolina in anticipation of a booming market for enslaved workers in the new "southwest" of Tennessee, Alabama, and Mississippi. This expansion of the slave trade was too much for Wilson to endure. The Presbyterian historian George Howe, who has been the primary source for all these deliberations, recounted that Wilson submitted an overture to the Presbytery, calling on the church to urge official representatives of the state government to adopt a plan for gradual emancipation. This policy proposal would have allowed children of enslaved parents to be freed on reaching adulthood. I have no doubt that Davis and Gilleland and others collaborated with Wilson. But the overture was defeated.[4]

By vote of the majority, the Presbytery deemed that this was not the right time for such a tactic, which would lead to unrest and disorder. How sobering this outcome is to me. Not being the "right time" is the same rationalization heard from the church during the years of the civil rights movement, when Dr. King wrote his "Letter from a Birmingham Jail." From the earliest moments in Presbyterian history in the South, it was never the right time to work for freedom.

Reverend Gilleland tried to submit to the ruling of his Presbytery but found himself increasingly troubled at being silenced on his moral convictions about slavery. He decided to appeal his case at the Synod, the next larger judicatory in the Presbyterian governmental system. At the next Synod meeting, held in what is today Morganton, North Carolina, he made his appeal. Again, the decision came down that sermons against

4. Howe, *History*, 608.

slavery and for abolition were not appropriate to a Presbyterian pulpit. Many pastors like Davis, Wilson, and Gilleland, while respected among their colleagues in Presbytery, could not exercise freedom of conscience in such a climate.

They responded to this censorship in different ways. Davis would remain in the Carolinas as a fiery leader of a group of Presbyterian congregations who removed themselves officially from the church on a variety of theological grounds and established an independent Presbytery. In 1805, Gilleland, Wilson, and a group of other lay leaders left South Carolina for Ohio, hoping to find more openness toward their antislavery views. Though even in Ohio the question of slavery could evoke bitter controversy, at least there, within the congregations of the Ohio Presbytery of Chillicothe, they were able to act on their convictions. With their help, an underground railroad for the escape of enslaved people from Kentucky and beyond was organized. Chillicothe Presbytery in Ohio would continue to advocate among their fellow Presbyterians across the South for the abolition of slavery. Abolitionist epistles written by Presbyterians in Ohio were delivered through the ecclesiastical channels of communication within the Presbyterian Church. The prophetic witness of the Chillicothe Presbytery and its members was one light shining in the darkness—a song line of hope and resistance.

CASTING THEIR LOT WITH SLAVERY

The Presbyterian Church in the South faced a theological turning point from which it would seemingly never recover. For those of conscience like Gilleland and Wilson, the only remaining option was to leave the South. (Wilson would go on to change his middle name to Gilleland—another gesture that confirms the value of mentors.) There simply was not the space to exercise one's freedom of conscience in a church that had wholeheartedly thrown in its lot with slavery. The ecclesiastical options for people of faith and conscience in a slave-holding society were becoming ever clearer. A southern Christian could "spiritualize" the social witness of the gospel by withdrawing into a private pietism that had nothing to say about injustice in the socioeconomic context of southern society. Or they could distort Scripture with sermons on the "curse of Ham" as justifying their white supremacy as an act of God. But as criticism mounted from churches in the North, southern church leaders were more likely to jump on the bandwagon with a complete embrace of slavery.

Clergy leaders like Davis, Gilleland, and Wilson were the exception rather than the norm. Far more prevalent was the altogether different stance of Presbyterians taken by men like the esteemed Presbyterian theologian Dr. Thornwell, a widely published apologist for slavery. There were others less well-known such as Rev. Zelotus Holmes, a northern Presbyterian who came south to serve a variety of Presbyterian congregations in the up-country, including Nazareth. Marrying a local woman from a planter family, he himself became a slaveholder. In regular correspondence with northern relatives over the years, Holmes was a tireless apologist for the benevolence of the slavery system. Thornwell, Holmes, and Reese would join a generation of Presbyterian theologians, educators, clergy, and laity who advocated for slavery as a benevolent institution ordained by God, justifying their position through a twisted interpretation of the Scriptures.

These Presbyterian leaders were not necessarily villains. They proceeded by their best lights. Many of them engaged in outreach to enslaved Black people. Seeing them as children of God, they proclaimed the gospel to them, led them in worship, and sometimes taught them to read and write until that became illegal. I can imagine that a few of them might have exhorted their white congregants to treat their enslaved people with kindness and compassion, even perhaps in private conversation, decrying cruelties committed against them. But the institution of slavery itself was for them morally neutral: a system like any ordained by God, which could be exercised with faithfulness, integrity, and virtue or not. Perhaps some of them even believed that slavery was against the will of God and yet they could see no way to remedy the situation, adopting a posture of waiting upon God to open a way toward resolution unavailable at the present.

What they were blind to then, as many of us are today, was the systemic nature of racism. The assumption of white supremacy pervaded the very system in which they and we "live and move and have our being." This moment among Presbyterians in the up-country of South Carolina reflects a watershed in the history of the church across the South. When the southern church lost the moral vision and prophetic voice of pastors and lay leaders like Davis, Williamson, and Gilleland, all debate about slavery was shut down. No longer was dissent possible within these congregations or within southern society at large. As dissenters left the region, the South would become hardened in its ideological commitment to slavery and increasingly radicalized in the face of criticism from the North.

ANDREW AND REBECCA PICKENS: ARCHETYPES OF THE SCOTS IRISH SETTLER

I recently returned to Old Stone Church and strolled among the graves of its cemetery. Near the church, I stood before the graves of Andrew and Rebecca Pickens, reflecting on why their story is both so fascinating to me and so very troubling. Their story is representative of my family's story as Scots Irish Presbyterians and of our complicated settler history in the up-country of colonial South Carolina. Like my Anderson ancestors, Pickens was a Scots Irish immigrant. Like them—like all human beings—he was searching for a better life. In his own life and personhood, Pickens would embody the struggle and conflict of that time and place of our shared history.

    Dr. Hatley, in *The Dividing Paths*, lays this out for us.[5] First there was Pickens the trader with the Cherokee, building wealth by bartering manufactured goods for deerskins. As a trader he exemplifies the early moments of colonial history when economic interaction with the Cherokee forged a tenuous coexistence between white South Carolinians and Native peoples. When the Cherokee War erupted in 1760, Pickens became a soldier who gained fame as an "Indian fighter" and, I suspect, experienced not just the physical scars of combat but the spiritual wounds of moral injury. Then, as a Patriot military commander in the bloody American Revolution, Pickens became, as it were, a "founding father" of South Carolina and the new nation. He was also the founder and a ruling elder of one of the oldest Presbyterian churches in the up-country, the Old Stone Church, which has become a shrine to colonial history. Pickens is also remembered as a "peacemaker" when he was called upon by the newly formed government of the United States to negotiate treaties with the Cherokee and several other major tribes of the Southeast. But remembering Pickens as an honorable man in his dealings with the Cherokee becomes more difficult when we acknowledge the history of broken and fraudulent treaties between the United States and Indigenous nations.

    Finally, as an honored military hero, an esteemed gentleman, and a beloved patriarch, Pickens fulfilled the southern masculine ideal of the planter by amassing enslaved workers and extracting from their forced labor his substantial wealth. School children in South Carolina are taught to admire Pickens as a historical figure who embodies the best of southern

---

5. Hatley, *Dividing Paths*, 202–3.

history. And yet traced through his life we find the dispossession of Indigenous people from their land and the gradual extension of the plantation economy of enslaved labor. Dispossession and enslavement went hand in hand. War against Indigenous peoples, land theft, fraudulent treaties, and the ever-advancing extension of slavery were simply phases of the same colonial process that we glorify as American history.

WRESTLING WITH THE LEGACY OF ANDREW PICKENS

Becky Pickens died in 1814. Andrew had her buried in the cemetery of Hopewell Keowee Presbyterian, now known as the Old Stone Church. Two-and-a-half years later, in his seventy-eighth year, Andrew Pickens would breathe his last as he sat in a chair beneath a few cedar trees in the yard of the Red House, sorting through papers and correspondence. By the time he was buried, the graveyard beside the Old Stone Church had already become a family cemetery for the Pickens family and other Presbyterian families, and the church building itself was on the verge of becoming a historical landmark. Only seven years after Pickens's funeral, the Hopewell congregation would build another structure within the town of Pendleton that was more convenient for most of its worshipers. Thereafter, the Old Stone Church would be used only for funerals and other special occasions.

Though they rarely worshiped there after 1824, the old sacred ground remained the place where Pendleton's Presbyterians buried their loved ones. One of the oldest graves in the cemetery is that of Osenappa, who died in 1794. Osenappa was thought to be a Cherokee, but this name is not linguistically Cherokee. Nevertheless, it has been passed down that Osenappa played a role for the Patriots in the Revolutionary War, though it is not known exactly what his contribution was. Osenappa's grave is marked by a pile of stones, and he is thought to be the only Native American buried in the cemetery. Although there were many African American slaves who were members of the congregation, none are buried there. Instead, they were buried in slave cemeteries on the plantations where they had lived and worked.[6]

The Old Stone Church soon became less a place of worship and more a shrine to northwestern South Carolina's early pioneers and to the

---

6. My source is the book *Old Stone Church*, published in 1972 by the Old Stone Church Commission (of which my grandfather had once served as chairman) in partnership with the Andrew Pickens and Cateechee chapters of the DAR.

virtues their descendants attributed to them. Near the graves of Andrew and Rebecca Pickens you can find the markers for Reverend Reese, the pastor of Hopewell Keowee who offered the rebuttal to Reverend Davis's denunciation of slaveholding. Like Pickens himself, the old edifice has served as a nostalgic reminder of the simple faith, conviction, and sturdiness of the area's earliest settlers.[7]

Major Robert Anderson, already widowed twice, would later marry Reverend Reese's widow. When Anderson died in 1813, his body was first interred on his plantation Westfield, on the opposite shore of the Keowee River from Pickens's plantation Hopewell. When Duke Power flooded the Keowee, his body was reinterred at Old Stone Church Cemetery, not far from the Pickens grave site.

My great-grandfather, George Edwyn Taylor, and his son, John S. Taylor Sr., both of Pendleton, helped coordinate the maintenance of the cemetery and the Old Stone Church itself, a memorial to the settler past of the South Carolina up-country. To this day the building and cemetery are carefully preserved and maintained. My grandparents and my aunt Hazael, along with other Taylor ancestors, chose to be buried in the graveyard of the Presbyterian Church that was relocated to the village of Pendleton. But my father, John S. Taylor Jr., is buried in the graveyard of Old Stone Church.[8]

A LAND ACKNOWLEDGMENT

Andrew Pickens and I have much in common. He was a Scots Irish Presbyterian ruling elder in the Presbyterian Church. And I, according to our Book of Order, am an elder as well as a minister of word and sacrament. I know as a person of faith, a Christian, and a Presbyterian that there is much that needs to be confessed about our complicity in the dispossession of the Cherokee people from their homeland and the subjugation of enslaved African workers. It is a painful and sinful history that I have traced in these pages. To repent this history, I believe, is to

---

7. Andrew, *General Andrew Pickens*, 309.

8. I will never forget the day of his funeral. It was raining cats and dogs and, in that deluge, I and the three other Presbyterian ministers traveling with me missed the turn to Old Stone Church and ended up arriving about half an hour late. There before us as we pulled up in the rain was a forlorn cluster of black umbrellas gathered around my father's grave. Surely one silent thought among the mourners was just how many Presbyterian preachers are required to find their way to the graveyard. My mother led a round of applause upon our arrival. I am confident my father would have joined in.

seek meaningful ways to repair the damage. Repentance—*metanoia* as defined by the Greek New Testament—is a turning around and going in the opposite direction. A contemporary theologian has written that repentance can also be a broadening expansion of one's worldview. By either definition, the Presbyterian Church of today has a long way to go to repent of its racism.

One initial action, a mere beginning step that demonstrates a repentant spirit within some faith communities today, is the practice of acknowledging whose land we are on. Among some faith communities at the beginning of a gathering, there will be a prayerful acknowledgment that this land before Europeans ever arrived here was the land of a First Nation. For many of us who live in the southeast, that First Nation is the Cherokee people. Perhaps this book is my initial step in acknowledging the land where I was born and raised as Cherokee land—and an initial step in fashioning a life of accompaniment to Indigenous people.

I have sought to trace the participation of the Presbyterian Church in this history of settler colonialism and its impact on the Cherokee Nation and on enslaved African workers. As I studied this period, it suddenly dawned on me with forceful clarity that the future of the American state and the fate of Native and African enslaved peoples was being hammered out in a power struggle between two of the most famous offspring of the Presbyterian Church in South Carolina—Andrew Jackson and John C. Calhoun. We have already described Jackson's deep roots in the Waxhaws Presbyterian Church that includes the traumatic events of the American Revolution, with young Andrew tending to the wounded Patriots who survived Tarleton's massacre near the Waxhaws church, and his then being wounded himself by a sword-wielding British officer.

But I only recently realized the extent to which Calhoun was formed in the culture of the Presbyterian Church. Recall that his parents, Patrick and Martha Caldwell Calhoun, were Scots Irish Presbyterians who also made the long journey of migration down the Great Wagon Road from Pennsylvania, with a stop in Virginia until they reached their destination at the Long Canes Settlement, right up against the Cherokee boundary. The trauma of the Long Cane massacre undoubtedly shaped Calhoun's identity. And the fact that his grandmother had been killed by the Cherokee in 1760 would no doubt color his relationship to them. At Long Canes Presbyterian, Calhoun must have heard sermons like the ones Jackson heard at Waxhaws, about the God who goes into battle with Gideon's sword. As a youth, Calhoun attended a classical academy run by the famous Presbyterian educator Rev. Moses Waddell, who would later move to Athens, Georgia, to save and reinvigorate what would become the University of Georgia. Waddell also founded the First Presbyterian Church of Athens (where I once served as associate pastor).

And then I learned this: Hopewell Keowee Presbyterian Church, the very congregation founded by Calhoun's aunt Rebecca Calhoun Pickens and his uncle Andrew Pickens, had a parsonage or, as it is called in the Presbyterian Church, a manse, named Clergy Hall. Built in 1803, Clergy Hall was a four-room house provided by the church for their pastor, situated very close to the Old Stone Church in Pendleton, South Carolina. At some point, Calhoun's mother-in-law purchased the house and surrounding farm. And then when she died, around 1830, Calhoun came to ownership. He expanded the size of the house by ten rooms, added extensive new acreage to his farm, and renamed it Fort Hill. When John C. and Floride Clemson Calhoun were dead and gone, Fort Hill would become the property of Thomas C. Clemson, who would ultimately bequeath it all for the establishment of what would become Clemson University.

John C. Calhoun, the most famous southern statesman, who served in Congress as both a House representative and as senator, who was secretary of both the departments of war and state, who was vice president under two administrations (Adams and Jackson) and ran for the presidency himself, this same Calhoun, the apostle of nullification, that led inevitably to the secession of the Southern slaveholding states and the Civil War, lived for many years in what was once the manse of Hopewell Keowee Presbyterian Church. I am not sure I can say what this means to me. But it seems somehow symbolic of the role that the Presbyterian Church has played in the tragedies of American and southern history that I have sought to describe here. It is as if the ideology of states' rights and white supremacy moved into the "Presbyterian House" and took up permanent residence there. We will return to this power struggle between Jackson and Calhoun in chapter 11: "A Reckoning with Settler Colonialism."

9

A Shaking of the Foundations

WE RETURN TO THE next stage of the struggle of the Cherokee and other Native peoples of the southeast to hold on to their land in the first decade of the nineteenth century. We recall that Dragging Canoe, the son of Attakullakulla, was strongly opposed to his father's willingness to accommodate American power or to assimilate within white culture. Dragging Canoe, along with his brothers, left his father and the Cherokee Overhill Towns, leading many others of his people to establish a stronghold of resistance in towns along Chickamauga Creek in southeastern Tennessee. It was then and there that a young Shawnee warrior by the name of Tecumseh came to know Dragging Canoe. Tecumseh was a member of a Shawnee band that was closely allied with the Cherokee-Chickamauga communities led by Dragging Canoe. Dragging Canoe must have been for the younger warrior Tecumseh not only a role model of courageous resistance against white power but a political leader who recognized the necessity of constructing a pan-Indian confederacy, strong enough to withstand the Americans. In 1792, Dragging Canoe was part of an all-night dance, celebrating the renewal of a military alliance with the Choctaw, Chickasaw, and other tribes. The next morning, he was found dead, having died of an apparent heart attack. A new generation of Native leadership emerged.

By the year 1810, Tecumseh, who had become a great Shawnee chief, was traveling on a wide north-south arc from Minnesota to Florida seeking to enlist all Indigenous nations in a covenant of mutual defense. In a council with the Creek Nation with a delegation of Cherokee in attendance, Tecumseh called upon separate tribes to come together in unity in a last-ditch armed effort to push back white settler expansion west of the Appalachians. One might wonder if there was a point in these council deliberations when Tecumseh looked upon the Cherokee in attendance and lifted up to them the memory of Dragging Canoe. Did he extol the courage of his spiritual elder, his warrior-mentor, in entreating the Cherokee to join his pan-Indian confederacy?

Tecumseh's political leadership as a war chief was paired with the spiritual leadership of his biological brother, Tenskwatawa, a one-eyed prophet and a recovering alcoholic who had journeyed in trances to the spirit world and had returned with a message of cultural renewal. To survive, Native peoples must throw off the influence of white civilization and return to Indigenous traditions and ways. Together, Tecumseh and Tenskwatawa laid out a political/spiritual program of resistance appealing to the Cherokee and all the southern tribes to join them in this life-or-death struggle. The decision posed by Tecumseh and Tenskwatawa was stark: armed struggle and cultural renewal or surrender and extinction.

What was the response to Tecumseh's call to resistance? The Creek Nation, like the Cherokee, was split between pro- and anti-American factions. Tecumseh must have been frustrated by the response of certain Creek and Cherokee leaders for when he left their council fires, he promised upon returning home to stomp the earth and shake the land and all of its inhabitants from their lethargy. The Cherokee knew well the cost of war if they fought again against the whites. But what did the prospect of assimilation into white civilization look like for the Cherokee? The United States in its "civilization" strategy with Indigenous peoples was pursuing a multifaceted campaign to "save the man by killing the Indian," (much like destroying the village to save it in the Vietnam War). This unrelenting pressure from the dominant white society that surrounded the Cherokee caused mounting stress on core values within Cherokee culture and revealed numerous fractures within their society about just what it meant to be Cherokee.

Here I rely greatly on the work of the historian William McLoughlin in his book *Cherokees and Missionaries, 1789–1839*. On this tumultuous period of change in Cherokee history, he writes: the Cherokee "were no longer sure of their place in the universe" and "had lost control of their destiny as a people." Official US policy sought to remove Cherokee men from their traditional vocation of hunting and defense and place them in the field as farmers. Simultaneously, the government intended to remove Cherokee women from the agricultural fields and place them in the home, pursuing domestic arts like spinning, weaving, and sewing. The Protestant work ethic, a core pillar of the teachings of the Presbyterian (and to a lesser degree the Moravian) missionaries working alongside of Cherokee communities, fostered a competitive, individualistic worldview that was at odds and in sharp contrast with the core values of the Cherokee: cooperation, sharing, and hospitality.[1]

This was most visible in the small mission schools established by missionaries. Though the number of Cherokee youths attending these mission schools was a small percentage of the larger population, the schools were a dramatic microcosm of the larger forces at work. Whatever good the Presbyterian missionary the Reverend Gideon Blackburn believed he was doing for Cherokee children and youth in the founding of his schools was undercut in the eyes of many Cherokees, who knew him for what he was: the eyes and ears of the US government. His reputation for partisan activities on behalf of the policy of removal and his real estate speculations in acquiring property within the Cherokee Nation would also raise suspicion.

In 1805, on the Fourth of July, Reverend Blackburn would lead the entire school of twenty Cherokee pupils in large canoes down the Hiwassee River to witness yet another treaty-signing between the Cherokee and the United States. Upon seeing the children singing Christian hymns, Governor Sevier of Tennessee remarked with much emotion to Blackburn: "I have often stood unmoved amidst showers of bullets from the Indian rifles; but this effectively unarms me. I see civilization taking the ground of barbarism, and the praises of Jesus succeeding to the war hoop of the savage."[2] These Cherokee children could have been performing for the very man who had murdered their parents and grandparents in a continuous war with the Cherokee from before the time of the Revolution through the 1790s. I would wager that no American had engaged in more barbarism than John Sevier, who rode his fame as an "Indian killer," to become the governor of the new state of Tennessee on lands stolen from the Cherokee. The mainline churches of the United States have only begun to investigate the shameful history of the Indian boarding schools. The Presbyterian Church has its own work to do.

Besides the external forces of white leaders pushing against Cherokee tradition, it was also becoming increasingly difficult for the Cherokee

---

1. McLoughlin, *Cherokees and Missionaries*, 82–84.
2. Posey, *Presbyterian Church in the Old Southwest*, 63.

desiring to remain faithful to their traditions to survive at all. Wild game was disappearing, and drought and pestilence threatened subsistence agriculture. Class divisions arose within Cherokee society and exacerbated tensions between the "progressives" (often from a mixed-race background and bilingual to some degree) ready to embrace white ways and the economically vulnerable "traditionalists" (typically full-blooded with minimal English fluency) who were finding their way of life increasingly precarious. Many of the material benefits of white civilization were hard to ignore. Myriad questions emerged about when and how one could assimilate into the white man's ways. What about using a plow and a spinning wheel or raising livestock? Should agriculture be focused on growing one's own food or raising a cash crop like cotton to sell?

Some Cherokee were becoming so successful at adapting to the white man's ways that they could afford to acquire slaves and were building prosperous plantations. Every choice to assimilate into white culture raised a question about the traditions of Cherokee passed down through the generations. Could a Cherokee remain Cherokee and adopt the Christian religion? What about the sacred dances and spiritual practices that had been passed down over countless generations? What about the teachings concerning the relationship to their fellow creatures? No question was more urgent or fundamental than the relationship to the land itself.

Those who made Indian policy in Washington saw owning private property as the key to "Americanize" (i.e., assimilate) Indians. They sought to move Cherokee families from a tribal culture of holding lands in common to American capitalism, with individual landowners having a stake in their own privately owned parcels. The American government declared that the value of land was finally defined as "real estate" to be bought or sold, owned, and developed by enterprising individuals. But for the Cherokee the land had multiple meanings: "Land as sustainer. Land as a moral obligation. Land as sacred. Land as self."[3] The Cherokee had already given up more than half of their homeland and what they had left was under constant assault from further settler encroachment.

The US government's allotment strategy, of granting private property to individual landowners within the Cherokee Nation, had a more insidious purpose. Granting land to individual landowners was the most direct way to deconstruct the reality of tribal sovereignty over land held

---

3. Kimmerer, *Braiding Sweetgrass*, 337.

in common. In this way, land not privately owned by Cherokee could be made available to individual white settlers who were relentlessly trespassing upon the boundaries established in treaties with the United States. Under this constant pressure, a few thousand Cherokee decided to sell their land to the United States government and voluntarily relocate to land purchased in the Arkansas territory. This first migration in the early 1800s exposed a rift in the Cherokee people that would only grow in the years ahead.

All these pressures upon Cherokee society caused fractures and tremors leading to a "shaking of the foundations" that was seemingly embodied in the land itself. In 1811, a series of earthquakes struck the continental United States. Now identified by geologists as the New Madrid Earthquakes, they originated in Missouri but could be felt as far north as Canada, as far south as the Gulf Coast, and as far east as the Cherokee homeland in North Carolina. Ten separate tremors and aftershocks were accompanied by claps of thunder, blitzes of lightning, wind, hailstorms, and the rising and sinking of tracts of land. There were Native leaders who remembered Tecumseh's prophetic words, promising when he returned home he would stomp the ground and shake the land and the lethargy of the Indians. These earthquakes rattled Cherokee society and seized the Cherokee imagination. Various prophets arose here and there across their mountain homeland, announcing a new vision that would bring deliverance to the Cherokee. The message of Tecumseh and Tenskwatawa had been heard by Cherokee prophets who spread the vision and stirred the people to resistance.

10

The Ghost Dance

Mooney briefly describes what happened next in the years of 1811–1812. The emergence of the Cherokee Ghost Dance religious movement was a watershed moment in Cherokee history, which Mooney considers only briefly. In response to this deepening crisis accompanied by natural disasters, Cherokee prophets emerged across their mountain homeland proclaiming a message of resistance and hope. These prophets spoke in councils of Cherokee towns, teaching that all those who had died from epidemic disease or been killed in war would be resurrected. The wildlife would be restored; the deer and buffalo would be abundant. Forest and rivers would flourish again, and the homeland would be secured. And all things would be as they once were.[1]

    The prophetic vision required a definitive answer, an either-or decision on what it meant to be a Cherokee. The prophets called upon the people to return to the traditional ways of the Cherokee and, with that, to renounce white culture and practices. This mandate varied from prophet to prophet and from village to village but included casting off the white man's alcohol, his livestock, tools, clothes, the acquisition of private property, and even a rejection of interracial marriage. One particular Cherokee prophet was specifically outraged about the fate of the ancient Cherokee village of Tugaloo. Tugaloo was a sacred town, this prophet believed, because it was there that the Cherokee had first received the gift of fire from the Great Spirit. But Tugaloo had been sold to the whites and its sacred mound desecrated; Tugaloo must be reclaimed and restored.

1. Mooney, *Ghost Dance Religion*, 89–90.

The apocalyptic vision of the Ghost Dance religion promised a great cataclysm yet to come. If the Cherokee wished to survive it they must leave their villages and go to a safe sanctuary in the peaks of the Smoky Mountains. The Cherokee prophets proclaimed a judgment against white people, sometimes described as total destruction, and other times a distinction was drawn between good whites and bad. When the storm of judgment had passed, the Cherokee people could return to their villages and begin a new age. When the cataclysm did not materialize, Mooney suggested, the Cherokee Ghost Dance movement dissipated and finally disappeared as a Native superstition. Did Mooney really understand the Cherokee Ghost Dance, and did it disappear? We will return to those questions shortly.

The Cherokee, with the exception of the Chickamauga towns, decided that their only realistic option was to beat the United States at its own game, working within the halls of power in Washington, DC, to advocate for their sovereignty. Cherokee leadership, learning how to utilize the white man's legislative and judicial systems, sought to defend the lands they still retained. Leaders like Chief John Ross were quick to invoke the Declaration of Independence as an ongoing mandate for human equality. To demonstrate their loyalty to the United States, the Cherokee volunteered a group of warriors to fight with General Andrew Jackson in his campaign against the anti-American "Red Stick" faction of the Creek Nation in the years 1813–1814. At the Battle of Horseshoe Bend, Jackson credited his victory over the Creek to the decisive action of his contingent of Cherokee warriors. What's more, it was the Cherokee warrior Junaluska who saved General Andrew Jackson's life during the battle.

In the north, many tribes aligned themselves with Tecumseh in his pan-Indian campaign to defend their civilization. That war culminated with Tecumseh's death in 1813 and the disintegration of his confederacy. Many Creeks migrated farther south and joined forces with the Seminole Tribe in northern Florida. General Jackson and an American army soon followed, and the first of three wars with the Seminole was fought between 1816 and 1818. This campaign quickly became a costly military disaster for US troops fighting in the swamps and wetland forests of Florida against a guerrilla army composed not only of Seminole but of formerly enslaved Africans. Africans, fleeing enslavement, had often found refuge in Florida among the Seminole and in the mountainous homeland of the Cherokee. Native tribes making common cause with escaped African people was another reason they had to be removed, from a southern white perspective.

GHOST DANCE REVISITED

James Mooney's career took a sharp turn in the year 1890. The Ghost Dance that he had documented among the Cherokee that occurred in 1810 had resurfaced again some eighty years later and was spreading like wildfire across the Indian nations of the prairie and mountains of the West. The Ghost Dance movement was highly threatening to the US government; its military leaders and policy makers feared it could lead to an all-out war across the West. Mooney, who had been working under the auspices of the newly founded US Bureau of Ethnology within the Smithsonian Institution in Washington, DC, was just about to get drawn into the eye of the storm.

John Wesley Powell, the famous western explorer and mapmaker, was the first director of the bureau, and he was determined to document the history and culture of Native peoples. As Mooney was completing his seminal work on the mythology of the Eastern Band of the Cherokee in North Carolina, he had applied to his boss, Director Powell, to continue his research with the western Cherokee Nation, located in Indian territory in what is now Oklahoma. Mooney was in fact en route to Oklahoma when the Ghost Dance movement erupted once again. Powell redirected Mooney away from the continuation of his work with the Cherokee in Indian territory in order to seize this opportunity to research what was happening with this new pan-Indian movement of the Ghost Dance religion.

So began Mooney's efforts to painstakingly document the Ghost Dance movement in its particular manifestations within many Indigenous nations, including the Kiowa, the Comanche, Arapaho, the Cheyenne, and the Lakota Sioux. Mooney recorded in detail the songs, dances, costumes, and other spiritual practices that characterized the Ghost Dance. He was even able to interview the Paiute seer Wovoka in his home in Nevada—recognized by many tribes as the chief prophet of the Ghost Dance movement.

In 1896, the Bureau of Ethnology, a department of the Smithsonian Museum, published Mooney's study of the Ghost Dance religion. (At some point, my grandfather John S. Taylor purchased copies of the bureau reports, particularly the two volumes that contained Mooney's work on the Cherokee spiritual traditions and separately in another volume the larger work on the Ghost Dance.) In his study of the Ghost Dance of 1890, Mooney traced its roots back in time to the story of Tecumseh and Tenskwatawa and their leadership of this pan-Indian confederacy. Mooney clearly believed the uprising led by Tecumseh and his brother was the precursor of this later Ghost Dance religious movement. This latest eruption of the Ghost Dance religion in the late nineteenth century also promised three essential things to Indigenous peoples, according to Mooney: the resurrection of their dead, the return of the buffalo, and the restoration of their lands.[2]

Not long after Mooney arrived on the scene, the massacre at Wounded Knee occurred, 132 years ago. We know the story or should. Mooney devotes more than forty pages in his book to narrating the massacre including Sioux testimony from survivors. He began with the story of Sitting Bull, who was murdered by Indian agency police as authorities attempted to arrest him for his involvement in the Ghost Dance movement. Shortly after Sitting Bull's killing, the Sioux surrendered and were marched to the Pine Ridge Reservation in South Dakota. The essential facts are these: On the morning of December 29, 1890, five hundred troops of the US 7th Calvary Regiment surrounded a group of Lakota Sioux where they had made camp at Wounded Knee Creek. The troops entered the camp to disarm the Lakota. During a brief scuffle between a soldier and a Lakota man who refused to surrender his weapon, the rifle fired, alarming the rest of the troops. The troops began firing on the Lakota. The attack lasted for more than an hour and left more than three hundred Lakota dead; over half of those killed were women, children, and elderly tribal members, and most of the dead were unarmed.[3]

After researching the Ghost Dance religion across the American West, what did Mooney make of it? As a pioneer of the new discipline of Native ethnography, Mooney had always described Native Americans with both scholarly objectivity and a sympathetic and a respectful heart. To his credit, Mooney largely avoided racist or romantic distortions so prevalent among other white documentarians working in Native ethnography. Mooney went so far as to make a comparative study of the Ghost Dance with other spiritual movements in religious history within the Judeo-Christian tradition, from biblical times, from the history of the

2. Mooney, *Ghost Dance Religion*, 843–46.
3. Mooney, *Ghost Dance Religion*, 843–84.

church to contemporary religious life including Shakers, Quakers, and Protestant revivalists. Director John Wesley Powell expressed concern about this and cautioned Mooney that there were many white people with influence, Christian leaders who would not welcome any comparison between what was widely considered Native "superstition" with more established, mainstream religious traditions within white civilization.

John Wesley Powell was probably right about the church then and maybe right about the church now. As a Presbyterian pastor, I am rooted in Protestant theological tradition. I wonder today how many within my church would be willing to engage in this comparative study that Mooney attempted. Would we be willing to compare our own beliefs about the resurrection of the dead with the Native hope in the return of all those who had been lost to genocide in the Americas? What of the cherished belief in the Christian church of the communion of the saints? Could this affirmation help us understand the Native belief that their ancestors are always with them to guide and protect the people?

I take strength from my Christian belief in the great cloud of witnesses that includes all those prophets, saints, and martyrs (and ordinary folk) of the past who came before us and accompany us in the present. In the liturgical calendar of the church, All Saints and All Souls Days are commemorated all over the Christian world. How different is my belief from that of the Cherokee people and their conviction that the *Nunnihi* were spiritual beings who defended and guided their people? The Christian's hope for the world to come has too often become an otherworldly heaven removed from the struggles of this life. We might have much to learn from the Ghost Dance vision of the restoration of nature's biodiversity and a renewed earth. What if we compared the Judeo-Christian belief in the promised land to the Native belief that it is the land underneath our feet which is sacred? What if Christians who lived under the sign of the sacred water of our baptism could grasp with the Cherokee that all waters are sacred?

Is it possible for me today to step out beyond my own worldview and with a humbler intention to consider the Ghost Dance religion not just with tolerance but with genuine respect? To approach the Ghost Dance with a willingness to honor a tradition other than my own without trying to appropriate it or explain it away? It is difficult if not impossible for me as a white Protestant to believe as a Native American might have in the Ghost Dance, but I too am inspired by the promise that the buffalo will return, and the good, good earth is restored, and its land and its plants, its air and water held as a sacred trust for the good of all living creatures. I too hope that all the countless dead who have been lost to oppression, violence, and poverty will be resurrected. And the domination of the empire defeated, and the curse of white supremacy forever removed, and a new beginning made possible for the reconciliation and healing of humankind.

I am indebted to James Mooney, and I admire him. Without his dedication and skill many of the traditions of the Cherokee would be lost forever. But he too had an interpretative lens that both revealed and concealed dimensions of Cherokee and Native life (as do I). The scholar Michael Elliott in his essay "Ethnography, Reform, and the Problem of the Real: Mooney and the Ghost Dance Religion" helped me understand how Mooney became aware of the limitations of his own methodology without being able to transcend it. On the one hand, Mooney is to be appreciated for placing the Ghost Dance religion within the wide spectrum of religious experience. On the other hand, he demystifies the Ghost Dance by simply reducing it to a desperate and futile self-delusion, a mere symptom of underlying causes of dissatisfaction. But as Elliott points out, Mooney does not take seriously the Ghost Dance religion as a vision of resistance.[4] In its early manifestation among the Cherokee in 1811 and its later expression in the 1890s among many western Indigenous tribes, Mooney failed to recognize how the Ghost Dance could be part of the solution to the problems faced by Native peoples and not just part of the problem itself. Mooney was blind to the political and spiritual dimension of the Ghost Dance religion, and maybe we still are today.

The Cherokee Ghost Dance of 1810–1811 was a precursor of the Ghost Dance religion that was tragically and violently suppressed at Wounded Knee in 1890. The historical arc between these two events reminds us that the struggle of one tribe, the Cherokee, to survive as a people, to remain on their ancestral homeland was the same struggle of all Native peoples in each decade from 1492 to 1890. The deep map of Cherokee history extends to other times and is connected to places in every direction across the continent. American history seen from the perspective of Native Americans was a never-ending cycle of resistance to conquest. The westward frontier of America was always a "zone of racial violence." War waged by the armies of the US government would be followed by Native peoples dispossessed from their lands. The Native

---

4. Elliott, "Ethnography, Reform," 228.

survivors were herded into smaller and smaller reservations that were entirely insufficient for survival. Government agents arrived to parcel out resources that had been promised in treaties. Basic supplies guaranteed by the government were delayed, reduced, siphoned off in corruption, or cut off altogether. Starvation was often close at hand. The buffalo were hunted to near extinction.

Missionaries came and established churches to convert the Indian from his heathen ways. Schools were built to complete the process of assimilation into white civilization. Soon it was decided that Native children could be more properly educated (meaning more effectively "Americanized") if they were entirely removed from their families on the reservations. Wrenching moments of government sponsored kidnapping ensued, when young children were sent to boarding schools where every effort was made to eradicate their Native identity. Long hair was cut. These children wore clothes that did not fit. Some may have learned to read and write in English, but if caught talking in their Native language they were punished. Yes, they may have acquired an agricultural or domestic skill. But these children were worked long hours of hard labor, exacted in return for all that their white schoolmasters had supposedly given them. And these children and youth were at great risk of even worse abuse. Beatings and sexual exploitation happened with regularity. And nearby these boarding schools, cemeteries with unmarked graves were gradually filled with Native children who graduated from these schools by death. It is a haunted history.[5]

Leslie Marmon Silko, the acclaimed Native American author based in Tucson, wrote *Almanac of the Dead* in 1992, the year of the Columbus quincentenary. This was Silko's offering of a radically different way to read five hundred years of American history from an Indigenous perspective. In my first reading of *Almanac of the Dead* shortly after publication, it was difficult for me to find my way into this apocalyptic vision of chaos and violence, played out in a decadent underworld centered around Tucson

---

5. Deb Haaland, a Laguna elder and Secretary of the Interior Department is helping our nation begin to heal from the terrible family separation policy that took children from indigenous families and placed them in boarding schools where systemic abuse occurred. The hearings that she is holding around the country are creating safe places for Native families to share their memories of trauma that continue to reverberate in harmful ways. For those readers who are ready to explore this American tragedy in greater depth one place to start is the book *Carlisle Indian Industrial School: Indigenous Histories, Memories and Reclamations*, edited by Jacqueline Fear-Segal and Susan D. Rose.

Arizona and the US-Mexico borderlands. After I thought I had finished writing this chapter, I decided to read it again. Silko wrote, "Generation after generation, individuals are born and then after eighty years, disappear into dust but in the stories, the people lived on in the imagination and in the hearts of their descendants. Whenever their stories were told, the spirits of the ancestors were present, and their power was alive."[6] The power of story and the presence of the ancestors. From Silko's Native perspective, stories serve the people as oral vessels in which the ancestors freely travel from long ago into the present. Stories are the embodiment of the Spirits who accompany the people through time.[7]

Near the very end of *Almanac of the Dead*, a Native seer by the name of Weasel Tail speaks to an assembly of healers:

> Today I wish to address the question as to whether the spirits of the ancestors in some way failed our people when the prophets called them to the Ghost Dance. Moody [referring to Mooney] and other anthropologists alleged the Ghost Dance disappeared because the people became disillusioned when the ghost shirts did not stop the bullets and the Europeans did not vanish overnight. But it was the Europeans, not the Native Americans who had expected results overnight . . . . [Mooney] and the others had never understood the Ghost Dance was to reunite living people with the spirits of beloved ancestors lost in the five hundred year war . . . . We dance to remember, we dance to remember all our beloved ones, to remember how each passed to the spirit world. We dance because the dead love us, they continue to speak to us, they tell our hearts what must be done to survive. We dance and we do not forget all the others before us, the little

---

6. Silko, *Almanac of the Dead*, 520.

7. Silko's book *Ceremony* concerns the spiritual journey of a Native veteran coming home from WWII shattered by the trauma of war. In the epigraph to *Ceremony*, Silko wrote:

> I will tell you something about stories.
> They aren't just entertainment. Don't be fooled.
> They are all we have, you see
> All we have to fight off illness and death.
> You don't have anything if you don't have stories
> Their evil is mighty
> But it cannot stand up to our stories
> So they try to destroy our stories
> Let the stories be confused or forgotten
> They would like that
> They would be happy
> For we would be defenseless then.

children and the old women who fought and died resisting the invaders and destroyers of Mother Earth! Spirits! Ancestors! We have been counting the days, watching the signs. You are with us every minute, you whisper to us in our dreams, you whisper in our waking moments. You are more powerful than memory![8]

---

8. Silko, *Almanac of the Dead*, 722.

11

A Reckoning with Settler Colonialism

THE GREAT REPLACEMENT THEORY

THE "UNITE THE RIGHT" march through Charlottesville, Virginia, on August 11–12, 2016, was a shocking sign of our times for most Americans. The violent spectacle of white nationalists carrying torches, shouting, "We will not be replaced," left many of us in disbelief at what we had come to as a nation. This distress was further compounded by the violence that led to the death of a counter demonstrator and by a president's declaration that there were "good people on both sides." We are left with one of the ironies of American history that continues today with a resurgent white nationalist movement that espouses the so-called great replacement theory, decrying what its constituents consider to be efforts to "replace" them with an infusion of people of color. But the replacement theory that was actually enacted in the reality of American history was the sustained campaign of the white, southern, planter class to replace Native Americans in the Deep South with enslaved African workers.

A turning point in my understanding of southern history came about when I discovered the book *Unworthy Republic: The Dispossession of Native Americans and the Road to Indian Territory*, by Claudio Saunt, a professor of history at the University of Georgia. Dr. Saunt was the highly anticipated keynote speaker at the annual convention of the Trail of Tears Historical Association meeting in Cherokee that I attended. I quoted Saunt near the beginning of this book in his declaration that this was the war the enslavers won. The critical point that I had not seen clearly until I read Saunt's book and heard him speak is this: the coordinated expulsion of Native peoples and the extension of the plantation economy and the institution of slavery were two sides of the same coin. These twin endeavors were not separate episodes in American history. They were part and parcel of the same driving force that formed the basis of southern ideology and the foundation of federal policy as the United States expanded westward across the continent.[1]

Planters in the South spent decades exhausting the soil of the southern Atlantic states. With the dispossession of Native peoples in the Deep South, they could exchange worn out lands in Virginia and the Carolinas for the fresh and fertile soils of Alabama, Mississippi, and Tennessee.[2] Even though most of the mountainous homeland of the Cherokee was not a prime location for cotton production, they too must go. Expulsion of the Cherokee was the first step in Indian removal across the Southeast. A policy of expulsion would be applied to them and to the other, so-called civilized tribes like the Creek, the Choctaw, and Chickasaw whose homelands were prime locations to produce cotton.[3] The impoverishment of the land under the cotton production of the plantation economy in the mid-Atlantic southern states made the expulsion of Native Americans "necessary" in the minds of the southern planter class to expand into lands not yet wasted.[4]

The heightened anxiety felt by white southerners over the tenuous control they exercised over hundreds of thousands of enslaved people was surpassed only by their desire to continue profiting from Native dispossession by opening up the Deep South to the production of king cotton. After advocating unceasingly to expel Native Americans from the South and replace them with enslaved African workers, white southerners of the planter-politician class faced the consequences of their actions, writes Saunt. The southern United States had become a volatile world on the verge of exploding in a maelstrom of violence.[5]

The ruling elite of the southern planter class had to first remove Native peoples from the Southeast to then extend the plantation economy, and the institution of slavery that undergirded it, into some of the richest

1. Saunt, *Unworthy Republic*, 44.
2. Saunt, *Unworthy Republic*, 194.
3. Saunt, *Unworthy Republic*, 54.
4. Saunt, *Unworthy Republic*, 32.
5. Saunt, *Unworthy Republic*, 245–46.

agricultural land in the world. This was something the white planter class of the South was very prepared to do. After all, white southerners were in the business of moving people. Millions of enslaved Africans were brought across the Atlantic to work on plantations in the South. After the Atlantic slave trade was abolished in 1808, the regional slave trade moved at least 200,000 enslaved people from the Atlantic states to the Deep South, what had been the territory of the Creek, the Choctaw, and the Chickasaw. This interregional slave trade was a second "Middle Passage." (The historian Edward Ball has called this the African Trail of Tears.) It was therefore not difficult to imagine transporting an estimated 60,000 Native Americans westward toward Indian territory to clear their lands for cotton production.[6]

THE "STATE'S RIGHT" TO ENSLAVE AND ABUSE

The official policy of the United States under the Washington Administration was the "civilizing" of Natives people, which meant assimilating Indians into white culture as farmers owning private property. But the prospect that the federal government would ever "civilize" Native Americans and make them citizens was terrifying to southern elites, lest the same enfranchisement might happen to their enslaved workers. Therefore, the political leadership of the southern states fiercely and repeatedly asserted the sovereignty and right of the individual state to determine treatment of Native Americans within their borders. The South's "colored" population whether free or enslaved, African or Indigenous, must remain within the sovereign control of the states.[7]

Under this states' rights agenda of southern powerbrokers, the civilizing policy of the US assuming the gradual assimilation of Native Americans into white society would be replaced by the even more overtly white supremacist conviction that racial coexistence between civilized whites and "savages" was impossible. The truth that was impossible to whites was not that whites and Natives could ever coexist peaceably and equitably but that whites and Natives could ever coexist on the same land, the land that belonged to Natives and was desired by whites.[8] Indian expulsion was brought about not by an inherent incompatibility between

6. Saunt, *Unworthy Republic*, 41.
7. Saunt, *Unworthy Republic*, 39–40.
8. Saunt, *Unworthy Republic*, 10.

racial groups or even by an irresistible tidal wave of white migration but by very specific legislative acts and policy decisions designed to dispossess them of their land and expropriate it for the advancement of the plantation economy.[9]

By 1817, the secretary of war under the Monroe Administration was none other than John C. Calhoun (the nephew of Rebecca Calhoun and Andrew Pickens). Calhoun established a Bureau of Indian Affairs within the War Department that transacted over forty treaties with Native peoples and funded many of the Indian schools that were administered by religious missionaries that have been described. Calhoun used a strategy of humanitarian appeal, bribery, bullying, and barely veiled threats to convince Indigenous nations that their best interests required them to give up claim to their lands in the east and move west beyond the Mississippi. Calhoun probably recognized that Americans' insatiable demand for land would eventually carry white settlers to those same Indian territories. By such time, perhaps, Indians would be thoroughly assimilated as American citizens or extinct.[10]

By 1824, Calhoun would join the Jackson administration as vice president. Jackson and Calhoun were of one mind when it came to expulsion of Native Americans to west of the Mississippi. They were also of the same mind on the preservation and expansion of slavery. Where they differed was the question of states' rights versus federal authority. Calhoun became the eloquent spokesperson for all southerners who believed in the absolute sovereignty of the individual state in its right to agree and abide by or disagree and not abide with a national policy or law. This came to a head in what historians call the "Nullification Crisis." On one side was Calhoun arguing on behalf of South Carolina and many southerners across the region that the state had the right to nullify any law with which it disagreed. And on the other side of the controversy was President Jackson doing his best to hold the Union together, arguing that federal authority must be preeminent if the United States was to remain a nation. Jackson was more than willing to bow to states' rights when it came to the rights of Native Americans in the southern states. But on nullification, he threatened war.[11]

9. Saunt, *Unworthy Republic*, 31.
10. Elder, *Calhoun*, 163.
11. Elder, *Calhoun*, 188.

By 1831, Calhoun broke ranks from Jackson, resigned as vice president, and was subsequently elected senator from South Carolina and continued to make his case for states' rights. It was a crisis moment of high tension that would lead some thirty years later to the secession of South Carolina, the creation of the Confederacy of Southern slaveholding states, and the Civil War. In this moment in the early 1830s Jackson managed to hold the nation together by isolating Calhoun and South Carolina. But in 1831, because of a Presbyterian missionary to the Cherokee practicing civil disobedience toward the state of Georgia, all this would come to a head, precipitating a constitutional crisis.

"WORCESTER, ADVOCATE FOR THE CHEROKEE NATION"

In its policy statement repudiating the Doctrine of Discovery, the General Assembly of the Presbyterian Church, PCUSA included a sketch of one Presbyterian minister, the Reverend Samuel Worcester, who was a missionary living and working among the Cherokee before, during, and after the removal:

> Samuel Austin Worcester (1778–1859), a Presbyterian minister who lived among the Cherokee people, played a crucial role in one of the most important cases regarding tribal jurisdiction in the United States, *Worcester v. Georgia*, decided in 1832. Worcester moved to Cherokee Territory in 1828, where he worked to translate the Bible into Cherokee using Sequoyah's alphabet and assisted Elias Boudinot in publishing the *Cherokee Phoenix*, the first Indian newspaper in North America. He opposed removal of Cherokees west of the Mississippi River, as Georgia took Cherokee lands and dismantled Cherokee government in the face of inaction by the federal government. Worcester was arrested and convicted for disobeying Georgia's law restricting white missionaries from living in Cherokee territory without a state license. Worcester knew that obeying the law would be tantamount to surrendering the sovereignty of the Cherokee Nation.[12]

Worcester was a part of a group of eleven missionaries who wrote a letter of protest to the state of Georgia and refused to get a state license. Worcester and the other ten were arrested in July of 1831, tried and

12. Presbyterian Church (USA), *Doctrine of Discovery*, 8.

convicted and sentenced to four years of hard labor at the state prison in Milledgeville, Georgia. Nine of the eleven agreed to accept Georgia's terms for a pardon and were released. Worcester and one other missionary, Elizur Butler, refused those terms. On appeal, the case (*Worcester v. Georgia*) went all the way to the Supreme Court and was decided in favor of the defendants and of course the Cherokee Nation. Writing the opinion for the majority, Chief Justice John Marshall ruled that Georgia, in imprisoning Worcester (and others), had violated the Constitution and interfered with treaties established between the US and the Cherokee Nation. Jackson's response as reported by Horace Greeley: "Well, John Marshall has made his decision, now let him enforce it."[13]

No matter the ruling of the Supreme Court, Jackson was determined to support Georgia in its case against the Cherokee for two reasons. First, supporting Georgia would advance the cause of the dispossession of Native nations in the southeast, a cause dear to Jackson's heart. And supporting Georgia in the midst of the nullification crisis, Jackson hoped, would keep Georgia in the fold of the Union, lest they throw their weight behind Calhoun and South Carolina. In the next few years, the Jackson Administration utilized a coercive "good cop/bad cop" strategy in its negotiations with Native representatives around the question of removal. Arguing for removal, the federal government declared that they were powerless to control the behavior of individual states, like Georgia, North Carolina, Tennessee, and Alabama, in how they treated their Native inhabitants.[14]

Jackson's most effective weapon wielded in this power struggle was this argument for removal: Native American communities must avoid finding themselves at the mercy of the state laws that were so oppressive and discriminatory toward Native peoples.[15] Expulsion from their homelands was portrayed as an expression of generosity and benevolence from the federal government and the only viable option to them. If removal to Indian territories was refused, the responsibility for the tragic consequences that would inevitably ensue would be squarely on the shoulders of Native Americans. In the face of strong opposition not just from Native peoples but within Congress and from the public, the Jackson Administration sought to portray its Indian removal policy as a humanitarian undertaking necessary for the protection of Native peoples.

---

13. Meacham, *American Lion*, 204.
14. Saunt, *Unworthy Republic*, 88.
15. Saunt, *Unworthy Republic*, 93.

COUNTING THE COSTS

But if the expulsion of Native Americans was nominally described by the Jackson Administration as a "humanitarian" undertaking, how would it be done in order to minimize human suffering and death? And who would bear the costs? One significant contrast between slave trade in African workers and expulsion of Native Americans was that the former was a vast commercial enterprise with many global partners and the latter, Indian removal, was administered by an inexperienced government bureaucracy. An estimated 15 percent of slaves died in the Middle Passage. This was calculated on the spreadsheets of enslavers as an acceptable rate of loss for a company. In other words, as enslavers determined their profit margin the death of countless Africans crossing the Atlantic was simply the cost of doing business. How exactly would a government bureaucrat in the Jackson Administration even calculate the "acceptable" percentage of lives lost for a supposed humanitarian undertaking?[16] And who would bear the costs? At the US treasury an army of accountants dutifully tallied the money accrued from the sales of the land taken from Native peoples and just as dutifully deducted the expenses that deporting these same people from their land would cost. Native peoples were not only dispossessed from their lands but had to pay the government back for the costs of being dispossessed.[17]

Did Jackson actually believe that he was offering Native Americans the paternal care of the federal government? Jon Meacham, in his biography of Jackson, answers: "Probably; the human capacity to convince oneself of something one wants to think true is virtually bottomless. Given the facts of Indian removal, it has to be."[18]

---

16. Saunt, *Unworthy Republic*, 42.
17. Saunt, *Unworthy Republic*, 212.
18. Meacham, *American Lion*, 318.

12

The Haunted History of the South

SOUTHERNERS' ATTRACTION FOR GRAVEYARDS is well-known. Rooted in part in an orientation to the past, and trained to honor our ancestors, southerners gravitate to the graves of our forebears with reverence and admiration. Like many others I too have lingered at the cemeteries and graveyards where my ancestors are buried, but increasingly this has left me a troubled conscience about those who went before me. I have a disturbed relationship with the dead; I am haunted by the violent history of Carolina. I am haunted by the many ways my colonial ancestors were integrally involved in the oppression of their enslaved African workers and in the dispossession of Indigenous people. Though not personally guilty of the sins of the past, I nevertheless remain deeply enmeshed in this history and bear some responsibility for how it shapes the present. I cannot encounter the history of colonial South Carolina as simply a timeline of objective facts. The ghosts who inhabit that history are alive and speaking.

Tiya Miles is one historian who takes ghost stories seriously. In her book *Tales from the Haunted South: Dark Tourism and Memories of Slavery from the Civil War Era*, she recognizes a discernible pattern to these ghostly phenomena. She defines ghosts as returned spirits of those who have died, manifested to the living in a recognizable form whether that be a shape, shadow, sound, or movement. Miles in her study of ghost stories describes them as souls that seem to be stuck, lost, or tortured, who return to the material realm because of unresolved tragedy or trauma. Ghosts emerge from the past to occupy the present in a mystical looping cycle of appearance and disappearance. She draws our attention to ghosts as a pattern of disruptive repetition that bends moments of chronological time, moments when the past punctures the placidity of the present to signal that something was wrong or missing and remains so.

In these ways, the ghost story can be understood as a popular form of historical narrative that is worthy of the historian's attention. Ghosts are historical entities, fragments of a remembered past that disrupt the now of the present. Ghost stories make it a point to render what is taboo, frightening, and alien to mainstream society, dredging up unsettling social memories for reexamination. Ghost stories testify to disturbing historical happenings that have often been excluded from conscious social memory.[1]

Miles has helped me to think about the phenomenon of haunting in southern history in a new way: as a dynamic within the collective psyche of the South. Ghosts are guides to our troubled past, metaphysical messengers who compel us to remember whether we want to or not. The messages ghosts bring can feel like bad news. The past they tell us is rife with wrongs, with traumas that must be named before they can be made right and healed—injustices that must be exposed in order to be redressed in the present.[2] The public historian who takes the experience of haunting seriously has a "sympathetic openness to hauntings, ghosts, gaps, seething absences, and muted presence."[3] Everything Miles has said about the American South being haunted by slavery, it seems to me, could and should also be said about America's relations with Indigenous peoples.

What comes to mind are the haunting words attributed to Chief Seattle to the governor of Washington Territory in the mid-1850s and recorded by a white writer, Henry A. Smith, for a newspaper in 1887.

> Every part of this country is sacred to my people. Every hillside, every valley, every plain and grove has been hallowed by some fond memory or some sad experience of my tribe ... their deep fastness at eventide grows shadowy with the presence of dusky spirit. And when the last red man shall have perished from the earth and his memory among white men shall have become a myth, these shores shall swarm with the invisible dead of my tribe. And when your children's children shall think themselves alone in the field, the store, the shop, upon the highway or in

---

1. Miles, *Tales from the Haunted South*, 15.
2. Miles, *Tales from the Haunted South*, 16.
3. Miles, *Tales from the Haunted South*, 21.

the silence of the woods, they will not be alone . . . . At night, when the streets of your cities and villages shall be silent, and you think them deserted, they will throng with the returning hosts that once filled and still love this beautiful land. The white man shall never be alone.[4]

In their book *Healing Haunted Histories*, the theologian Ched Myers and the educator Elaine Enns have helped forge a path for activists, educators, and public historians doing this kind of work of historical excavation. They recognize that these famous lines attributed to Chief Seattle may have been "enhanced" by the white reporter who recorded his speech for publication. But the textual ambiguity of "who said what" in the passage, which is an unavoidable mixture of Seattle's and the reporter's words, only confirms the disturbing truth of Chief Seattle's prophetic utterance: the white man will be haunted by Indigenous presence. It may be that any enhancement the reporter did is more evidence that he was already experiencing the sense of being haunted by Seattle, by the past.

Indian ghosts appear in novels of iconic American authors like Washington Irving, James Fenimore Cooper, Herman Melville, and Edgar Allen Poe. One of the most popular figures on the American stage of the nineteenth century was Metacom, the ghost of "King Philip," the Indigenous leader of the eponymous war across New England that came close to destroying the English-speaking colonies of that time.[5] On stage, the specter of Metacom would deliver his jeremiads against the sins of the nation, sending chills up the spines of thousands who attended nightly performances. In the documentary *Woodlands Dark and Days Bewitched*, produced in 2021 about the genre of horror films, the Ojibwe journalist Jesse Wente remarks on the number of US horror films that are set on Indian burial grounds. He says: "I sort of like it, because if non-Indigenous people are going to be afraid of the Indian burial ground, then I got some news for you. It's all an Indian burial ground."[6]

To be haunted, the scholar Avery Gordon suggests, is a different way of knowing and writing about the historical world. To be haunted and to write from that location is not a methodology or a consciousness that

---

4. Myers and Enns, *Healing Haunted Histories*, 36–37.

5. A book I wish had been available to me just a bit sooner is *Ghosts of King Philip's War* by Thomas D'Agostino and Arlene Nicholson, which explores the landscape of New England and the "permanent physic scar on the land that still resonates in the many haunted places where wartime tragedies took place" (synopsis).

6. Jenkins, "Wisdom of Folk Horror," 50.

you can simply adopt. Following ghosts is about making a contact "that changes you and refashions the social relations in which you are located. It is about putting life back in where only a vague memory or a bare trace was visible to those who bothered to look."[7] Haunting is a "structure of feeling, an emotional presence, a quantum entanglement, an exchange of noisy silences and seething absences."[8]

One such ghost story is associated with the Conestoga massacre in Lancaster, Pennsylvania, the location of which is a structure of the workhouse/jail which has survived and is today the Fulton Theater, a refurbished concert hall and a mainstay of a thriving downtown. In his book, Brubaker describes an event in 1997, when hundreds of Native Americans and citizens of Lancaster gathered to dedicate a plaque at the site of the massacre and honor the dead. As part of the ceremony, Natives beat drums, danced, sang, burned sage and cedar, and recited poetry. One participant, who claimed Cherokee ancestry, testified that he felt a wind suddenly rise and subside during the ceremony and believed it to be a Native ancestral spirit. The playwright in residence at the Fulton returned to his office after the ceremony, and on top of a desk filled with files and office clutter he placed a braid of sweetgrass. When he returned the next day to his office, everything on his desk was scattered about the room, except for the sweetgrass. Benjamin Franklin's prophecy proved true. It seems that Lancaster is home to Indigenous spirits. Hopefully they have found some peace by what happened in 1997 and then later in 2010. Brubaker reported in the local Lancaster newspaper, the *Scribbler*, that a regional gathering of Presbyterians, Mennonites, and Quakers apologized for the 1763 massacre of Conestoga Indians and asked for forgiveness.[9]

But when I write of being haunted by ghosts, I am really not trying to prove a particular ghost story or pursue a spectral appearance of some kind. Nor do I fully embrace the phenomenon of the paranormal so popular in our media today. Being haunted for me is to feel the presence of an absence. It is sensing at the very edge of semantic availability that "something is to be done."[10] Discerning what that "something to be done" might be is the restlessness that informs this writing, the impetus that drives my telling of this story. The way of the ghost is haunting, and

7. Gordon, *Ghostly Matters*, 22.
8. Gordon, *Ghostly Matters*, 200.
9. Brubaker, *Massacre of the Conestogas*, 149–51.
10. Gordon, *Ghostly Matters*, 202.

haunting is a very particular way of knowing what has happened or is happening yet.[11] Only when we, the descendants of our settler ancestors, are able to internalize a more conscious awareness of our collective past can we begin to heal that haunted history. Some expression of lamentation is called for, an audible sign of collective grief.

Only when we, the descendants of settlers, can grieve together the oppression and violence of our history can we move forward. That "thing that must be done" is a collective acknowledgment by white society in the United States of the destruction waged against all Native peoples of this continent and against those our forebears enslaved. Only then will we be able, as Americans, to heal our haunted history, allowing for the possibility of peace for their dead, for our dead, and for ourselves.[12] Then, perhaps we can begin or continue a conversation about what it would take to repair this history in the present. We have so much to learn and so far to go. To come to know ourselves is to recognize that American history has deposited in each one of us "an infinity of traces, without leaving an inventory. With no inventory we erase behind ourselves any traces of genocidal past."[13] It is an ongoing ethical necessity to challenge forgetting. And to remember.

---

11. Gordon, *Ghostly Matters*, 8.
12. Gordon, *Ghostly Matters*, 19.
13. Myers and Enns, *Healing Haunted Histories*, 42.

13

Healing the Family Tree

MUCH COULD BE MADE of Tyger Jim's and Polly's legacy to their descendants. Their five sons all served in the Civil War. Some of their wartime correspondence to their families has been preserved in a volume entitled *Upcountry South Carolina Goes to War: The Letters of the Anderson, Brockman, and Moore Families 1853–1865*. In May of 1865, near the very end of the war, Tyger Jim and Polly were victims of violence. A federal cavalry unit in pursuit of Jefferson Davis passed through their farm and plundered the place. Later that same day, Yankee stragglers came upon the farm and demanded to know where their gold and valuables were hidden. To obtain this information they placed a rope around Tyger Jim's neck and hoisted him three times over a beam in a shed. When he still would not divulge the location of any valuables, they beat him severely and left him for dead. Tyger Jim crawled to a hiding place in the cleft of a rock along the Tyger River and was later found by family and nursed back to health. He lived to be eighty-six years old and died on June 24, 1870. Polly had passed away in 1856. They are buried together in the graveyard at Nazareth Presbyterian Church.

THE MARRIAGE OF MARIA ANDERSON AND JEFFERSON GILREATH

Our Anderson history traces lines of descent from Tyger Jim and Polly that carry Anderson kinfolk in every direction. Tyger Jim's son, William Washington Anderson, would marry Jane Cauble of Greenville in 1846. Their youngest daughter, Maria Worthington Anderson, would marry

Jefferson Davis Gilreath, whose family history of Scots Irish settlers closely mirrors that of the Andersons. As told before, some of my Gilreath ancestors left Wilkes County, North Carolina, in 1788 with their leader Ben Cleveland and settled on the S. Tyger River. Cleveland moved on to the Tugaloo River where he was awarded land seized from the Cherokee for his service in the American Revolution.

In subsequent volumes of this family history writing project I intend to explore in depth other branches of my family tree, focusing on the stories of six ancestors who each embody a dimension of southern history from the early nineteenth century, through the Civil War and Reconstruction. One of these is Perry Duncan (PD) Gilreath, Jefferson Gilreath's father. PD was a Confederate veteran who refused to surrender at Appomattox. Breaking free from the federal troops that encircled the Army of Northern Virginia, Gilreath was part of a cavalry unit that accompanied Jefferson Davis and his Confederate cabinet fleeing Richmond. In that fateful year of 1876, which ended the period known in Southern history as Reconstruction, Wade Hampton was elected governor of the state (recall the story of the Hampton massacre) and Gilreath was elected sheriff of Greenville, a position in which he served for over twenty-five years.

Even today Gilreath is remembered in Greenville County and celebrated as "High Sheriff," the epitome of the honorable lawman. And yet it is indisputable that he was elected in the most corrupt and violent election in US history. How did he understand and respond to that critical moment in American history? How did my ancestor use his authority and power as sheriff? And does his story teach us anything about how the criminal justice system became a new kind of slavery? Those are some of the questions I intend to wrestle with in a subsequent volume. My great-grandfather Jefferson Gilreath made a living first as deputy serving with his father, Perry Duncan Gilreath, when he was high sheriff. When Perry Duncan retired, his son Jeff was elected to replace him.

THE ENSLAVED AFRICANS IN THE GILREATH FAMILY TREE

As with my work on the Andersons, I have also worked on the Gilreath line of descent. Two discoveries have shocked me to the core that pertain directly to our story here. First was the discovery of African Americans who are descended from my Gilreath ancestors. I have reached out to them, and they have shared genealogical information that confirms our common ancestors. The second shock was a detail included in the information provided to me: a brief reference to the tragic story of a Native American woman, probably a Cherokee. Her story and the story of her enslaver is woven into the Trail of Tears.

Knowing that my Gilreath ancestors once inhabited the area where I now live in Elkin, North Carolina, I was curious one day when I met an African American elder by the name of Gilreath. I was able to contact her, and she referred me to other relatives out of state who knew more about their genealogical history. A round of phone calls led me from one member of the family in the DC metro area, to another relative in Atlanta, and finally to a woman living closer to home, Ms. Mae Jeffries Cole of High Point, North Carolina. Each was gracious to me and willing to share information on their family. All acknowledged that they were getting up in age and no longer able to organize family reunions that had been held for many years. Ms. Cole in particular provided concrete evidence that we are branches of the same family tree, descended from my ancestors William and Mary Gilreath, who had eight children. John was born to them in 1752, and some of these African American Gilreaths claim him as the line from which they come. Others claim the third-born son, Alexander. My branch of the family tree extends from the youngest-born son, Jesse, who migrated with his parents to South Carolina in 1788.

Our common lineage is before me in black and white. Underneath these genealogical branches is the violent reality of white sexual violence inflicted on Black women. I can think of no other way to interpret this information than to say that several of my Gilreath ancestors, perhaps William the patriarch, and certainly the two sons John and Alexander, exercised their power over enslaved African women by raping them. From this violence endemic to the slavery system, new branches of the family tree were born. This is a dense fact that it will take me some time to unpack. To get inside this reality that I have ancestors who probably sexually exploited the women they enslaved, I returned to a book I first read decades ago: *Slaves in the Family* by Edward Ball. He too grapples with the starkness of this reality and its possible ambiguity within his family history. Amid the vast and obvious inequities of slavery and the power imbalance between white men and enslaved black women, Ball wondered, was it possible that sometimes in some ways there could be mutual desire and shared intimacy between the enslaver and the enslaved? The following story makes it very plain that exploitation was the rule.

A SHOCKING REVELATION

Ms. Cole, one of the African American Gilreath descendants, sent me genealogical information about her ancestors that included a line of descent from the family of Samuel Stokes. Samuel was born in Petersburg, Virginia, in 1826, the child of an Indian enslaved woman (unnamed) and a white father, Montford Stokes of North Carolina—his mother's enslaver. The straightforward genealogical information that was shared with me had a note written to the side recounting a tragic narrative: "Samuel's Native American mother went to a nearby river and tightly wrapped her baby in a blanket, to smother him. She then walked into the river and drowned herself. The child did not die but was found by the Stokes family and raised in their household until he was an adult." This was Samuel Stokes who remained an enslaved offspring. What scale of suffering and abuse and overwhelming despair would be so unbearable that it could propel Samuel's mother, a Native woman, perhaps a Cherokee, to kill her child and take her own life? What would it have meant for Samuel to be raised in the white family that had driven his despairing mother to consign herself and her newborn son to death in order to escape enslavement?

Montford Stokes, the alleged white father of Samuel Stokes and likely the source of his mother's anguish, went on to pursue a career in politics. He represented Wilkes County (the county next to mine) in the statehouse and eventually became the governor of North Carolina. Following his tenure as governor, Stokes's political ally and friend President Andrew Jackson appointed him to be an administrative overseer of Jackson's Indian removal policies. He moved to Oklahoma and spent the rest of his life there. Horrifying possibilities linger like ghosts. How did this man, Montford Stokes, so treat this unnamed Native woman that she would rather kill herself and her child than remain in his power? And given this history, what evil prerogative did he exercise as he administered the dispossession and resettlement of the entire Cherokee people?

These were the traumatic origins of Samuel Stokes—part Native, part white, but still enslaved. He would marry Nancy, an enslaved African woman in Wilkes County, North Carolina, in 1854. They remained in bondage until the end of the Civil War. Samuel and Nancy had twelve children. Their fifth child, a son named Montford Sidney Stokes, was born in 1864 and married Hattie Gilreath, at age nineteen, in January of

1883. Here two lines of descent merged in the genealogical information provided to me by Ms. Cole.

TRAUMATIC ECHOES

This brief reference to an enslaved woman who sought to end her baby's life and her own rather than live in slavery brought another story to mind. Toni Morrison's *Beloved* is the story of a formerly enslaved woman named Sethe haunted by the ghost of a daughter she killed rather than allowing her to live in the degradation of slavery. Morrison shared that, in her research, she had run across a reference to an enslaved woman by the name of Margaret Garner. In January of 1856, Margaret Garner and her husband and four children escaped from Kentucky to Ohio. When a slave hunting posse was about to recapture them, Margaret killed one child and sought to kill the others, rather than allow them to be taken back into slavery. Morrison testified that she was haunted by this tragedy. And *Beloved* grew out of this haunting. *Beloved* has appeared on some lists of books to be banned as too traumatic to be read by white school children.

MILL ROCKS

Jeff and Maria Gilreath had five daughters, including my grandmother Hazael and my great-aunts Mary, Jane, Elizabeth, and Earline. My great-aunt Earline (Earline Gilreath Hungerford White) and I became better acquainted near the end of her life when she was still living out at her parent's homeplace—an old three-story country manor called Mill Rocks in Greenville County, not very far at all from the Tyger River. This was the homeplace built by Maria and her husband Jeff Gilreath for their five daughters. It has been a gathering spot for my extended family for generations. I regret that I did not know my grandmother Hazael very well before her death, so Earline became a surrogate for me.

Feeling a greater need for rootedness in my family history and cherishing Earline as the last of her generation, I would visit her there and much enjoyed her lively company. Sitting before a fire on the lowest floor, we would enjoy a toddy together and go fishing for memories. Aunt Granny, as we called Earline, was at that age not always able to easily remember and retrieve answers to specific questions. But if you were patient and could handle your bourbon, eventually the fishing line would give a tug in the pool of her memory, and she would pull up a beautiful recollection about our family history.

GILREATH MILL

Across the road from Mill Rocks stands a state historical landmark, Gilreath Mill. An old, preserved grist mill, it served the surrounding community up until the 1950s. On grinding days such a mill became a gathering place where farmers from miles around would congregate, some overnight, to await their turn. Music, food, and conversation enlivened the waiting. Rummaging around on the top floor of the mill structure, I was pleased to find old flour sacks adorned with the Gilreath logo, a red rose. These flour sacks have become treasured keepsakes, hanging on the walls of various family members' homes. A large iron wheel still stands that was turned by the creek that runs under Gilreath Bridge and down the length of the front yard of the home. You have met my grandmother Hazael. You have met my great-aunt Earline. Now let me introduce you to another daughter of Maria and Jefferson: Jane, the third-born daughter of Maria Worthington Anderson and Jefferson Davis Gilreath.

Gilreath Mill Photo

Gilreath Mill Drawing

THE *KEOWEE TRAIL PAGEANT* OF 1921 REVISITED

As mentioned at the beginning, on Friday, November 11, 1921, a remarkable drama was performed at the Greenville County Fairgrounds. Entitled the *Keowee Trail Pageant*, it starred Jane Worthington Gilreath. According to the *Greenville News*, an estimated thirty-five thousand people attended afternoon and evening performances and watched a cast of over two thousand performers dramatize the early colonial history of South Carolina and its interactions with the Cherokee Nation. My grandfather was a member of the executive committee, and as a member of the history committee, he helped to write the pageant narrative. Jane Gilreath, a direct Anderson descendant who was also a member of the executive committee, played the Cherokee maiden, Cateechee. The *Greenville News* gave her rave reviews as the "radiant and captivating" Cateechee. But it hardly needs to be said that Janie, a Scots Irish Anderson descendant, was no Native American.

Mariah and the Five Gilreath Sisters, from Left to Right—Elizabeth, Hazael (My Grandmother), Mariah, Mary, Jane, Earline

Janie Gilreath as Cateechee (*Keowee Trail Pageant* Brochure)

THE LEGEND OF "CATEECHEE"

The central drama of the pageant is the story of Cateechee and her desperate nighttime journey from Keowee to the colonial fort at Ninety-Six to warn her lover Allan Francis, a Scots Irish trader, and the white settlement of an impending attack by the Cherokee. My grandfather wrote the historical sketch in the program describing Cateechee as a Choctaw maiden who had been captured by the Cherokee and was living in Keowee as a prisoner. She is the heroine of the story for warning the whites of danger. The attack ensues, but the settlers are victorious over the Cherokee. Cateechee is rewarded for her loyalty and courage by being liberated from Cherokee captivity in her marriage to her Scots Irish lover.

The legend of Cateechee goes on to suggest that, along her night ride down the Keowee Trail, the creeks she crossed were named to signify the number of miles to the white settlement she must traverse to deliver her warning. My grandfather, who had a historian's eye for detail, possessed a copy of Hunter's map depicting these creeks. I am quite sure that he recognized that these creeks had already been designated as landmarks along the Keowee Trail some thirty years before the Cherokee War, in which Cateechee supposedly intervened on the side of the colonists. And yet her legend continues to have staying power, passed down from generation to generation in South Carolina folklore.

COLONIAL SOUTH CAROLINA HISTORY IS CELEBRATED

In the pageant, six primary episodes were performed on stage depicting South Carolina history from 1730 to the American Revolution. The program indicates that the first scene was a Cherokee village in which two dances were performed. A later scene was a treaty at Saluda Old Town negotiated between the colonial governor of South Carolina and the Cherokee chief Attakullakulla. The script of the Cherokee chief was the actual speech as recorded at the time. One scene depicts the Scots Irish settlement of the Waxhaws with a chorus singing and children playing. Another scene shows the establishment of Fort Prince George and the Scots Irish settlement at Long Cane, with a portent of the massacre that would later befall them.

I was surprised to find in the program's historical sketch an actual reference to the circumstances at the beginning of the Cherokee War of 1760. The Cherokee, returning from the French and Indian War, appropriated horses that belonged to Virginia settlers: "They were secure in their knowledge that they had aided their white friends and, in their childlike simplicity, believed it was only fair to take whatever fancy dictated and fate might put in their way." The program declared that despite the colonists fair treatment of the "childlike" Indians, the Cherokee turned against the English. However, the war that ensued finds no mention at all. Although Mooney's book on Cherokee history, myths, and legends is cited as a primary source, the pageant indulges in another historical inaccuracy. The white actor playing the Cherokee chief Attakullakulla is adorned in the classic Great Plains Indian headdress made of eagle feathers, one no Cherokee ever wore.

Another scene was a dramatization of the Battle of Kings Mountain, a decisive turning point in the American Revolution. The drama depicted a Scots Irish Presbyterian parson by the name of Reverend Doak who, on the eve of the Battle of Kings Mountain, offered a prayer that God would grant the Patriots a victory over the British who would fight with "Gideon's Sword." For the program, my grandfather penned the kind of prayer that he imagined Doak might have uttered. Dancing and singing then celebrated the ultimate triumph of Patriot forces over Lord Cornwallis and the British.

The historical figures depicted on the stage include many that have appeared in this narrative: Henry Laurens, Andrew Pickens, Francis Marion, Thomas Sumter, and many other South Carolina military leaders I have not mentioned. The pageant program, more than fifty pages long, culminates with a photo of Old Stone Church, which serves as a sacred shrine to South Carolina's colonial past. I am certain my grandfather had a hand in inserting this photo in the program.

A CELEBRATION OF AMERICAN PROGRESS

Digging into this story, I learned that pageants like this were quite the thing in US culture in the first half of the twentieth century. Artistic directors from the Northeast were in great demand to orchestrate such historical pageants, in which local communities fleshed out celebrations of American progress. The final episode of the *Keowee Trail Pageant*, entitled "Vision of the Years," was a series of processional pictures that brought the audience from the past to the present. In a written prologue entitled "By the Carolinian" we find these words: "The carefree slave is happy at his task, while in the white-pillared mansion of his master spacious hospitality welcomes all." To the orchestra's rendition of "Dixie," a parade of actors crossed the stage, representing the accomplishments of South Carolina in education, health, and industry. Actors also personified patriotic values. Then came a memorial to the soldiers of all wars, including Confederates, who were given an honored place beside veterans of other American Wars: the Revolution, the War of 1812, the Mexican War, the Spanish American War, and the American Legion of those who served in World War 1.

The credits at the end of the program demonstrate the wide range of participants in the *Keowee Trail Pageant* in 1921. In Greenville, some two hundred community organizations participated in the production, with over two thousand cast members wearing costumes sent from New York at great expense. Many others were employed as members of the orchestra, chorus, and stage crews. Twenty-two committees were organized to carry out this performance, and the event involved girls' and boys' clubs from the mill villages of the upstate and service clubs like Rotary and Kiwanis. Student groups were recruited from area colleges like Clemson, Wofford, Converse, Furman, and others. Veterans' organizations participated. Local schools sent classes of children. I admire the community spirit and organizational ability the pageant demonstrated almost as much as I regret the many ways its interpretation of history fails to do justice to the full story: the devastating impact the settler colonialism of my Scots Irish ancestors and other settlers had on the Cherokee Nation.

As I look over the pageant program for the Keowee Trail and read its accompanying essay on the history of the early settlers on the frontier and their conflicts with the Cherokee, it is obvious that this tale has been romanticized and simplified to satisfy the appetites of generations of white South Carolinians like me, being taught to see in our history only what we want to see. Through the legend of Cateechee, we have been served up a story line that blesses white supremacy in the romantic image of an Indian maiden who forsakes her "savage" people to preserve and advance white civilization. The *Keowee Trail Pageant*—largely narrated by my grandfather—celebrates the Cherokee by erasing them. No mention is ever made of racism, land theft, war crimes, or the deportation of thousands of Cherokee women, men, and children in the forced death march of the Trail of Tears. At the same time that the pageant was performed in 1921, the Eastern Band of the Cherokee in North Carolina were resisting federal pressure to subdivide tribal lands into parcels of private property, undermining the collective identity of the Cherokee Nation.

"THE CONTEST FOR SOUTHERN MEMORY"

In *Monuments to Absence: Cherokee Removal and the Contest over Southern Memory*, the historian Andrew Denson describes a similar pageant held in Chattanooga in 1938, first organized to celebrate the seventy-fifth anniversary of the nearby Civil War Battle of Chickamauga. Somewhere along the way, the pageant organizers realized that 1938 was also the one hundredth anniversary of the Cherokee Trail of Tears, which had been launched from the same area. They decided to include both events in the commemoration of the founding of the city of Chattanooga. This pageant also included a Cherokee woman as the central actor in the drama. This time she was identified not as Cateechee but as Nancy Ward, the niece of Attakullakulla who had married a white trader and was buried nearby. The DAR had established a monument to Nancy at her grave site, near Denton, Tennessee. As we have seen, Nancy Ward did in fact advocate for peace in tribal councils where war was being debated.

Cateechee in the *Keowee Trail Pageant* and Nancy Ward in the later Chattanooga pageant are both depicted as allies and helpers—almost as co-founders of white society. For the creators of these pageants these Indigenous women, by giving their higher loyalty to protect white settlers, foreshadow the disappearance of their people. With no more than this backward glance, both women are assimilated into the larger narrative of the progress of white civilization. And of course, the Chattanooga pageant makes no mention of Dragging Canoe, the son of Attakullakulla, who unlike his father never gave up fighting for his people and homeland. Dragging Canoe and many Cherokees like him established a new settlement of Cherokee towns that became known as the Chickamauga Cherokees. All the Chickamauga towns were in the vicinity of what would someday become Chattanooga.

DAUGHTERS OF THE AMERICAN REVOLUTION

Turning now and then to the biographical sketches in my trusty *History of the Anderson Family*, I noticed that both my great-grandmother Maria and my grandmother Hazael were members of Daughters of the

American Revolution (DAR). My grandmother was for fourteen years the registrar of the local Greenville chapter. I paid little attention to this credential until later, when the work of the DAR kept popping up in my research. First there was the marker dedicated to Keowee Town, where my grandfather spoke on the history of Keowee. And then, on the field trip with Dennis Chastain, we passed through the impressive campus of the Tamassee DAR mountain boarding school. In my reading, I noticed that it was the DAR that sponsored other historic markers here and there, like the grave of the Cherokee leader Junaluska, near Robbinsville, North Carolina, or the grave of Nancy Ward near Chattanooga, Tennessee. This seemed a bit odd because we know that the Cherokee fought not on the side of the Patriots but on the side of the British.

Assuming that the DAR was a network of history-minded women who were linked by genealogy to the American Revolution, I got curious and decided to dig into what they were all about. I was shocked at what I found. In "Defenders of Patriotism or Mothers of Fascism? The DAR, Antiradicalism, and Un-Americanism in the Interwar Period," Simon Wendt outlines a disturbing pattern in the DAR's history. Once the Wilson Administration brought the United States into World War 1, the DAR jumped in full bore with patriotic fervor in support of the war effort. Support for the US military became an abiding pillar of their charter. And following the Russian Revolution (1917–1923), so did anti-communism. National leadership began railing against the dangers of communism and encouraged local chapters to blacklist suspicious sympathizers of un-American activities. Who might these un-American citizens be? People like W. E. B. Du Bois, the African American scholar and activist who did so much to truthfully reinterpret American history. He wrote in his classic work on Black Reconstruction: "Nations reel and stagger on their way; they make hideous mistakes; they commit frightful wrongs; they do great and beautiful things. And shall we not best guide humanity by telling the truth about all this, so far as the truth is ascertainable?"[1]

By the 1920s, the DAR had a membership of 140,000, composed largely of middle-class, educated, Protestant women like my grandmother. Its founding values affirmed patriotism, religious faith, private property, the family with a father as its head, and the Anglo-Saxon contribution to American history. In defending these "American" values, the DAR decried immigration, class warfare, feminism, pacifism, and socialism.

---

1. Du Bois, *Black Reconstruction in America*, 714.

Criticism of the DAR arose both from within the organization and outside it, repudiating its values as un-American and arguing for a more pluralistic and inclusive vision of the nation. Undeterred, in 1939, the DAR decided to exclude Marion Anderson, the famed African American singer, from performing in their Washington, DC, Constitution Hall. As many of us know, Ms. Anderson was then allowed to sing in front of the Lincoln Memorial to an integrated audience of seventy-five thousand. Her historic performance was one of the great triumphs of the early civil rights movement. For the DAR, it was a disgraceful defeat.

Now I did not intend to pick on my great-grandmothers or the DAR. I share their appreciation for history and am genuinely grateful for their work in erecting historical markers. My grandmother was the definition of a gentle person, never drawing attention to herself. I wish I could have known her better. But this detour confirmed for me the importance of how and why we tell the story of our nation. And how it is that good and kind people live and move within ideological systems and cultural assumptions that shape and define us in ways that hurt all of us. From their website, the DAR appears to be a vibrant organization to this day. They seem to have invested effort in atoning for their exclusionary past. I wonder, though, if their understanding of American history has evolved since those days when my great-grandmothers were members. The America of the present is determined in part by the America of the past and how we understand that history.

South Carolina, as is the nation, is poised to commence a new round of anniversary celebrations commemorating the events of its colonial and Revolutionary War history. The state is gearing up for the two hundred and fiftieth anniversary of the American Revolution with plans to offer battlefield road trips for history-minded tourists and educational resources for school children. Will these commemorations be any different from those of previous generations, where remembering was a kind of forgetting? Will the telling of the history of our nation's history be yet another erasure of the struggles of Indigenous and enslaved peoples, as was the case with the *Keowee Trail Pageant* in 1921 or the Chattanooga pageant of 1937 or, nationally, the Columbus quincentenary of 1992?

With all that we now know it would seem that there is no going back to the way white folk have told the story of our nation in the past. Yet today the obstacles to truth-telling have never been more formidable. Angry folk who call for the banning of books are afraid of how their children might be made "uncomfortable" with the truth of our nation's history. Politicians animate their base supporters with misleading tirades about "wokeness" and critical race theory. Southern governors badger school boards about teaching Black history. Can white America, as the historian Dr. Eddie Glaude said recently, face the monster in the mirror of our history? Will our nation ever face up to the truth? Will we remember what has been willfully forgotten? Will we "re-member" a "dismembered" history in such a way as to put the history of our nation back together again? When I began this project I didn't realize how pivotal its timing would be. But perhaps this book is my offering to the conversation that will certainly intensify as we approach the two hundred and fiftieth anniversary of the American Revolution.

TRAIL JOURNAL: CONTINUING ALONG THE CHEROKEE PATH

It has become clear to me that the Keowee Trail does not end at Keowee. As I walk the trail in my imagination, it carries me deeper and deeper into Cherokee history. All that occurred along the Keowee Trail led inexorably to the Trail of Tears, the forced deportation of Cherokee people in a death march that killed thousands. Years ago, I went on to the Qualla Boundary, the Cherokee Reservation, and got a motel room along the Oconaluftee River in the heart of the reservation of the Eastern Band of the Cherokee. While there, I attended the famous drama *Unto These Hills*, which tells the Cherokee story. This show first debuted in 1950, and since then millions of American tourists have filled the mountainside theater to see it. The performance is centered on the historical figure of Tsali, a Cherokee warrior who resisted removal.

The legend of Tsali, the dramatic centerpiece of the performance, is recorded in Mooney's history.[2] The story concerns the moment when General Winfield Scott's federal troops were rounding up Cherokee communities and herding them to concentration camps to await their deportation on the journey west. The military operation was almost finished. In fact, the soldiers who captured Tsali, his wife, and their children were among the last in the area, having just returned from a distant patrol in South Carolina. When a soldier, pushing the family along with bayonets, knocked Tsali's wife to the ground, Tsali retaliated and killed him. In the ensuing struggle, another soldier was killed and a third was wounded

---

2. Mooney, *Myths of the Cherokee*, 157–58.

but survived to tell the tale. Tsali and his family made their escape into the farther reaches of the wilderness. The incident became a headline in newspapers across the country. The government's need for saving face meant that these Cherokee must face justice. The legend of Tsali suggests that General Winfield Scott agreed to curtail his round-up of other Cherokee refugees hiding in the mountains if Tsali would turn himself in and face the consequences of his actions. But some historians have concluded that by that point, Scott had already decided to bring the military operation to a close. The unwelcome media attention caused by the incident demanded a face-saving resolution.

Tsali actually may never have surrendered. He may have been recaptured by federal troops with the assistance of Cherokee. But in Cherokee legend he comes across as a Christ figure who sacrifices himself so that some of his people might remain in their mountain homeland. Tsali, it is told, went to his neighbor, Standing Wolfe (*Oochella*), and consulted with him about what must be done. Both knew that any prolongation of US occupying troops would certainly mean that others hiding in the mountains might succumb to hunger and the elements. And so, Tsali and Standing Wolfe came to an agreement: eventually, Tsali turned himself in and faced the consequences of his resistance. He was executed in what is today Bryson City, North Carolina, by a firing squad composed of his fellow Cherokee. It was this last detail that seemed to me the final indictment of the cruelty of US power. But there may be another possible interpretation. Perhaps, rather than Scott's army forcing the Cherokee to shed the blood of their brother, it was the Cherokee who themselves decided that they would carry out the hard and heavy work, bringing the impasse to a close by taking responsibility for the execution of Tsali. There is a measure of truth in both interpretations. Whether this provided a sliver of consolation to Tsali, only he could know, but the narrative of his heroic sacrifice has become an origin story for the Eastern Band of the Cherokee.

Like so many others, I am drawn to the Tsali legend. I am not overly troubled by the demythologizing that historians must do. But as history, it is true enough that in his story we catch a glimpse of the resistance of countless Cherokee families as they were forcibly rounded up. Cherokee families who were allowed time to carry only what they could place on their backs. Cherokee families who watched in horror as white men waited in the wings, poised to plunder their farms and seize their lands even before they were marched away forever. That Tsali fought to preserve his family in his homeland and died for it is all the history I need to know.

The Journal of the Reverend Daniel S. Butrick

While I was in Cherokee, I visited the Cherokee Museum, taking my time with this excellent exhibit. In the museum bookstore I purchased a copy of the *Journal of Reverend Daniel Butrick*, a Presbyterian missionary who accompanied the Cherokee on the Trail of Tears and recorded his experiences of the day-to-day sufferings of the people as they walked to Oklahoma. Butrick fascinates me. Apparently, he was convinced that the Cherokee were a lost tribe of Israel. However dubious this theory would be to a biblical scholar today, it allowed Butrick to weave the story of the Cherokee into what was for him the sacred story of the Bible. And it motivated him to a passionate study and preservation of Cherokee culture, its spiritual traditions, and other antiquities. Whatever racial, cultural, or theological assumptions Butrick had as a missionary, these must have been stripped away and remolded in his solidarity with the Cherokee on the Trail of Tears. The history of the Christian church in relation to Indigenous peoples of the Americas is one of deep complicity with genocide. As a person of faith, I need to acknowledge that and at the same time find some hope in individual stories of other people of faith who stood up to conquest and suffered for their faithfulness.

Walking with the Cherokee on the Trail of Tears, Butrick experienced in body and soul their suffering as his own. I wonder how that experience changed his faith. As a Christian, could he reimagine Christ's journey to the cross as the very path he was walking with the Cherokee? By his faith was he able to affirm that the suffering of the Cherokee was part of the suffering of the crucified Christ? Butrick represents for me a model of accompaniment, a way of supporting peace and justice in the world by walking with those on the margins of society, those pushed down by the forces of domination. Accompaniment means walking alongside, not leading or following. It means being with the suffering of another without necessarily having the power to solve the problem or to be able to rescue them from their pain. It means witnessing the struggles of others and not trying to judge or direct those struggles. I hope and pray that this writing project will be received by the Cherokee as an expression of accompaniment.

Kituwah

As I left the reservation, I spotted a historical marker that indicated this valley was the location of Kituwah, the mother town of the Cherokee people. Here was the point of origin where the people first emerged from the earth. I pulled over and parked and walked to the edge of a big field. The sacred mound of Kituwah there is now little more than a slight rise in the ground. The Eastern Band has Kituwah again in its possession and holds an annual sacred festival there. The place of Kituwah holds a sacred presence that can be felt deeply even by the non-Cherokee. But I did not know if it was permissible for me to explore. I did not want to trespass where I did not belong. Understanding what Kituwah means to the Cherokee and how it feels to me to be there, my further exploration of this sacred site would have to wait for another day. I drove on to Bryson City and saw the historical marker signifying the place of Tsali's execution.

Horace Kephart

While in Bryson City, I went hunting for the grave of an author I greatly admire—Horace Kephart. I knew that Kephart had moved to the Smokies in 1904 after a nervous breakdown and had been restored to some measure of health in his beloved mountains. Beginning life anew, he lived in Bryson City and was the author of *Our Southern Highlanders*, one of the great classics of American literature, documenting the culture of the Scots Irish settlers who inhabited the southern Appalachian Mountains. Kephart was one of the first to seek to describe the "Indigenous" culture of this mountain people, who occupied a place like contemporary ancestors of times past and were fast disappearing. Kephart understood, though, that the Cherokee were the true Indigenous people of the Smokies. He also wrote *The Cherokees of the Smoky Mountains*, which is less well-known but expresses his deep respect and admiration for the people who lived in the mountains long before the white settlers arrived. But Kephart's greatest achievement was as one of the primary leaders of the movement to establish the Great Smoky Mountains National Park, rescuing at least some of his beloved Blue Ridge Mountains from the massive clear-cutting of logging companies during that time.

In a cemetery on a bluff overlooking the town of Bryson City, I walked among the graves until I found his tomb with a memorial tablet attached to a boulder. Kephart died in a tragic road accident in 1931. My visit to honor his grave was the least I could do to show my admiration for this historian, naturalist, and conservationist. In spite of his alcoholism, his separation from a wife and family that he loved and who loved him, Kephart was able as a writer to transcend his brokenness and recreate historical narratives that define Indigenous life in these mountains.

From Bryson City, I made a slight detour up to Robbinsville to another grave and memorial dedicated to the memory of the Cherokee leader Junaluska. According to public memory, as mentioned before, Junaluska saved the life of General Andrew Jackson at the Battle of Horseshoe Bend during the Creek War of 1813. Junaluska's heroic act was remembered as a poignant contrast to President Jackson's betrayal of the Cherokee in his death-dealing removal policies. Junaluska is reported to have said, "If I had known Jackson would drive us from our homes, I would have killed him that day at the Horseshoe."[3] Daughters of the American Revolution had engraved a boulder at the site of Junaluska's grave commemorating his courageous service to Andrew Jackson.[4] In what the historian Andrew Denson called a "repatriated memorial," the Cherokee community of Snowbird commissioned a series of seven panels around the grave telling in fuller detail the remarkable story of Junaluska.

Captured in 1838 by federal troops under General Winfield Scott, Junaluska, like many of his Cherokee contemporaries, was forced on the long death march to the new Indian territory. Junaluska returned after a few years, walking back to the southern highlands, in effect reversing the Trail of Tears. Sometime after that, the United States offered him citizenship and North Carolina gave him a plot of land to live on. In his book *Monuments to Absence*, Denson writes that Junaluska's grave is an example of how history is often a contested space. The Daughters of the American Revolution memorialized Junaluska as "a gesture of respect but also as an act of possession."[5] As an assimilated citizen, Junaluska is reduced to a minor footnote in the unfolding history of the United States. The Cherokee community of Snowbird responded to that characterization and revised it to show Junaluska as an Indigenous leader of his people, in determined resistance to removal. Since that time, the Eastern Band has acquired the site, which has become the destination of a pilgrimage route for Cherokee youth, retraced not westward in the direction of removal but eastward, in the purposeful motion of Junaluska's return.

3. Mooney, *Myths of the Cherokee*, 164.
4. Denson, *Monuments to Absence*, 223.
5. Denson, *Monuments to Absence*, 223.

Primeval Forest

Robbinsville is not far from the Joyce Kilmer National Forest, so I decided I had to gaze once again at giant trees that inhabit this lost cove of old-growth woodland. The forest is aptly named for the poet Joyce Kilmer, whose poem "Trees" was memorized by many school children of my generation ("I think that I will never see / A poem as lovely as a tree . . . Poems are made by fools like me / But only God can make a tree"). The poem has become a cliché, but it takes on new meaning in this forest. I walked among poplar trees almost as large as the fabled redwoods of the West Coast and as old as 450 years (contemporary to the events described in these pages). Here it is easier to imagine the ancient forests that flourished from the Atlantic Coast all the way to the Mississippi River until they were cut down by European settlers.

Apparently, logging companies made three separate attempts to harvest the trees of this beautiful cove. One attempt failed because the company went bankrupt during the Depression. Another attempt was stymied by a stretch of bad weather that made the forest even more inaccessible. And the third attempt, so the legend goes, was forestalled by a revolt of the very loggers hired to do the deed, who refused to cut down such magnificent trees. Again, I give thanks for the life's work of Horace Kephart in preserving the Smoky Mountains from clear-cutting. But before him, before all of us, there was and continues to be an Indigenous people who understood that the trees are human beings' elder siblings, who must be respected and cherished.

Sitting in the forest at Joyce Kilmer, one is naturally inspired to imagine the grandeur of the primeval forest that spread from the Atlantic Coast of North America west to the Mississippi, so dense that the proverbial squirrel could travel that entire expanse without setting a foot on the ground. And surely there is great truth to this ecological vision. The westward advance of European civilization in North America was enacted as one massive logging operation that felled millions of trees. But whatever our longing for a nature untouched by human hands, the myth of the "primeval wilderness" is just that—a myth. North American forests prior to Columbus were not untouched by human hands, but rather were carefully managed by countless woodland Native communities like the Cherokee, who not only preserved them but utilized them through a careful use of fire.

Native use of fire went far beyond the "smoke signals" dramatized in TV westerns of the 1950s that I grew up with. Ethnohistorians have estimated that Native peoples employed fire in dozens of ways to enhance their forest ecosystems. Native peoples like the Cherokee and their ancestors had for generations practiced using fire to manage their forests, including clearing space for village sites and agricultural fields and maintaining their trail routes. They learned that canebrakes, from which they harvested cane for a multitude of uses, could be enhanced by periodic burnings that revitalized that ecosystem and allowed for regenerative growth, as would other crops, such as wild strawberries. With fire, Indigenous people carved pastures out of woodlands and attracted game such as deer and bison. In the fall, they burned off the scrub of a forest understory to make harvesting chestnuts easier. Early Europeans who traveled through the Carolinas, like De Soto, Lawson, and Bartram, left descriptions of the landscapes that provide evidence of the ways Native Americans used wildland burning to shape their environment. Bartram was not alone in describing the ease of travel in open forest floors cleared from undergrowth. The "spacious high forest and flowery lawns" he admired were no doubt managed and shaped by the Cherokees' careful use of fire.

Tree Rings Are a Deep Map

As I walk through Joyce Kilmer Forest, I gaze at magnificent trees that were standing when all the human history that I have been describing was actually happening. I stop at a tree that has fallen across the path and has been cut through to allow passage. Perhaps you too have had the experience of walking along a forest trail and coming upon a fallen tree, have observed the tree rings that layer the trunk across its width. I plop down on a fallen tree to rest and gaze on the trunk that has been cut to clear the trail. I count the rings of the tree, the circular artwork inscribed across the width of the trunk. I recall that each of these rings represents a layer of growth that reveal the history of the tree from its earliest beginnings. Perhaps some of us are aware of how much science can now ascertain about the lifetime of the tree from analyzing the number and texture of its rings.

I first learned about dendrochronology, the scientific study of tree rings, while I was living in Tucson. Andrew Ellicot Douglass, a scientist at the University of Arizona, founded the very first laboratory of tree ring research in America there in 1937. Ironically, Douglass was an astronomer and not a botanist by training. As an astronomer, he had discovered some correlations between tree rings, Earth's climate patterns, and sunspots and cycles of solar activity. Around 1914, an archeologist at the American Museum of Natural History was planning a region-wide survey of Native American ruins in the desert Southwest and had heard a lecture by Douglass on his tree ring research. He contacted Douglass to inquire if he could date timbers found in archeological ruins according to their tree rings. To answer that question, Douglass's career from that point on went veering off in a new direction. Years later, Douglass was able to verify the ages of timbers excavated at none other than Pueblo Bonito, the central complex at Chaco Canyon in northern New Mexico. Tree ring research pioneered by Douglass broke open the field of archeology and our understanding of the history of Native America.

Dendrochronology as a scientific discipline has spread far and wide and is not only able to use tree rings to date the trees but can read them like a book or a map, like windows in time that reveal disturbances that have impacted the tree over its lifetime—hurricanes, drought, insects, disease, fire, and human impacts of logging. If I knew how to read tree rings like a dendrochronologist, I could look at the trunk of this tree in Joyce Kilmer and tell you much about its history and that of the forest to which it belongs.

Tree rings seem to me to be a wonderful metaphor for understanding the history of a growing human being. At the core of who we are is the ring of our time in our mother's womb, then our earliest experiences as an infant, a toddler, a child. Then comes our growing into adolescence, the wonders and challenges of discovering our own bodies, the exploration of relationships beyond our family with people different from ourselves, the evolutions of awareness, to a sense of calling and meaningful work in the larger world. Interwoven through all these stages of growth and development are the seasons of want and plenty, the times of thriving and the scars of hardship. Rings tell of our experiences of the larger world, of the other, larger circles enclosing more of life and a widening embrace of creation.

Extending the metaphor to greater depth, we might see ourselves as occupying a ring of growth that is founded on the rings of generations past—the family tree—a synonym of genealogy. My identity is far more than what has occurred to me in my lifetime. I too am only a ring layer, a living extension of a deeply rooted tree that preceded me and will survive me. This Anderson family history that I have been excavating is much like a tree with its rings of growth, and in those rings we can detect an unfolding story of which I am only one ring in a long succession of growth and development.[6]

The Valley Towns

After my time of reverie in Joyce Kilmer's primeval forest, I continued my journey the next day through the Nantahala Gorge. *Nantahala*, the Cherokee word for "land of the noonday sun," is a fitting name for this gorge, with its steep cliff sides that allow sunlight to reach the valley floor only at noon. Driving alongside the Nantahala River, I recalled white water rafting adventures from previous visits in which I was baptized in the river several times. I was unable to find anyone who could tell me the location of two significant Cherokee towns nearby, but I did find the place where Bartram met Attakullakulla along the river. I drove on into the beautiful area around the town of Andrews, North Carolina, which was once the heart of the Valley Towns, spread out along the Hiwassee River. At what is today an airstrip serving the area, there was once a ceremonial Cherokee mound and the council house of a thriving Cherokee town. The mound was unceremoniously bulldozed to make the airstrip. All around are lush cornfields that hearken back to the time when the valley was the breadbasket of the Cherokee Nation.

Getting a little lost, I made a phone call to Brett Riggs, who got me back on course in my exploration and helped me find the grave of a Cherokee hero, John Welch. Welch was a prosperous Cherokee farmer in the Valley River area, near present-day Andrews, who was able to secure an exemption from removal because of his marriage to a white woman. The Welch farm became a center of Cherokee resistance as he and his family provided food for Cherokee hiding in the mountains and kept fugitives informed of the movements of federal soldiers seeking their capture.

Finally, Welch boldly traveled to Fort Cass, one of the roundup camps where Cherokee were held until removal—now in Eastern

---

6. I recently returned to the Museum of the Cherokee in South Carolina in the town of Walhalla to spend some time with the museum's director, Luther Lyle. He could barely contain his enthusiasm as he showed me his latest acquisition—a large tree trunk on which he traced significant moments in Cherokee history situated at approximate rings.

Tennessee. When Welch went there to assert his rights and claims, he was arrested by General Winfield Scott, commander of the federal forces carrying out the removal operation, and imprisoned at Fort Cass. There, like many of his people, he suffered severely. His health was broken, and he went blind, but his will to resist remained steadfast. Released after the removal operations concluded, Welch returned home and continued to work on behalf of his people. The land he made available to remaining Cherokee became known as Welch's Town.[7]

At a waste and recycling center near Andrews, North Carolina, I parked my car, approached a worker, and asked about the whereabouts of Welch's grave. He immediately stopped what he was doing and escorted me behind some industrial trash bins into a scraggly patch of woods. In the thick of it he pointed out the well-tended grave of John Welch and told me that Cherokee visited at least once a year to make sure the grave was weeded and cared for. The Cherokee do not forget to honor their ancestors.

On a return trip to Cherokee to attend a Trail of Tears conference, I had the good fortune of getting to know Dr. Lance Greene, an archeologist and scholar of Cherokee history who has written a book on Welch as representative of one Cherokee community in active resistance to removal. His research conclusively demonstrates that the resistance to removal was not simply a matter of a handful of Cherokee running away from soldiers to hide in the mountains. Rather, it was a carefully planned strategy to carve out sanctuaries where Cherokee could remain in their homeland.

Fort Butler

I continued down the valley and reached Murphy, a thriving little mountain town in the farthest western corner of North Carolina. There I located the Cherokee Museum and saw its impressive exhibits. My first order of business was to find the location of the site of Fort Butler, the prison camp in Murphy where the Cherokee were concentrated before removal. A local historian happened to overhear my queries at the museum's information desk about how to find it, and volunteered to take me there, indicating that it was not far but was a little hard to find. Twisting and turning up a hill in Murphy, we came to the inauspicious site of Fort

7. Denson, *Monuments to Absence*, 41.

Butler on the hilltop overlooking the Hiwassee River. I am hopeful that the historically minded in the town of Murphy would like to do more to commemorate this historic site, and perhaps that will yet happen, but now, it feels like a neglected place that cries out for memorialization.

Leaving Murphy, I headed east toward Haysville through a spectacularly beautiful valley of rolling hills and pastures and views of the river. I was looking in vain for the Peachtree mound, which I think is on private property. But as I turned around to get back on track, I discovered along the way a historical marker to a Cherokee boarding school run by Baptist missionaries. The Baptists did not approach Cherokee culture exactly the way the Presbyterians did. The Baptist mission located in the Valley Towns, run by the minister the Reverend Evan Jones, was similar to other mission schools in creating a model farm, a blacksmith shop, and grist mill, as a means of sustaining the school and providing vocational training for their students. But the Valley Mission was different under the leadership of Reverend Jones. He learned the Cherokee language, translated the New Testament into Cherokee, and taught his students in their mother tongue. Among his students were future leaders who would oppose removal. When removal finally came, the school was dissolved.

Reaching Haysville, I dawdled in their historical museum right on the town square. Behind the museum was a replica of a Cherokee dwelling worth seeing. This was a hardy structure made from clay and river cane that reminded me a little of the adobe construction of Indigenous lodgings in the desert Southwest. Haysville was the location of Fort Hembree, another Cherokee concentration camp. Standing in the locations of Fort Hembree and Fort Butler, I found it difficult to register my own feelings about these historical locations of great suffering for the Cherokee people. I remembered a similar feeling when, as a college student studying in Europe, I visited Dachau, the Nazi concentration camp outside Munich. I could not absorb the reality of that place then, nor can I now. There are those who would react negatively to referring to the internment camps the US government used for Native peoples in the southeast as "concentration camps," resenting the comparison to the death camps of Nazi Germany. But concentration camps they were: that was precisely their function. In these compounds, breeding grounds for disease, many Native people died—abused, ill-housed, sick, hungry, and exposed to the elements.

Isabel Wilkerson, in her book *Caste*, is not the first or only scholar to point out Hitler's studious fascination with the system of segregation in the South as a model for the Nazi program of racial purification in Germany. Hitler also praised the United States' near genocide of Native Americans. Susan Neiman writes: "Hitler took American westward expansion, with its destruction of Native peoples, as the template he said was needed to provide Germans with the room to live."[8] After all, long before Nazi policy makers debated the final solution to the "Jewish question," the policy makers of the United States debated the "Indian question." The outcome of those policy debates was the near extinction of Indigenous people, a distinctly American holocaust. The people of Germany today are far ahead of the citizens of the United States in facing their history and reckoning with the magnitude of the evil of racial oppression. I hope that this book will be one small contribution to moving the country I love toward a truthful reckoning with our history toward Native peoples.

Returning toward Murphy, I made a quick stop at the famous John C. Campbell Folk School. I harbor a dream of returning someday to take a class on basket weaving or wood turning. On their campus they have nurtured a canebrake of our southern bamboo. Walking there helped me visualize the flora that once abounded across the Southeast. The historian Claudio Saunt describes how the Cherokee used river cane: for "housing, fencing, forage, constructing fish traps, grinding flour from seeds, and treating various ailments. From cane, the Cherokee crafted furniture, wove mats and baskets, fabricated musical instruments, built rafts, and treated various ailments. Before the arrival of European firearms, they employed cane for making weapons like the blowgun and even armor." Part of the tragedy of being uprooted from the land you have known for centuries is the loss of a deep knowledge of the habitat gained over countless generations. The use of river cane is just one example of the Cherokees' multigenerational expertise in flora and fauna. As the Cherokee sought to rebuild their lives in the Indian territories beyond the Mississippi river, cane was nowhere to be found.[9]

What had already been a long day got longer as I headed out of Murphy on the historic Unicoi Turnpike, an ancient trade route that connected English traders with the different settlements of the Cherokee Nation. The turnpike also became the route of the Cherokee who were deported by the US army from the Valley Towns on the Trail of Tears. As I drove along, the turnpike became a gravel road and seemed to go on

---

8. Neiman, *Learning from the Germans.*
9. Saunt, *Unworthy Republic,* 197–98.

endlessly up and down over mountains. Finally, I emerged from the forest at a remote Tennessee crossroads and found yet another little museum, staffed by a lovely matriarch who was a fountain of historical information and eager to share it. I regret that by this time, exhausted by the journey, I was less interested in all that I might learn from her. Continuing on my way, I was chased by a massive storm system—pouring rain, thunder, and lightning—as I drove toward Fort Loudoun.

Fort Loudoun today is an impressive replica of the colonial fort. Across the lake is the Tellico Blockhouse, the site of another village, mission school, and a trading post. Near the fort is the Sequoyah Museum, commemorating the Cherokee genius who created the written Cherokee language. Sequoyah's linguistic accomplishment revolutionized the Cherokee Nation, providing them with a written alphabet and language that was immediately accessible to most of the Cherokee people. Many of the sites of the Overhill Towns today are, like Keowee and other Lower Towns in South Carolina, submerged under lakes that resulted from vast hydroelectric projects decades ago. The location of Chota, the mother town of the Overhill Cherokee, is marked by an impressive display on the edge of a lake. But it was here, somewhat like Bartram, that I just ran out of steam and decided to turn around and head home. A proper exploration of the Overhill Towns and their history will require another journey to this beautiful area in eastern Tennessee.

A Cherokee "Trail of Tears" Pilgrimage?

There was a purpose to my wanderings through Cherokee country. I was hoping to discern a pathway for a penitential pilgrimage for my fellow Presbyterians, acknowledging our church's and our nation's complicity in the dispossession of the Indigenous peoples of the southeast. The purpose of such a pilgrimage would be to honor and understand Cherokee history, culture, and spirituality, past and the present. To understand and grieve the injustice of Indian removal and the Cherokee Trail of Tears. To examine the complex legacy of Christianity within Cherokee history. To confront the ongoing legacy of white supremacy within us and in American race relations and articulate a path of repentance from this racism. To seek a new beginning in the church's encounter and relations with Indigenous peoples.[10]

---

10. This pilgrimage has not yet been accomplished. The pandemic happened and this

The Trail of Tears has a unique place in the telling of American history. Sometimes, white historians have been willing to acknowledge it but only as a tragic aberration of US history rather than the very pattern of dispossession of Indigenous people, carried out brutally and continuously, upon which our nation was built. The Trail has so often been sanitized and rendered innocuous as a story about the disappearance of Indians in the distant past. Even the name "Trail of Tears" obscures the full measure of the dispossession of Native peoples from their land. Claudio Saunt accurately describes the full measure of the dispossession of Native peoples through active synonyms: forced migration, ethnic cleansing, deportation, extermination, genocide.[11]

---

and other difficulties prevented us from undertaking this pilgrimage. Since that time, I have continued to think about it and have had time to question some of my own assumptions. What role should Cherokee people play in this pilgrimage? I need to be wary of the white do-gooder syndrome that plunges ahead with oblivious good intentions. And I am aware that the Cherokee, like other communities of color, grow weary of the needs of white people to unload white guilt or seek cheap grace. Even more troublesome is the desire of white folks to appropriate Native spiritual traditions for themselves.

I am convinced that white people have our own work to do, and we cannot continue to ask Indigenous or other communities of color to hold our hands and bless us while we do that work. Apologies for what has been done in the past are not the culmination of a process of reconciliation but merely the beginning point that should lead to meaningful and tangible expressions of reparations and repair. I have wondered if my fascination with Cherokee history is like the other "monuments to absence" that the historian Andrew Denson so ably clarified, a romantic portrayal of Indian disappearance. What do I have to offer, what can I do to continue walking this path? At the very least I need to make for myself the pilgrimage along the Trail of Tears. The writing of this book has felt very much like a pilgrimage. And it is a pilgrimage that I will continue into the future.

11. Saunt, *Unworthy Republic*, xiii.

14

Doing History

ONE OF THE JOYS of this writing process has been the discovery of an academic historian whose research and writing has opened up fresh vistas, new perspectives on the trail I have been following. Reading a brilliant history like Claudio Saunt's *Unworthy Republic* can be like inviting a distinguished historian into your home as a resident scholar and, through leisurely conversation, having him fill in gaps and make connections in the larger narrative you are weaving. The bibliography at the end of this book is not an obligatory afterthought for me. It is a grateful listing of mentors who have blessed me with their hard work and eloquence. Before I define the work of what "public history" has come to mean for me and distinguish how it differs from academic history, I want to acknowledge my own indebtedness to the many historians mentioned throughout, from whom I have learned so much.

WHAT IS PUBLIC HISTORY?

So, what is public history? My grandfather was an example of a public historian, as he advocated for the erection of historical markers, helped to organize historical pageants, and was called upon to speak at public occasions of historical significance. It turns out that after the spectacular success of the *Keowee Trail Pageant* in 1921, my grandfather sought to capitalize on the public's interest in local history. He wrote a letter to the editor of the *Greenville Piedmont*, calling for the creation of a historical society focused on upstate South Carolina. Recognizing that the state historical society headquartered in Charles Town was perhaps understandably focused more on the history of the low country, he lamented that in the up-country many historic sites were being lost through neglect. "There are many places within a short automobile ride of Greenville, which are of great historical value, and which at present are unmarked, many of them scarcely known. The site of Fort Prince George is marked only by a mulberry tree, which is said to have been planted by the British soldiers of its garrison. A few years ago, when I first visited the site of this old fort, the lines of its fortification were to be plainly seen. When I was there this summer on my most recent visit to this historic spot the earthworks had been entirely obliterated by the plow and the elements." He further noted a similar neglect at the site of the fort at Ninety-Six.

Alongside the copy of this opinion letter was an action plan for creating such a society that is an impressive vision of how to begin. I don't know if he generated this himself or if he derived it from research he did, or if this action plan was published.

1. Send letters to schools, colleges, universities, libraries, and newspapers telling of your organization, your aims, and inviting suggestions from them.
2. Send letters to other historical associations and ask for a report of their work.
3. Seek information about old landmarks and points of historic interest, old legends from early history, old manuscripts owned by families, stories of early setters, old pictures and relics, historical data about your area.
4. Personal visits when possible to these points of interest to inspire the community to mark these places on special holidays or anniversaries.

And so on, he recommended working with the state board of education, the founding of a museum or art gallery, and promotion of filmmaking and more historical plays. Apparently his advocacy was successful, and the Upper South Carolina Historical Society was created, and he served as president. In the sixties, it was reorganized as the Greenville Historical Society and exists to this day.

My trail mentor Dennis Chastain, who is constantly giving lectures and presentations on the Keowee Trail, is a public historian. Luther Lyle is another prime example, the founder of the Museum of the Cherokee in South Carolina. Public history is the work of history done outside of a traditional academic setting by those who may not possess the normal credentials of an academic historian. Public history is applied history, put to work in a variety of settings to address concerns and questions in a real-world historical context. Public historians may be museum professionals, cultural resource stewards, archivists, conservationists, local historians, and community activists—in short, all those for whom the interpretation of history is a necessary dimension in their work. Most broadly speaking, public history is a social movement that includes an even wider range: anyone who might make a pilgrimage to a battlefield, visit a museum, watch a documentary, volunteer with a historical society, or research their own family history.

I certainly did not think of myself as a public historian, not even in 1992, when I was working on the Columbus quincentenary, or more recently when I was involved in efforts in several North Carolina communities to commemorate lynchings of African Americans. Or, even more recently, when I journeyed to Alabama with a group of Presbyterians to immerse myself in civil rights history in Birmingham, Montgomery, and Selma. In fact, the first time I remember hearing the phrase "public historian" was over coffee with a colleague of mine on the faculty of the Wake Forest School of Divinity. I was quizzing her about her experience of taking students on a historical tour of the Cherokee Trail of Tears.

As I mentioned earlier, I have wanted to design such an experience for Presbyterians as a kind of penitential pilgrimage. She offered a wealth of insight and experience about the challenges to such an undertaking, and in the course of our conversation, she may have said something like, "... your work as a public historian." This startled me. Is that what I am? It felt like a naming experience in which you feel your identity invoked more deeply, calling you to a particular kind of work. At that point in my life, it felt primarily aspirational. But then I realized that this vocational identity was something I have been pursuing for years. What's more, it was a vocation modeled for me by my grandfather. He and I have come to widely different conclusions about the history of the South. Nevertheless, he forged a path that I am following, and for that I am grateful. However, the conversation between us is far from finished. His influence on me and the differences in our understanding of southern history extended into the American Civil War and Reconstruction.

There is another way in which public history can be distinguished from much of academic history as it has been practiced in the past (though that is rapidly evolving). Public history may be more interdisciplinary in content and rely on collaborative efforts within the community. The collaborative nature of public history is especially inherent in the "deep map" approach of time and place that I have pursued here, which invites, indeed requires, multiple perspectives and various angles. Because public history is applied history for the good of the public, it aims to equip and empower communities with connection to their past. Knowledge of the past becomes applied history especially when we are seeking greater awareness of how the past defines the present for good or ill. Many public historians may in fact seek to interpret how the past has defined the present in order to open up different possibilities for the future in contemporary struggles for equity and justice.

The racially enlightened public historian is fighting for an oppressed past, as the scholar Avery Gordon argues in her book *Ghostly Matters*, by carefully excavating it out of a homogenous history of white, nationalist civilization. Public history, as I have come to embrace it, is the struggle to reclaim what is seen as dead history, successfully buried in forgetfulness, repressed by collective amnesia, but is nonetheless alive and operating in the present even if barely visible. Indeed, to fight for an oppressed past is to make this past come alive as the lever for the work of the present: obliterating the sources and conditions that link the violence of the past to the present, ending that history and setting in place a different future.[1]

A PHILOSOPHY OF HISTORY

As an aspiring public historian, I have a simple philosophy that guides my work: history is not a straight line. Time is not linear. It is a curious thing that most human beings who think and live in time have so completely accepted, if unconsciously, the notion that time is a straightforward progression from past to present to future with hard, fixed boundaries separating distinct zones of time. It's curious because all the realities that define time are in fact circular: the daily spinning of the Earth in and out of the sun's light, the annual rotation of our planet around our star, and perhaps on a grander scale of deep time, the rotation of our solar system around the Milky Way Galaxy, requiring millions upon millions of years. It is curious but understandable that we perceive time as linear since we lack perspective and cannot easily see the curve in time's circumference.

---

1. Gordon, *Ghostly Matters*, 66.

History, like time, has a circular shape that is hard to perceive except from a distance. There are times when history feels like nothing more than a futile repetition of forces—when, with the author of Ecclesiastes, we feel that there is nothing new under the sun, that all is futility. The circular shape of history often does appear to devolve into vicious cycles of violence that seem to go on wreaking havoc for generation upon generation, making us question if humankind has made any progress whatsoever. And then there are moments when history can also ascend in a wide arc that promises change and even future possibilities of transformation. History depicted as a spiral recognizes simultaneously the repetitive nature of time and the possibility of novelty, creativity, and progress. Similar to the Reverend Martin Luther King Jr.'s proclamation, the arc of history is long, but it bends toward justice.

History as a spiral also suggests that there can be moments in the present that, while seemingly far removed chronologically from a more distant past, can in fact be proximate to one another, next door if you will. Side-by-side moments in a circular, spiraling history can exert a magnetic influence between them. How often have I felt this during this writing process over the last few years. We have lived through a period when our democracy has faced multiple authoritarian threats and a resurgence of racism, hate, and xenophobia. The veil has been torn aside and we have seen the ugliest part of our national character. Alongside this, we also see the best that we can be. The borders between the past, the present, and the future are not solid, hard walls but porous boundaries that waver and shift.

Temporality is the human condition. Each of us knows the finitude of a human life, circumscribed as it is by our birth and our death. But temporality is more than the limits of an individual life span. To be a mortal creature is to live in time, to be embedded in history. To be fully human is to know that history lives in us and that we live in history. To be fully historical beings is to bring greater awareness to the ways in which the past ripples through our present and how unknown possibilities spring from our present toward the future. To live in the present moment is to exist inside a temporal halo formed by the horizons of past and future. The past and the future permeate each other inside of a porous present, a wavering now. It is this wavering present that is open to a great circle of being, of those who went before and those who will come after.

With this significant anniversary of the American Revolution approaching, we have yet another opportunity to focus our attention as the people of the United States on the whole truth of our nation's history. I certainly hope that the Keowee Trail will become a central narrative in the way we understand the history of the Carolinas and the multifaceted encounter between white settlers and the Cherokee. I believe the deep map approach is one way to capture many different perspectives in a variety of modalities. At the beginning of this narrative, I mentioned my indebtedness to Deborah Kirk, the Cherokee scholar who introduced me to the deep map way of interpreting history. Everything about her vision of a deep map approach to the Cherokee Trail of Tears could be applied to the Keowee Trail.

I hope that what I have offered here makes it abundantly clear that the Trail of Tears began with the Keowee Trail; they are part and parcel of the same historical reality. Imagine a documented route along the Keowee Trail that pilgrim travelers could utilize, available online for greater context, perspective, and commentary at each step and landmark along the way. Dennis Chastain tells me that the State Commission for the Sesquicentennial Celebration of the American Revolution has asked him to establish the GPS coordinates of the Keowee Trail as it crosses the state. This is an important and necessary first step. On that basis, one could dare to imagine a deep map online resource for the Keowee Trail, accessible to all and receptive to new contributions from local communities.

Perhaps a first step toward that end could be planning for a consultation to be held during the commemoration at a place like Ninety-Six, or the Cherokee Museum in Walhalla, South Carolina, or at the Nikwasi Initiative in Franklin, North Carolina. Maybe Clemson University, which resides in Cherokee territory, might play a convening role, offering hospitality and historical expertise to representatives from all along the trail. This would be an opportunity for various stakeholders and professionals including parks and recreation staff, archeologists, historians, community development officers, and other interested lay people to gather and brainstorm ideas about a long-range plan for the Cherokee Path.

I have been deeply encouraged by the ways museum professionals have expanded the interpretive lenses of our history to include communities of color and their significant contributions to the American story. I am confident that there are many within a new generation of museum professionals of today who would be among the first to say that there is more to be done, that the work must continue. May those cultural stewards of historic sites find ever more creative ways to interpret the significance of landmarks in their care, recognizing that these sites are becoming pilgrimage destinations for many US citizens who long to know and are ready to learn our full history. May local historians bring fresh eyes to how they help interpret history through the stories of particular times and places, deepening a sense of belonging and inclusion that springs from a shared history and a common legacy.

Many communities in the Carolinas have already discovered the socioeconomic benefits for developing trails, including my hometown of Greenville with their wildly successful Swamp Rabbit Trail. (My grandparents as young adults used to take the Swamp Rabbit Train to the North Carolina mountains to escape the summer heat in Greenville.) My current home, Elkin, the official Trail Town of North Carolina, is the trail head for the Overmountain Victory Trail leading to Kings Mountain. The Mountain-to-Sea Trail across North Carolina runs through Elkin. And many are enjoying kayaking our blue trail: the Yadkin River. Would there be similar interest in the communities along the Keowee Trail to develop a local strategy for respectful commemoration of the story of the Cherokee in the Carolinas? This book is my prayer that it may be so.

Beyond my own fascination with the Keowee Trail, I hope that more academic historians will emerge from what has been the relative safety of academic life to join the fight for an oppressed history. Academic historians are well aware of the growing political pressure to adapt their "product" to reflect a one-sided version of American history. We need all the help we can get in pushing back on the whitewashing of our collective history. We need professional historians more willing to get their hands dirty in the struggle for a truthful reckoning with the story of our country. While I remain indebted to the scholarship of academic historians, like Tiya Miles and Claudio Saunt, and all the historians associated with the 1619 Project, I hope others will flex their muscles in applying their historical research and writing to the needs of local communities and our larger society. The same should be said about church historians. I hope and pray that there will be colleagues in my Presbyterian church and other denominations who will inquire more honestly into the mixed legacy of the historical journey of the church in US history. The church's support for slavery and for Native dispossession has yet to be fully named, confessed, and atoned for.[2]

---

2. Thankfully this work has been carried on by such historians as Dr. Erskine Clarke, retired professor of religious history at Columbia Theological Seminary in Decatur, Georgia. And that critical perspective is continued by another historian at Columbia, Dr. William Yoo, with the outstanding book entitled *What Kind of Christianity: A*

It has been several years since I have visited Mepkin Abbey, my spiritual retreat and the place where my trail journal began, at the plantation home of Henry Laurens along the Cooper River, near Charles Town. I finally returned needing to nourish my connection to the monastic community there. And I've been very curious to see their truth and reconciliation memorial that I heard was in the works, as I mentioned earlier. As I walked past what was the location of Laurens's original manor, I crossed over a ravine on a footbridge the monks have built that leads to the Laurens family cemetery. There in front of the cemetery is a path in the shape of a figure eight around which are situated various commemorative stations. The texts below are a sampling from those stations that I think best captures the spirit of the memorial.

The Meditation Garden of Truth and Reconciliation at Mepkin Abbey:

> Station 1: Crossing Over
>
> We ask that you reflect upon the First Peoples on the American continent for whom this land is sacred and that you consider the millions of individuals who crossed over multiple waters as part of their journey to this place. consider how these peoples continue to transform the landscape of our continent. consider our diversity as Native Americans, Europeans, Africans, Hispanics, and Asians.
>
> With a shared past, our points of contact were often antagonistic, which led to harsh and brutal actions; some peoples were forced to labor, which led to suffering, isolation, and in the earliest of cases, annihilation. We each carry forward the pain of this history in distinct ways as we converge as one American people. Christian theology teaches that suffering may also be transformative—if we focus on how it may unite us with Christ's passion in His final hours. Embracing our shared suffering may help us develop a more genuine empathy for each other and support our observation of the second commandment: "Love your neighbor as yourself" (Matthew 22:39).
>
> Station 2: Our Worlds Meet
>
> We come to this place from differing origins. Our shared truth is that we are all here now choosing to help each other.
>
> There is pain in our shared past. Many of these diverse ancestors built lives together while others killed the indigenous and

---

History of Slavery and Anti-Black Racism in the Presbyterian Church. Reading this book should be required reading for all ordained leaders, clergy, and lay elders alike.

enslaved for bounty, stole their legacies and land, and destroyed their lives. But we have endured and remain.

The lives we have built together have been mixed with joy and pain. Here we remember our ancestors, their stories, and their experiences. Our races and cultures have mixed together.

We can choose to focus on a movement of Truth, Forgiveness, Reconciliation, and Healing to live together in Peace and in the Light of God.

Station 6: Truth, Forgiveness, Reconciliation, and Healing

In our respective spiritual journeys, each of us may ask ourselves if our capacity for love and trust will ultimately triumph over our capacity for fear and hatred.

Our nation has a complicated and troubling past, but we are not solely defined by it. Although incomplete knowledge of the past may bias, shape, and limit our present understanding, a better vision for our shared future is possible.

Crucial to our potential for facilitating reparative social justice and seeking redemption are our emotions of compassion and empathy. We are capable of inquiry, new discovery, and of collective and individual growth. As humans, possessing the faculty of reason and free will, we are able to learn, adjust, and adapt. We are capable of correcting falsehoods and superstitions with facts when new reliable information is provided. We are able to develop a well-formed conscience and choose Christ the path to a redemptive future.

For then "You will know the truth, and the truth will set you free" (John 8:32).

Finally, I hope that every family will become more curious about their origins and come together to dig into the stories of their past. The potential for family history goes far beyond collecting genealogical information. Family history can be a means of recognizing the traumas that reverberate from the past to the present. In facing those traumas, I believe we will be able to claim new possibilities for healing, growth, and resilience. When white folks scratch the surface of our family history, we begin to dismantle whiteness as our defining cultural identity. We reclaim a more authentic and complex multiethnic lineage that reaches out in many directions, making connections with others who once seemed so different.

In *Healing Haunted History* by Myers and Enns, the authors describe three lines of inquiry woven together like a braid for those of us who engage in exploring our family history.

Bloodlines: Our blood not only carries white cells that fight off infection and red cells that carry oxygen to every part of the body, but our blood also carries our genetic blueprint, our DNA, that we inherited from our ancestors and that tells us who we are. This first area of inquiry is a focus brought to bear on the family and genetic bloodline of our ancestors. Some of us may possess a family tree that depicts the flow of generations, genealogies that track births and deaths and provide a factual foundation from which to begin. Some extremely fortunate families like mine have ample documentation of their histories in the form of letters, journals, and articles about their ancestors. European Americans are coming to understand that this is another example of white privilege, the possession of documentation around which we can give substance to the family narrative. Other families, especially within communities of color including those who have experienced slavery, displacement, violence, or even genocide may not have ample documentation and must resort to imaginative and creative means to reconstruct narratives that have been rendered invisible or lost. And some, like the descendants of enslaved ancestors, have little choice but to utilize the records of their ancestors' enslavers. Exploring bloodlines may also include people with whom we do not share genetic lineage, such as people who journeyed with our ancestors in meaningful ways. Bloodlines includes more than genealogy or even exact genetic heritage. It is an embodied story that may include people and places alongside our families.

Landlines: The second area of inquiry creates a space in which we can map the immigration journeys of our ancestors. We seek to understand the push and pull of historical forces that motivated their families to leave one place and migrate to another. Were our ancestors refugees from violence or disaster? Were they seeking freedom of religious expression or searching for entrepreneurial opportunity? Were they already in America facing the onslaught of settlers coming from afar or were they kidnapped and forced into enslaved labor? How did our ancestors get here and how did they respond to the ones they encountered? Who was in the place of our origins before our ancestors arrived and who followed them? How have these immigration journeys been inscribed in the history of the land? How does the land itself hold the traumas of racial violence?

Song lines: The final area of inquiry is symbolized in the ancient aboriginal tradition of song lines. This practice of some Indigenous people enabled them to navigate long journeys because they had been taught songs that could be sung identifying landmarks along the route as a kind of map, a sung map. Song lines in the context of a writing project like this one will be sought in stories from the past that uplift and inspire us about the potential for justice and compassion. These stories may be found in our ancestors, or in others who embody a social vision that promises equality and human flourishing that gives hope for the future. These song lines may be heard in our family narratives or in those of people quite different from our ancestors. These song lines might be expressed through belonging in alternative traditions or by participation in movements for change. Identifying these song lines of goodness and resilience has the potential to bring us forward from the past to face the present with courage and the future with greater hope.

I hope each one of us will come to recognize our place in history as temporal beings, to understand that we who live today are connected to a long line of ancestors who came before us and equally to a line of descendants reaching into a hopeful future where all our differences can be affirmed and celebrated as part of a magnificent, multicolored fabric. And that each one of us can see ourselves, not as an object of history, determined by circumstances beyond our control, but as a subject of history with agency to construct a future. And may we together build a more perfect union, a multiracial democracy with liberty and justice for all.

15

Coming Full Circle

THE STORY OF THE Cherokee people began with the sacred town of Kituwah where, according to tradition, they first emerged from the earth. It seems fitting that this story I have been weaving would end here at Kituwah as well. As I described earlier, the second day of the Trail of Tears conference 2022 was to be a pilgrimage through the Cherokee cultural corridor that included a visit to Nikwasi and an all-too-fleeting view of Watauga and Cowee. We left Cowee and made our way through the mountains until we came again to the Mother Town of Kituwah. A Cherokee elder who had come from Oklahoma to be a part of this conference said, "We have all heard that to be here is like coming home. But it is more profound than even that. To be here is like coming back to the very beginning of our people."

Once before, I had driven through this beautiful valley and stopped to read the historical marker dedicated to Kituwah. Knowing that this sacred site had been returned to the Cherokee Nation, I had not been sure if further exploration would be trespassing. But now, on this return trip, I knew we were welcome, and I was eager to soak up the ambiance of the place. There is a spiritual quality of timelessness at Kituwah, what my Celtic ancestors from Scotland might have called a "thin place" where the boundary between the temporal and the eternal is thin or porous. Here is the point of origin for the Cherokee people; here they emerged from the earth as the principal people. Here the sacred fire was maintained in the council house on what was once a twenty-foot-high mound in the center of the village. From this fire, the separate fires of each Cherokee family and other villages were maintained. Here in this place are layers of

Cherokee history sitting lightly one upon another, including the stories of a great Cherokee chief by the name of Yonagusta.

THE GREAT CHIEF YONAGUSTA

When the Cherokee had lost almost all of their homeland, they somehow hung on to Kituwah through the courageous effort of leaders like the great chief Yonagusta. Yonagusta was born in 1759, on the eve of the Cherokee War of 1760–1761. (His name means "Drowning Bear"—how I wish I knew the story behind that.) He came of age during the continuation of that war in the American Revolution. He most certainly would have fought as a warrior against the forces of General Rutherford, whose North Carolina militia invaded Kituwah and the Out Towns along the Tuckasegee River and destroyed them. Yonagusta was a strikingly handsome man at six foot, three inches, with a strong build and a gift for oratory. His adopted son was the famous Will Thomas, a white trader who championed the cause of the Cherokee, beginning with his advocacy in the halls of power in Washington, DC. As it became clear that his diplomatic effort to protect Cherokee sovereignty would fail, Thomas assisted Yonagusta and other Cherokee communities in purchasing land that could become their private property. Even after the treaty of 1819, when the Cherokee were being pressured to cede all their remaining land along the Tuckasegee River, Thomas was able to purchase and set aside 640 acres, including Kituwah, for Yonagusta.

Two stories must be passed down concerning Yonagusta. We know that the introduction of alcohol by white civilization had a devastating impact upon Indigenous peoples and, in particular, on Cherokee culture, destroying far too many Cherokee families. Yonagusta did not escape this addiction, which caused his health to collapse. Finally, he fell into an alcohol-induced coma. Thinking he was dead, the Cherokee began to mourn him, but twenty-four hours later, he regained consciousness and declared that he had been to the spirit land and had returned with a message. He would never again drink alcohol, and he was determined to lead his people to sobriety. The Cherokee communities who respected his leadership and vision became a "temperance society" in the best sense of that word—a community in recovery.

The second story, related to us by Horace Kephart, concerns the translation of the Bible into Cherokee. When a translation of the Gospel of Matthew was brought to Kituwah country, Yonagusta insisted that it be read to him before he allowed it to be available to his people. After hearing a couple of chapters, the old chief dryly remarked, "Well, it seems to be a good book—strange that the white people are not better, having had it so long." In the year 1839, one year after removal, when Yonagusta was about eighty years of age, he sensed death was near and decided to speak one last time to his people, urging them never to leave their country. Having issued this exhortation, he wrapped himself in a blanket, lay down, and died.[1] Kituwah was beloved of Yonagusta. His spirit is a part of that sacred place.

SITTING BY THE TUCKASEGEE

Cherokee women treated us to their singing and Cherokee men even invited us to join them in dances. Before dinner was to be served to all of us underneath a big tent at Kituwah, I took a stroll down a beaten path. To one side was a corn field, to the other the faint remains of the original mound, which had been plowed down by white farmers who once owned the land. The path took me to the edge of the Tuckasegee River, and I enjoyed the "Long Man" once more, his quiet current flowing past me in the evening light. The voice of a woman behind me, a Cherokee leader from Oklahoma, asked me if I would mind having some company. "Of course, not," I responded. As we admired the river flowing past us, I shared with her that "going to the water" was the aspect of Cherokee spirituality and tradition that I most appreciated. Though I can never know exactly what going to the water might have meant for the Cherokee long ago or what it might mean for them today, intuitively, I believe it was a recognition that water is life: a sacred resource that sustained them and provided for them, a beautiful current running through their lives, a medium of cleansing and rebirth.

When I think about the journey that I have been on in writing this book, some of the most important characters in this story have been the rivers that define the landscape: the Keowee, the Tugaloo, and the Chattooga feeding into the Savannah. The Reedy and the Saluda. The French Broad. The Little Tennessee. The Yadkin. Recall that two of my Anderson ancestors were named after rivers: Tyger Jim and his cousin Enoree Jim. Such is the nature of the river that flows around us and through us. Growing up in the mountains of the Carolinas I was significantly shaped by the sensual experience of water. Just up the road from my hometown

---

1. Kephart, *Cherokees of the Smoky Mountains*, 31.

of Greenville near our family cabin in western North Carolina, there are many spectacular waterfalls in what is now Dupont State Forest. Since I was a child, I have hiked to one waterfall called Bridal Veil where scenes from the movie *Last of the Mohicans* were shot. You can climb down underneath and behind this waterfall and yet remain somewhat dry. As a thunderous flow of water passes over and all around you feel that you are inside a water world; you feel as if you have become the water itself. We human beings are made up, after all, of 60 percent water.

What is a watershed? It is a region or area of land draining into a river. There are two thousand watersheds in the United States. All of them include multiple sub-watersheds of smaller rivers and streams flowing around us and, in the water we drink, through us. Water is the architect that designs the shape of the earth we live on. Water finds its way, carving contours in the land. You can see this clearly hiking anywhere in the Blue Ridge Mountains. As you walk along trails you will notice springs turning into streams, all flowing down, carving pathways as they follow the course of gravity, flowing together, rivulets becoming modest creeks, then more fulsome streams, until they become strong and mighty rivers, finally finding their way toward the unity of oceans.

Remember John Lane, the kayaker on Lake Keowee that I mentioned at the beginning of this narrative. As a naturalist, he has taught countless school children—and me—that a watershed is our ecological address: the location of the life community we are a part of is sustained by water. This life community doesn't just mean the human species but all life: the Appalachian brook trout that needs the cold, clear water of shaded mountain streams or the bog turtle that requires deep, muddy wetland areas. Other members of the watershed community include the kingfisher and the heron, the beaver, and the deer. The rivers themselves as living beings have their requirements for vitality and, I believe, their inherent right to a sustainable life.

My own life pilgrimage, which has brought me to this point, is a story that could be told by water. I have heard antiracism educators speak of the need for profound change in the "groundwaters" of our culture, the aquifer of our collective consciousness. I hope that what I have done here will be one small contribution toward detoxifying the groundwaters of our ecosystem.[2]

---

2. I fell in love with flowing water in the mountains of Carolina. But it was not until I moved to the desert Southwest that I began to fully appreciate water. In the desert you cannot take water for granted. You cannot go hiking for any distance without a good supply of water. And when you see a ribbon of green life cutting through the desert,

THE RESILIENCE OF THE CHEROKEE PEOPLE

At Kituwah, after dinner under an open tent, we heard from Tom Belt, a Cherokee elder and coordinator of the Cherokee Language Program of Western Carolina University, which seeks to preserve and revitalize the Cherokee language and culture. He was born in Oklahoma but returned to the Qualla Boundary of the Eastern Band in the early 1990s. After hearing him, it was not difficult to imagine that it was the spirit of Yonagusta that was speaking through him. Standing just a few feet from me, he addressed our assembly in a humble monotone, which could tempt his hearers to miss the import of his words. Never changing that cadence, his words nevertheless began to carry a growing power, such that you wanted to write down all that he was saying, lest you forget. Only afterward, riding back to Cherokee in the bus, could I jot down a few remembrances of what he said to us, preserving only a weak paraphrase here.

It went something like this:

> We remember the Trail of Tears and the removal of our people from their land not because we relish victimhood and/or wish to dwell on the suffering of our people in the past. We remember the Trail of Tears to lay claim to the resilience of our people then and now, their courage to move forward and build a new future. We could have given up after removal. But we didn't. What held us together as a people, what they could not take from us, is our identity. We are people of this place. Our strength is in knowing who we are. We are people of this place. Our purpose is to be here. To care for this land, our home.

Perhaps it was in this moment, as I listened to this wise Cherokee elder speak to us from his heart, that I began to realize the full value of an

---

whether cottonwood trees or cactus, you know that water is present. In the desert as nowhere else, you know that water cannot be taken for granted. Water is life. Water is sacred. When I left the desert Southwest and returned to North Carolina, it seemed to me that the abundance of water resources in our state could make it very easy to take water for granted. My new home of Elkin has a river running through it, the Yadkin River. My house looks out on the river. I began to learn more about the wonders of our Yadkin River and the surrounding watershed. Shortly after moving back to North Carolina, I had the opportunity to start a nonprofit organization to preserve and protect the watershed of Elkin Creek, the water source for my community in the town of Elkin. Over a ten-year period, Watershed Now has been working with our local schools, our town council and staff, and area landowners and farmers to conserve our creek as a vital resource that deserves our care and protection. We believe that you cannot save something until you love it, and you can't love it until you know it.

ethics of remembering that calls the past into the present for the sake of a different future.

In Tom Belt's words I heard a deep determination to protect and preserve the sacred landscape of the Cherokee Nation. If I heard him correctly, sacred landscape certainly means the treasured town sites like Kituwah, Cowee, and Nikwasi that have thankfully been reclaimed under the sovereignty of the Eastern Band of the Cherokee. But what I believe he was saying to us is that the landscape held sacred by the Cherokee includes all the Blue Ridge Mountains homeland. The Great Spirit herself hovers over these mountains, making them blue, blessing all her creatures with love and life. I believe that the Cherokee people, who are so deeply rooted in their mountain homeland, will do everything within their power to care for the land that has been entrusted to them by their Creator.

I share their love for these, our Blue Ridge Mountains. I too call them my home. And I know I have much to learn from the Cherokee about what it means to belong to the land and to exist in right relationship to all our relations, our fellow creatures who share this place. Our shared love of this land widens beyond it, to enclose the earth and all the cosmic elements from which we are all made. The earth and fire, wind and water, sun and moon and the starry night sky. I want to believe that there is a role for allies in the white community who are ready to learn what it means to become "Indigenous," who can support this life's work to preserve and protect our common home. And I hope that what I have done here will be a helpful contribution to a deep map of this sacred landscape.

Something more needed to be said but I couldn't find the words; it was not mine to say. Robin Kimmerer, from the Potawatomi Nation, in her book *Braiding Sweetgrass*, speaks from a heart of hard-won wisdom when she wrote about the losses Native peoples have experienced in the dispossession of their lands, their culture, their very children:

> In the face of such loss, one thing our people could not surrender was the meaning of the land. In the settler mind, land was property, real estate, capital, or natural resources. But to our people, it was everything: identity, the connection to our ancestors, the home of our nonhuman kinfolk, our pharmacy, our library, the source of all that sustained us. Our land where our responsibility to the world was enacted, sacred ground. It belonged to itself; it was a gift, not a commodity, so it could

never be bought or sold. These are the meanings people took with them when they were forced from their ancient homelands to new places.[3]

With understandable fear and trembling, Dr. Kimmerer holds out an invitation to us. From the history she knows in her bones as a Native woman and scholar, she is keenly aware how white people can turn the most sacred things into commodities in our relentlessly commercial culture. She knows all too well that her words might be yet another occasion for exploitation. But in her book, she risks an invitation to all of us born from settler society to become more Indigenous. She writes, "After all these generations since Columbus, some of the wisest Native elders still puzzle over the people who came to our shores. They look at the toll on the land and say, 'The problem with these new people is that they don't have both feet on the shore. One is still in the boat. They don't seem to know if they are staying or not.'"[4]

Understanding our rootlessness, our social pathologies, our cultural homelessness, she offers us this possibility of coming home. Can we as a nation reckon with the destructive legacy of settler colonialism? Can we as a nation of immigrants shed our colonial settler identity and learn to live here as if we are staying, with both feet on the shore? Even so, she wrestles in her heart with contradictions: "Immigrants cannot by definition become Indigenous. Indigenous is a 'birth-right' word. No amount of time or caring changes history or substitutes for soul-deep fusion with the land."[5]

Drawing on her deep and broad understanding of plants as she does throughout this remarkable book, she finds an example of a foreign plant that has become "naturalized": successfully transplanted into a new earth community. The plant's scientific name is plantain, and, having been introduced by European settlers, its popular name is "white man's footstep." Over time measured in centuries, Natives learned of the fine qualities of this plant, its healing properties, and its contributions to cuisine. And unlike other invasive plants like kudzu, it did not take over the ecosystem but blended in, finding its place to generously contribute.

Perhaps settlers could be so naturalized as to become more Indigenous to their homeplace.

3. Kimmerer, *Braiding Sweetgrass*, 17.
4. Kimmerer, *Braiding Sweetgrass*, 207.
5. Kimmerer, *Braiding Sweetgrass*, 213.

> To become naturalized to place is to throw off the mindset of the settler and to live on and in the land as if this land feeds you, as if these are the streams from which you drink, that build your body and fill your spirit. To become naturalized is to know that your ancestors lie in this ground. Here you will give your gifts and meet your responsibilities. To become naturalized is to live as if your children's future matters, to take care of the land as if our lives and the lives of all our relatives depend on it. Because they do.[6]

She asks us: What happens when settlers truly become native to a place? When we finally make it a home? To become Indigenous is to grow the circle of healing to include all of Creation.

Kimmerer's last hopeful word was a gracious benediction to me and my Celtic ancestors. She said that all of us, no matter where our ancestors come from, were once "Indigenous" somewhere.[7] That is a word of blessing that reaches deeply into my own Celtic ancestral journey that began so long ago in the Scottish Highlands.

GIVING THANKS FOR NATIVE AMERICA

It is a national tradition and part of the cultural heritage of many in our country on every Thanksgiving Day to remember all the ways in which God has blessed us and to give thanks. The focal point of this Thanksgiving celebration has often been found in the collective memory of the first pilgrims at Plymouth who celebrated their existence in the New World. Faced with complete unfamiliarity with the challenges of the New World, with devastating waves of disease, and with periods of famine that almost extinguished the pilgrim community, their governor, William Bradford, set aside a day of thanksgiving to celebrate the miracle of their continued existence.

This memory is especially poignant to me not just because of all the Thanksgivings that were celebrated at my grandparents' home in Greenville. Thanksgiving has a special meaning for me because through my grandmother and her Anderson family lineage, I am a descendant of Gov. Bradford, who initiated this first thanksgiving celebration. (Bradford was also the author of *Plymouth Plantation*, what many scholars believe is the first history of North America.) Most of us know that without the aid and

---

6. Kimmerer, *Braiding Sweetgrass*, 215.
7. Kimmerer, *Braiding Sweetgrass*, 377.

support of the First Americans offered to the pilgrims, there would have been no thanksgiving celebration. But do we know that it was not just because their Indian neighbors brought gifts of food that the pilgrims were able to celebrate the original Thanksgiving feast. Without the ongoing aid and support of Native Americans, the first colonists would simply have not survived at all. Since that first Thanksgiving, Native Americans have given and continue to give gifts to the culture of our nation and to the world that have become so much a part of who we are that the givers of the gifts have been forgotten.

The very sad and tragic truth about the First Thanksgiving is the reality that this beginning point in the encounter between Europeans and Native Americans was not only the first encounter but the high point in that relationship. It went downhill fast from there. Never again would Native Americans experience anything like mutuality and respect from the first undocumented aliens from Europe. My ancestor William Bradford, the governor of Plymouth Colony, a few years after the First Thanksgiving, would witness and rejoice in the brutal massacre of hundreds of Pequot Indians—men, women, and children—carried out by the pilgrims with fire and sword. Thereafter, Thanksgiving was often celebrated by the pilgrims as gratitude for what they believed was God's wrath unleashed on their enemies.

About this clash between two vastly different civilizations that makes up the story of American history, the anthropologist Jack Weatherford writes, "The Indian civilizations crumbled in the face of the Old World, not because of any intellectual or cultural inferiority. They simply succumbed in the face of disease and brute strength. While the Indians had spent millennia becoming the world's greatest farmers and pharmacists, the people of the Old World had spent a similar period amassing the world's greatest arsenal of weapons. The strongest but not necessarily the most creative or the most intelligent won the day."[8] In closing, I want to lift up some of the enormously significant contributions that Native Americans have made to our nation and to our world for which I am grateful. And I want to reaffirm why I believe Native American and Indigenous peoples all over the world offer us our best hope for the future of our planet.

---

8. Weatherford, *Indian Givers*, 252.

I am much indebted to the work of the anthropologist Jack Weatherford and the research that he has put together in the book *Indian Givers*.⁹ Weatherford teaches us that yes, Native Americans brought food to the first Thanksgiving feast celebrated by our pilgrim ancestors. But it was their agricultural expertise that taught the pilgrims and other colonists up and down the East Coast how to successfully grow the food that they needed not only to survive but to become self-sufficient. Irrigation, terracing, mixing crops, crop rotation, and organic fertilizers are just a few examples of the kinds of agricultural expertise that Native Americans taught to the colonists. Native Americans helped Europeans overcome their distaste for shellfish, clams, oysters, and mussels that were repugnant to the first European immigrants.

The contribution of Native Americans went even further than this. The introduction of Native American foods to the diet of Europeans would bring about a food revolution that would cure Europe of episodic famines that had devastated the Old World for centuries. The exportation of the potato by itself saved hundreds of thousands of people from starvation. The potato and other American foods like corn, beans, tomatoes, peppers, and squash would become the mainstay of European agriculture and food consumption. But it was not just the food itself but how it was prepared that made such an impact on colonial America and on Europe. The use of spices and chilies changed the culinary habits of Europeans. Anyone who enjoys barbecue should know that it is a derivative of a Native way of preparing meat. Cajun and Creole foods were again a mix of African, European, and Native American cuisine. Been to an athletic event game lately? "Popcorn, peanuts, get your popcorn peanuts." Both are Native contributions. You hikers carrying trail mix: Indians taught us how to go on long journeys carrying seeds and dried fruit for sustenance. Along with these foods came other gifts that Europeans have not handled as well: things like sugar, chocolate, and tobacco.

The next great gift of Native America to our nation and to the world came in medicine and the healing arts. Native Americans possessed knowledge of natural pharmaceuticals that had been passed down for centuries. Native Americans had a natural remedy for almost any condition, from constipation to goiters, to headaches, to burns, to fevers. The only diseases they seemed to have no remedy for were those brought by

---

9. Weatherford takes as his title an early pejorative name for Native Americans and turns it on its head. But we must acknowledge that even the referential term of Indians is not universally accepted among Native peoples.

the Europeans themselves, like smallpox which swept away millions of Indians in the first century after contact.

The first European immigrants did not hack their way through an impenetrable wilderness. They followed a well laid-out transportation system of trading paths, navigable rivers, and in some cases, as in the desert Southwest, actual paved roads traveled for centuries by Native Americans. Much of today's interstate system is laid out exactly along the old trading paths of Native nations. The Incan Empire in the Andean Highlands was traversed by a highway system that rivaled that of the Roman Empire. New archeological evidence suggests that the First Americans may have navigated in boats down the Pacific Coast of the continent, from generation to generation until they reached South America. Natives who settled in the Pacific Northwest were adept at hunting whales on the open seas. Native contributions of the canoe and the kayak and the raft helped early European immigrants navigate the vast waterways of America. Native Americans were the pathfinders of a vast continent. They did not carry maps for long journeys across hundreds and hundreds of miles because, as some believe, they memorized the directions as songs to be sung as they traveled. Their maps were songs sung along the journey.

The importance of the Indians in shaping contemporary cultural geography in America is clearly shown in the names of American rivers, mountains, cities, and states. The first white colonial settlers in America tended to name everything after their place of origin like New York, New England, or New Jersey, or after their benefactors as in Virginia, the Carolinas, and Georgia. As we know, the Spanish had a proclivity for naming everything after saints. As Amitav Ghosh has observed, "Renaming was one of the principal instruments with which colonists erased the prior meaning of conquered landscapes."[10] It appeared for a while that Indigenous names would be entirely dropped, and the map of America would read like the map of a scrambled Europe. To the contrary, Indian names have held on with great tenacity in states like Tennessee, named for the Cherokee Overhill Town called Tanasi. What about other states like Massachusetts, Mississippi, Minnesota, Texas, Utah, Kansas, and the Dakotas? And there are too many towns and cities to name like Poughkeepsie, Tallahassee, Roanoke, Nantucket, Chicago, and Tucson.

As familiar as they were with the earth beneath their feet, their knowledge of the stars was unsurpassed. Go to Casa Grande in southern

---

10. Ghosh, *Nutmeg's Curse*, 49.

Arizona and learn about an ancient observatory that charted the courses of the stars. Go to the Great Kiva at Chaco Canyon in north New Mexico and see how the light of the sun at the seasonal equinox lights up the center of the sacred space of the Great Kiva. After all, looking at the night sky was the chief nighttime entertainment of Native Americans, that and storytelling: two pleasures that most contemporary Americans have largely forsaken.

I will never forget the two days I spent wandering around the ancient Mayan city of Tikal in Guatemala. If you have ever seen the pyramids of Tikal, or for that matter the great mounds of the Mississippi Basin, you cannot help but be impressed by the architectural achievement of Native Americans. Archaeologists are still unable to explain how it is that the massive stone blocks that make up walls of ancient Incan cities and temples could have been so precisely cut and fitted to the millimeter. Though the architectural designs of Indians never caught on with British North America, in what was Spanish colonial America in the desert Southwest the architecture of the Pueblo Indians continues to combine an appealing aesthetic elegance with functional simplicity well suited for desert living.

Perhaps one of the greatest contributions of Native peoples to American culture and the most forgotten is in the political domain. The first colonists were amazed and baffled by the egalitarian democracies that they encountered among Indian nations. Yes there were chiefs, but these chiefs, at least in North America, never had power over the people. They functioned as wise elders, as leaders among other members of councils who sought consensus in the decisions affecting the tribe. Colonists were filled with consternation at the equal place and status afforded women in many tribes. We tend to think that the sources of inspiration for American democracy were primarily the city-states of ancient Greece, or the humanism of the Enlightenment, or the emphasis on individual liberty among the Puritans. But the witness of democratic egalitarianism of Native American tribes was an important influence on the evolution of American political culture. That the Iroquois Confederacy was a concrete model and inspiration for the American form of government is an almost completely forgotten aspect of American political history.

So many of the things that Native Americans have contributed to the planet have been so thoroughly incorporated into our global culture that the Indigenous origins of these gifts are all but forgotten. Every Thanksgiving should be an occasion to give thanks for all that Native Americans have contributed to the culture of our nation and to the world. America is uniquely what it is today, not just because of what Europeans did when they came to this continent, but what was given to us by the First Americans. American culture is a unique blend of the culture that was here before 1492 with everything that followed.

Perhaps the gift we most need to receive from Native Americans is their spiritual legacy. Christians have somehow come to believe that dominion over creation given to us according to one deeply wrong interpretation of the creation story in Genesis is a license for us to dominate the earth; to lay waste to land, sky, and waters; and to exploit our fellow creatures. Native Americans understand that creation is a precious gift given by the Great Spirit to all earthly creatures who are siblings to one another. And today all over the world, Indigenous communities are the forefront of a global effort to save our planet from environmental destruction. Five hundred years ago, Europeans came and first encountered Native Americans. We came, we saw, we conquered. More than five hundred years later, can we finally encounter Native Americans, the First Americans who are wise teachers from whom we have so much to learn? Can we encounter and learn from Native Americans about living on the land in the way that the Great Spirit intends? Let us give thanks for all that Native Americans have given us to make our country what it is today. And may we follow their lead in fighting to save our planet.

Postscript: The Anderson Diaspora

BEFORE WE LEAVE ALL my assorted Anderson ancestors including Tyger Jim and Polly Anderson and all the rest, I want to tell a story about a serendipitous series of revelations and connections that led to a meeting with a long-lost cousin of Tyger Jim. I was poised to begin a new job as co-pastor at St. Mark's Presbyterian in Tucson, Arizona, in 1993. Just prior to leaving to drive from South Carolina to Arizona, I received a note from the Reverend Will Campbell, the well-known renegade Baptist preacher, civil rights activist, and author. Will was congratulating me on my call to St. Mark's. The note in Campbell fashion stated dryly that he didn't know of many "big steeple" churches that were worth their salt, but from what he could tell St. Mark's was one of them and he wished me all the best. How in the world did Will Campbell learn about my call to St. Mark's and why had he felt moved to write me?

In high school, I had read a couple of Campbell's books. One of them, *Brother to a Dragonfly*, made a strong impression on me. The book was in part the story of Will's beloved brother and his tragic struggle with alcoholism. The book also gives us a sense of Will's growing involvement in the civil rights movement from his days as a chaplain at Ole Miss to his work with the National Council of Churches and their civil rights advocacy. During my years as an undergraduate at Wake Forest, I had also seen Will Campbell, Wake alumni, perform a concert, strumming his guitar and telling stories about the civil rights movement and southern culture. But I had never met the man.

Getting a note from Will Campbell was a big thing for me. As I was driving from South Carolina to Arizona, heading west on I-40 toward Tucson, near Nashville I realized that I might be in the vicinity of Will Campbell's home. I took an exit and found a phone booth, dialed directory assistance, and got Will on the phone. Why yes, he lived a few miles from that very spot, and I was welcome to come by. He would be behind the main house in the log cabin that served as his study. Well, I found him inside that log cabin, and we had a lovely conversation for an hour or two, and then I headed on my way. I had a long way to go.

It was probably then that I learned of his friendship with a member of my new congregation whom I had not yet met. Will had known Sue Minter since the early days of the civil rights movement, when she and her husband David were run out of Mississippi because of their racial justice work. I surmised that it was Sue who had prompted Will to reach out to me as a personal favor to her. Shortly after I got settled in Tucson and began to get acquainted with members of my new congregation, I reached out to her. She was an aged but lively widow. Her husband David, a physician, had been dead for several years. And she owned up to asking Will to write me a note. I can't remember exactly what she shared with me about what happened in Mississippi—just something about getting thrown out of the state.

She also mentioned that her husband David had South Carolina ancestors.

With a look of amused wonder, and a roll of her eyes, she said aloud the name of one of them: "Tyger Jim Anderson."

"Tyger Jim Anderson," I exclaimed. "We are cousins!"

The fact that Dr. Minter and I were distant cousins established a familial affection and rapport with Sue, but otherwise I was not that curious about what exactly had happened to the Minters in Mississippi or how David Minter and I were related.

It was years later, long after Sue's death, that I read Will Campbell's next book, *Providence*, the story of one square mile of land in Mississippi as told through many historical layers. In the opening chapter Will describes how, in 1955, he and Dr. Mac Bryan, a professor of ethics at Wake Forest, had decided to try to visit a biracial farming community called Providence that was literally under siege by the white community in Tchula, Mississippi. This was the community that the Minters had been a part of, along with Eugene Cox and his wife Lindsey. David and Sue ran a free medical clinic and Gene and Lindsey oversaw the farming. They were living in community with other black men and women trying to build something for the common good.

Will and Mac, having heard of the trouble surrounding this community, decided they would try to make contact and offer support. Driving through the woods at night, they passed through a group of hostile and armed white men, manning a checkpoint set up by the White Citizens Council to monitor the coming and going from Providence Farm. Later, over a long night of conversation, Mac and Will got the full story from the Coxes and the Minters. How a rumor had been circulating around Tchula that at Providence black and white children were allowed to swim together in the local swimming hole; and how the White Citizens Council had called a larger community meeting where the interracial character of Providence Farm was widely denounced by those in attendance, all save one. A Presbyterian minister by the name of Rev. Marsh Calloway was in attendance that night and spoke up forcefully as a kind of character witness for the Minters and the Coxes and criticized the White Citizens Council's attempt to run them out of the county. Calloway was not only shouted down that night but, soon afterward, the Session of his Presbyterian Church fired him, and the Presbytery voted their approval of the firing as justified. The Minters would end up leaving Mississippi and moving to Tucson. I don't know what happened to Reverend Calloway.

In *Providence*, Will Campbell tells the story of the Minters and the Coxes and the biracial community they tried to build as just one layer in the history of Providence, that square mile of Mississippi land. In his book, Campbell also sought to tell of the Choctaw Indians who had lived and thrived there for eons until their lands were stolen from them and their tribe, along with the Cherokee, were removed to Oklahoma. Campbell told of the southern plantation that had occupied the site and had been worked by enslaved Africans. He related the story of the work that the Minters and the Coxes and their black friends tried to accomplish during the era of the civil rights movement, and after that, how Providence reverted in a sense to its original state as a forest preserve.

What Will Campbell accomplished with *Providence*, telling the story of the historical layers of one small place, roughly a square mile in Mississippi, has been an inspiration for what I am trying to do with this narrative about up-country South Carolina. A deep map that traces bloodlines, that inscribes landlines of migration. That recalls song lines of resistance and struggle. Layers of history in a particular time and place. Cultural archeology. A deep map of the Keowee Trail.

I will always treasure that brief interaction with Will Campbell, and I will always regret that I did not take any courses at Wake Forest with Dr. Mac Bryan, who himself is a local legend. And I fondly remember my friendship with Sue Minter. In the little book *The Anderson Family History*, published in 1955, from which I have drawn so much material for this narrative on my Anderson ancestors, I discovered a short paragraph describing Dr. David Minter and his wife Sue and their work in health care in Mississippi. Dr. Minter is there among a multitude of descendants of Tyger Jim and Polly Miller. This history of the Anderson family was first published right at that moment David and Sue were still at Providence Farm, just before being expelled from Mississippi. I am proud of my kin and of the family narrative that is still being written. There in the Anderson family history is the smallest mention of a newborn boy—John Stuart Taylor III, born July 23, 1954—born just in the nick of time to be barely a footnote in the family story.

Epilogue: The Unfinished Revolution

THE MOST RADICAL IDEA enshrined in the Declaration of Independence is not the right to revolution, but the claim that "all men are created equal." The most profound principle of freedom the Declaration espouses is that the basis of every political institution is human equality; indeed that equality is the foundation of human society. How was this vision of human equality to be understood, interpreted, and implemented in this new American Republic? For the vision of equality from the outset did not include women. The implications of this ideal were a matter of great debate in the original Continental Congress. The affirmation that all men are created equal, and therefore King George must go, got no argument from the gathered assembly of white men. There was consensus around freedom as the right to revolution. However, if the statement was that all men are created equal and therefore slavery must go, our founders were plunged into a conflict that went right to the heart of this new nation. Certainly, the slave owner patrician class of the southern colonies, of which Jefferson was the most prominent representative, did not wish to apply the ideal of human equality to the institution that undergirded their economic lives. Many in the northern colonies, not just those that built and sold and manned the ships that plied the slave trade, realized that they too had a vested self interest in the continuation of slavery. And what about the Indigenous people, here eons before the first European settlers, were they equal to white men? Apparently not.

The genius of the Declaration is that the colonies got what they wanted in the short term, independence from King George, but they also got in the fine print something else they did not necessarily want, something they weren't sure they were ready for: a commitment to the equality of all people. All men are created equal. We cannot hear that phrase without feeling the irony of it. We wonder how it is that our Founding

Fathers were able to make this universal affirmation and at the same time exclude from its application all women, all people of color, all who were different from themselves.

The great irony of Jefferson's Declaration of Independence was that, in its original application, some were more equal than others. We know that Jefferson knew better. The transcendent intellect and conscience of the man who articulated the moral vision of a nation was nevertheless grounded in the fallible assumptions of his culture and in the concrete circumstances of his self-interests. He owned slaves upon whose labors his livelihood depended. We know that he was deeply agitated by the example of one of his neighbors in Charlottesville, a plantation owner who sold his plantation, moved to Ohio, emancipated his enslaved workers, and gave them each acreage and a mule. Jefferson could have acted in a way consistent with his love of freedom and freed his enslaved, but he did not.

Indian removal implemented in the policies of the Jackson administration in the 1830s was originally envisioned by Jefferson. Without condemning Jefferson, we can simply state that he did not embody the freedom that he espoused. He was a contradiction. What we face in Jefferson, our great Founding Father, is the painful contradiction that every white American faces in themselves, the contradiction between our stated ideal and the reality. For that reason, Jefferson is the quintessential white American, the perfect metaphor for the greatness and the shadow of the American character. The work of historians like Annette Gordon Reed, who has documented the relationship between Jefferson and Sally Hemings and the biracial community of Monticello, takes us to the very center of the contradiction in Jefferson's life, character, and vision of human equality.

And so, what began on July 4, 1776, when our nation came into being, has been a part of our national story ever since. We have fashioned at the very heart of our national identity a fundamental moral compromise. The nature of this compromise was to allow and tolerate a gap between our professed vision and the actual reality. This gap has grown wider and wider until at times one could say it bordered on national schizophrenia. On the one hand we have America as democracy, the self-conscious image of ourselves as a nation founded on the principle of equality. But lurking just beneath full awareness, in the shadows of our self-understanding, is a very different reality: America as empire.

EPILOGUE: THE UNFINISHED REVOLUTION

When I speak of America as empire, I am referring to that nation that espouses the false gospel of manifest destiny, which proclaims the inherent right of this nation to intervene in and control the destinies of other peoples, to crush other revolutions if they pose a threat to our status quo. America as empire believes that might makes right. America as empire is founded on racist assumptions about the superiority of white civilization. America as empire is motivated and driven by an insatiable greed to consume, control, to own, to exploit, to extract. Every generation of Americans has had to struggle with this dual identity. Many times, we have tried to make peace with it by invoking the pious rhetoric of virtue, opportunity, and freedom while hiding from ourselves the realities of exploitation, greed, and violence. In the soul of our nation, America as democracy is locked in a permanent revolutionary struggle with America as empire.

It is America as democracy that I love and respect. This is the America that I long for and believe in, that makes its claim upon me as a citizen. I give my loyalty to America as revolutionary democracy. By the power invested in me as a citizen of a revolutionary democracy, by the power invested in me by the Declaration of Independence, I declare that America as empire does not have my consent. I join my lot with all other citizens in saying, "We defy you." I join myself with the freedom struggles of communities of color who have been excluded, dominated, exploited. I join myself with all who struggle in hope for the realization of a truly multiracial democracy. I believe we will yet overcome America as empire. And we will continue to discover and claim that the true American, the patriotic American, is still a revolutionary. That is the promise of democracy and the ongoing American Revolution that I celebrate, and that I hope and pray will triumph over empire in the struggle for the soul of this nation.

The American Revolution is not over. The Revolution was not finished when British power was overthrown and we won our national independence. That is when the revolution in a sense began. If the Declaration of Independence was simply the announcement to the British Crown that we are a new government, then it is of profoundly limited historical value, a document to be filed somewhere in our national archives. But the Declaration is much more than that. Fundamentally, this document is addressed to every new generation of the American people themselves. The vision of freedom, the goal of equality, the hope of justice for all, is unfulfilled in this country and still faces us. The Declaration of

Independence is a standard for the future which calls us to struggle, to embody in our national life the freedom and equality that we are founded upon.

The citizens' right to revolution is not the prerogative of those who demean our elections, or who suppress our right to vote, or who undermine other institutions of democracy, or threaten political violence. The right to revolution is the citizen's responsibility to continually refashion our institutions to make them more just, inclusive, and fair to all. The revolutionary activity of the citizen is always to challenge those who govern to be more responsive, more accountable to the common good. The Declaration of Independence asks every American citizen to take up our permanent right, our responsibility, for an ongoing revolution. It is ongoing because this American Revolution is yet unfinished. The work of building a multiracial democracy is before us and calls us to imagination, courage, and hope.

Acknowledgments

MY LIFE IS RICHER for having undertaken this book, in large part because of friends, family, and colleagues who have offered inspired collaboration along the way. First I want to say thanks to members of my family for their encouragement, especially my siblings Buffie and David, my cousin Mary, who is my go-to family genealogist, and her daughter Sarah Jane, who put together the book cover. Our beloved Aunt Hazael joined our ancestors years ago, but she was and is the one who has instilled in us an appreciation of our family history, and we still miss her. Next I am grateful to Dennis Chastain and Luther Lyle for all that I learned from them about the Keowee Trail and the Lower Towns of the Cherokee. Dr. Brett Riggs, an archeologist at Western Carolina University, has done so much to help many to understand and appreciate the precious legacy of Cherokee history. Ched Myers has been a friend and mentor throughout my life and career. Appreciation to him and Elaine Enns for the tool kit they provided so many of us in their book *Healing Haunted Histories*. In the arduous process of learning how to write a book, I am indebted to a trio of editors, Joyce Hollyday, who helped me take my dream of writing a family history and begin to shape it into a tangible plot line; Jacqueline Lancaster, who hung in there with me in the trenches of writing when I was tempted to give up in frustration; and most of all Dr. Susan Hardy Aiken, whose friendship, scholarly wisdom, and brilliant editing has made all the difference. Finally, a prayer of gratitude to my grandparents John and Hazael, who I hope would offer their blessing upon this venture. From the bottom of my heart, I thank you all.

Bibliography

Amanpour and Company. "Will Congress Follow Through on Its Promise to Seat a Cherokee Delegate?" PBS, September 5, 2023. YouTube video. https://www.youtube.com/watch?v=ZOFLvHv5SNg.
American Battlefield Trust. "Ring Fight." n.d. https://www.battlefields.org/learn/revolutionary-war/battles/ring-fight.
Anderson, Edward. *A History of the Anderson Family, 1706-1955*. Columbia, SC: The R. L. Bryan Company, 1955.
Andrew, Rod, Jr. *The Life and Times of General Andrew Pickens: Revolutionary War Hero, American Founder*. Chapel Hill: University of North Carolina Press, 2017.
Ball, Edward. *Slaves in the Family*. New York: Farrar, Straus and Giroux, 1998.
Boyd, Colleen, and Carl Thrush, eds. *Phantom Past, Indigenous Presence: Native Ghosts in North American Culture and History*. Lincoln: University of Nebraska Press, 2011.
Brackett, Richard Newland, ed. *The Old Stone Church*. Clemson, SC: Old Stone Church and Cemetery Association, 1972.
Brubaker, Jack. *Massacre of the Conestogas*. Charleston: History, 2019.
Calloway, Colin G. *The Indian World of George Washington*. New York: Oxford University Press, 2018.
Campbell, Will D. *Providence*. Marietta, GA: Longstreet, 1992.
Cashin, Edward J. *William Bartram and the American Revolution on the Southern Frontier*. Columbia: University of South Carolina Press, 2000.
Clarke, Erskine. *Our Southern Zion: A History of Calvinism in the South Carolina, Low Country 1690-1990*. Tuscaloosa: University of Alabama Press, 1996.
Corkran, David H. *The Cherokee Frontier: Conflict and Survival, 1740-46*. Norman: University of Oklahoma Press, 2016.
Craig, Tom Moore, ed. *Upcountry South Carolina Goes to War: Letters of the Anderson, Brockman, and Moore Families 1853-1865*. Columbia: University of South Carolina Press, 2009.
D'Agostino, Thomas, and Arlene Nicholson. *Ghosts of King Philip's War*. Haunted America. Mount Pleasant, SC: Arcadia, 2024.
Dallmeyer, Dorinda G., ed. *Bartram's Living Legacy*. Macon, GA: Mercer University Press, 2010.
Dennis, Jeffrey W. *Patriots and Indians: Shaping Identity in Eighteenth Century South Carolina*. Columbia: University of South Carolina Press, 2017.
Denson, Andrew. *Monuments to Absence: Cherokee Removal and the Contest over Southern Memory*. Chapel Hill: University of North Carolina Press, 2017.

Dorton, Mitzi. *Chief Corn Tassel*. Georgetown, KY: Finishing Line, 2022.

Du Bois, W. E. B. *Black Reconstruction in America 1860–1890*. New York: Free Press, 1962.

Dunaway, Wilma A. "The Southern Fur Trade and the Incorporation of Southern Appalachia into the World-Economy, 1690–1763." *Review (Fernand Braudel Center)* 17 (1994) 215–42.

Dunbar-Ortiz, Roxanne. *Not "A Nation of Immigrants": Settler Colonialism, White Supremacy, and a History of Erasure and Exclusion*. Boston: Beacon, 2021.

Duncan, Barbara Reimensnyder. "Going to Water: A Cherokee Ritual in Its Contemporary Context." *Journal of the Appalachian Studies Association* 5 (1993) 94–99.

Duncan, David Ewing. *Hernando de Soto: A Savage Quest in the Americas*. New York: Crown, 1975.

Edelson, Max S. *The New Map of Empire: How Britain Imagined America before Independence*. Cambridge, MA: Harvard University Press, 2017.

Edgar, Walter. *Partisans and Redcoats: The Southern Conflict That Turned the Tide of the American Revolution*. New York: HarperCollins, 2001.

Elder, Robert. *Calhoun: American Heretic*. New York: Basic Books, 2021.

Elliott, Michael A. "Ethnography, Reform, and the Problem of the Real: James Mooney's Ghost-Dance Religion." *American Quarterly* 50 (1998) 201–33.

Fear-Segal, Jacqueline, and Susan D. Rose, eds. *Carlisle Indian Industrial School: Indigenous Histories, Memories and Reclamations*. Lincoln: University of Nebraska Press, 2016.

Fraser, Charles. *A Charleston Sketchbook*. Rutland, VT: Charles E. Tuttle, 1959.

Ghosh, Amitav. *The Nutmeg's Curse: Parables for a Planet in Crisis*. Chicago: University of Chicago Press, 2021.

Gordon, Avery F. *Ghostly Matters: Haunting and the Sociological Imagination*. Minneapolis: University of Minnesota Press, 2008.

Green, Lance. *Their Determination to Remain: A Cherokee Community's Resistance to the Trail of Tears in North Carolina*. Tuscaloosa: University of Alabama Press, 2022.

Haaland, Deb. "Opinion: How We Expunged a Racist, Sexist Slur from Hundreds of Public Lands." *Washington Post*, September 28, 2022. https://www.washingtonpost.com/opinions/2022/09/28/remove-racial-slur-federal-land-native-american/.

Hatley, Tom. *The Dividing Paths: Cherokees and South Carolinians through the Era of Revolution*. New York: Oxford University Press, 1993.

Heller, Karen. "Interior Secretary Deb Haaland's Charged Mission of Healing." *Washington Post*, July 17, 2023. https://www.washingtonpost.com/lifestyle/2023/07/17/deb-haaland-road-to-healing/.

Howe, George. *The History of the Presbyterian Church in South Carolina*. Vol. 1. Columbia, SC: Duffie & Chapman, 1870.

Jenkins, Philip. "The Wisdom of Folk Horror." *The Christian Century* 140 (2023) 48–50.

Kephart, Horace. *The Cherokees of the Smoky Mountains*. Gatlinburg, TN: Great Smoky Mountain Association, 2010.

Kimmerer, Robin Wall. *Braiding Sweetgrass: Indigenous Wisdom, Scientific Knowledge and the Teaching of Plants*. Minneapolis: Milkweed, 2013.

King, Duane H., ed. *The Memoirs of Lt. Henry Timberlake: The Story of a Soldier, Adventurer, and Emissary to the Cherokees, 1756–1765*. Cherokee: Museum of the Cherokee, 2007.

Lane, John. "Keowee." In *Bartram's Living Legacy*, edited by Dorinda G. Dallmeyer, 381–91. Macon, GA: Mercer University Press, 2010.

Lawson, John. *A New Voyage to Carolina*. Chapel Hill: University of North Carolina Press, 1967.

Least Heat-Moon, William. *Prairyerth: A Deep Map*. New York: HarperCollins, 1999.

Log College Press. "Samuel Doak's 1780 Sycamore Shoals Muster Sermon and Prayer." *Log College Press* blog, September 26, 2022. https://www.logcollegepress.com/blog/2022/9/25/samuel-doaks-1780-sycamore-shoals-muster-sermon-amp-prayer.

McLoughlin, William G. *Cherokees and Missionaries, 1789–1839*. Norman: University of Oklahoma Press, 1995.

———. "New Angles of Vision on the Cherokee Ghost Dance Movement of 1811–1812." *American Indian Quarterly* 5 (1979) 317–45.

Meacham, Jon. *American Lion: Andrew Jackson in the White House*. New York: Random House, 2009.

Menakem, Resmaa. *My Grandmother's Hands: Racialized Trauma and the Pathway to Mending Our Hearts and Bodies*. Las Vegas: Central Recovery, 2017.

Miles, Tiya. "The Narrative of Nancy, a Cherokee Woman." *Frontiers: A Journal of Women Studies* 29 (2008) 59–80.

———. *Tales from the Haunted South: Dark Tourism and Memories of Slavery from the Civil War Era*. Chapel Hill: University of North Carolina Press, 2015.

Miller, Robert J. *Native America, Discovered and Conquered: Thomas Jefferson, Lewis and Clark and Manifest Destiny*. Lincoln: University of Nebraska Press, 2008.

Mooney, James. *The Ghost Dance Religion and Wounded Knee*. New York: Dover, 1973.

———. *Myths of the Cherokee and Sacred Formulas of the Cherokee*. Nashville: Charles and Randy Elder, 1982.

Myers, Ched. *Who Will Roll Away the Stone? Discipleship Queries for First World Christians*. New York: Orbis, 1994.

Myers, Ched, and Elaine Enns. *Healing Haunted Histories: A Settler Discipleship of Decolonization*. Eugene, OR: Cascade, 2021.

Nabokov, Peter, ed. *Native American Testimony*. New York: Penguin, 1991.

Neiman, Susan. *Learning from the Germans: Race and the Memory of Evil*. New York: Farrar, Straus and Giroux, 2019.

Newell, Philip J. *Sounds of the Eternal: A Celtic Psalter*. Grand Rapids: Eerdmans, 2002.

Ostler, Jeffrey. "The Shameful Final Grievance of the Declaration of Independence." *Atlantic*, February 8, 2020. https://www.theatlantic.com/ideas/archive/2020/02/americas-twofold-original-sin/606163/.

Pinckney, Roger. "Zambezi Dirt: Embracing Africa, Embracing Each Other, Embracing Ourselves." In *Bartram's Living Legacy*, edited by Dorinda G. Dallmeyer, 394–402. Macon, GA: Mercer University Press, 2010.

Posey, Walter Brownlow. *The History of the Presbyterian Church in the Old Southwest 1778–1838*. Louisville, KY: John Knox, 1952.

Presbyterian Church (USA). *Doctrine of Discovery: A Review of Its Origins and Implications for Congregations in the PC(USA) and Support for Native American Sovereignty*. 2018. https://facing-racism.pcusa.org/site_media/media/uploads/facing_racism/doctrine-of-discovery-report-to-the-223rd-ga-2018-finalized-copy_as-approved.pdf.

Raphael, Ray. *A People's History of the American Revolution*. New York: Perennial, 2002.

Reed, Philip J. Review of *"Reformed and Evangelical across Four Centuries*: The Presbyterian Story in America." *Presbyterian Outlook*, October 26, 2022. https://pres-outlook.org/2022/10/reformed-evangelical-across-four-centuries-the-presbyterian-story-in-america/.
Richie, Fiona, and Doug Orr. *Wayfaring Strangers: The Musical Voyage from Scotland and Ulster to Appalachia*. Chapel Hill: University of North Carolina Press, 2014.
Rosen, Jeffrey, and David Rubenstein. "Why Did Jefferson Draft the Declaration of Independence?" National Constitution Center, April 13, 2015. https://constitutioncenter.org/blog/why-did-jefferson-draft-the-declaration-of-independence.
Rouse, Parke, Jr. *The Great Wagon Road: How Scotch-Irish and Germanics Settled the Uplands*. Richmond, VA: Dietz, 1992.
Rozema, Vicki, ed. *Cherokee Voices: Early Accounts of Cherokee Life in the East, Winston-Salem*. Durham: John F. Blair, 2002.
Saunt, Claudio. *Unworthy Republic: The Dispossession of Native Americas and the Road to Indian Territory*. New York: Norton, 2020.
Silko, Leslie Marmon. *Almanac of the Dead*. Reprint. New York: Penguin, 2006.
———. *Ceremony*. New York: Penguin, 2006.
Sturges, Mark. "A Deep Map of the South: Natural History, Cultural History, and William Bartram's Travels." *South Atlantic Review* 79 (2014) 43–67.
Teach Tennessee History. "Fort Loudoun." n.d. https://teachtnhistory.org/File/Fort_Loudoun.pdf.
Tortora, Daniel J. *Carolina in Crisis: Cherokees, Colonists, Slaves in the American Southeast, 1756–1763*. Chapel Hill: University of North Carolina Press, 2015.
Truettner, William, H., ed. *The West as America: Reinterpreting Images of the Frontier, 1820–1920*. Washington, DC: Smithsonian Institution, 2001.
Van Dorn, Mark, ed. *The Travels of William Bartram*. New York: Macy-Masius, 1928.
Walker, Melissa. *The Battles of Kings Mountain and Cowpens: The American Revolution in the Southern Backcountry*. Critical Moments in American History. New York: Routledge, 2013.
Waxhaw's History. "Ordeal of Touch." Facebook, February 17, 2022. https://www.facebook.com/waxhawshistory/posts/the-suspicious-death-of-a-waxhaw-ministerthe-death-of-the-rev-william-richardson/2520403828092208/.
Weatherford, Jack. *Indian Givers: How the Indians of the Americas Transformed the World*. New York: Fawcett Columbine, 1988.
Wendt, Simon. "Defenders of Patriotism or Mothers of Fascism? The Daughters of the American Revolution, Antiradicalism, and Un-Americanism in the Interwar Period." *Journal of American Studies* 47 (2013) 943–69.
Woodmason, Charles. *The Carolina Backcountry: On the Eve of the Revolution*. Edited by Richard J. Hooker. Chapel Hill: University of North Carolina Press, 1953.
Yoo, William. *What Kind of Christianity: A History of Slavery and Anti-Black Racism in the Presbyterian Church*. Louisville, KY: Westminster John Knox, 2022.
Zinsser, William. *Writing to Learn*. New York: Harper, 2008.

www.ingramcontent.com/pod-product-compliance
Lightning Source LLC
Chambersburg PA
CBHW031804220426
43662CB00007B/518